PROFITING FROM REAL E

PROFITING FROM REAL ESTATE REHAB

Sandra M. Brassfield

John Wiley and Sons, Inc.
New York • **Chichester** • **Brisbane** • **Toronto** • **Singapore**

This book is dedicated to my children:
Lori, Rob, and Denise.

In recognition of the importance of preserving what has been
written, it is a policy of John Wiley & Sons, Inc., to have
books of enduring value published in the United States
printed on acid-free paper, and we exert our best efforts
to that end.

This publication is designed to provide accurate and
authoritative information in regard to the subject
matter covered. It is sold with the understanding that
the publisher is not engaged in rendering legal, accounting,
or other professional services. If legal advice or other
expert assistance is required, the services of a competent
professional person should be sought. *From a Declaration
of Principles jointly adopted by a Committee of the
American Bar Association and a Committee of Publishers.*

Library of Congress Cataloging-in-Publication Data

Brassfield, Sandra M.
    Profiting from real estate rehab / by Sandra M. Brassfield.
      p.   cm.
    ISBN 0-471-54857-X (cloth) : — ISBN 0-471-54858-8
(paper) :
      1. Real estate investment. 2. House buying.   3. House selling.
    4. Dwellings—Remodeling—Economic aspects.   5. Housing
rehabilitation.   I. Title.
    HD1390.5.B73   1991
    332.63′243—dc20   91-15775

Printed in the United States of America

10 9 8 7 6 5 4 3 2 1

Acknowledgments

Real Estate Rehab Group, Ltd.—Experts in residential real estate, with experience in a variety of projects, including residential real estate, finance, reconditioning, and marketing.

Michael F. McCormick, Sr., CEO, Real Estate Rehab Group, Ltd., Tax Management Group—San Diego, California, a special thanks, as this project would never have been completed without his commitment to it. His tenacity, resources, and vision made this happen.

Francis Scorza, Instructor—San Diego, California, for his diligent rewrite and editing of the various drafts of this book and his contribution of "hands-on experience" examples for the text.

Jim Stacy, Realtor—Seattle, Washington, for his inspirational writing which he generously allowed to be shared on several pages of this book.

Judy Reed, Senior Vice President, Security Pacific Bank—Seattle, Washington, for her personal support of me in this effort and her professional contribution to the financing programs listed in this book.

Christine Wells, Manager of Information Systems, Tax Management Group—San Diego, California, who showed those of us involved in the project what patience and hard work were about. For her 100 or so input revisions of this manuscript, thank you.

Sam Kephart, Aerie Lion Group—San Diego, California, thank you for being the spark plug that kept the energy flowing on this project through all its ups and downs.

Contents

PROFITING FROM REAL ESTATE REHAB

Introduction to Real Estate Rehab

All the steps and techniques given in this book relate to residential rehab of one to four units per parcel. One very important reason to begin the business of rehab for profit with single-family, duplex, triplex, or quads (1 to 4 units), is that this is where the lending community offers the most choices for financing. We will not cover multifamily rehab of four or more units, commercial rehab, or mixed-use property rehab in this book. However, we *will* incorporate general first-time investor principles and information that you will need, if and when you decide to expand your rehab project options.

I have found that the three areas of rehab that are of interest to most people inquiring about the field are:

1. *Purchase/rehab/resale as a business.* This is commonly referred to by real estate people as "flipping property." The object is to get in, rehab, resell quickly, and obtain your profit. This is the highest risk option, but can be built into a full-time business and has been successfully done by many people.

   The ideal here is to get proficient enough to be able to do several projects simultaneously. They can grow into a main source of income.

2. *Homeownership.* Some individuals want to live in a house as a residence and improve it. This is called "sweat equity" rehabbing. Their interest is in creating the profit and tax writeoffs in utilizing the home as a primary residence, while they also build profit in

the improvements that they make. The average time line for turn-around is 1 to 2 years and, if done correctly, can yield the same profit as two "flipper" projects. Special areas needing attention relate to understanding the relationship between certain improve-ments and added value, and improvements vs. repairs.

3. *Real estate for income.* The smallest group of inquirers has always been those who want to buy/rehab/and hold, to build a portfolio of real estate for income. It is less risky than "flipping," can provide the stream of income of a business, and, in many high-cost parts of the country, offers the most profit. The reason for this is that quality residential units, one to four per parcel, can have the best resale value because they can be sold to either new in-vestors or buyers who want or need helper units to qualify for financing.

Whichever of the above reasons has motivated you to explore rehab for profit, the steps outlined in this book will apply in getting you to that goal.

We will review these steps in depth and in the order in which you need to proceed, from desire to execution of a successful project.

STEP 1—RESEARCH YOUR LOCAL REAL ESTATE MARKET

This is accomplished by regularly reading the local or city newspapers. They will become a continuing source of information on changes in local trends, interest rates, and resources. Begin a clipping file for various topics to keep for reference. Subscribe to the local business newspaper. In every medium or large-sized city, there is a publication that special-izes in business items only. A large portion of this publication will be devoted to real estate and, just as this publication is required reading for real estate professionals wishing to stay current, it will need to become part of your research also.

STEP 2—GATHER YOUR RESOURCES

We will discuss the various professionals that you will need on your "team," but it is worth noting here that, no matter how self-sufficient you want to be, you will find the road to profits in this business a lot less fraught with pitfalls if you acknowledge that you will need a team of professionals to help you.

STEP 3—CONDUCT SPECIALIZED RESEARCH ON AREAS OF YOUR COMMUNITY

One of the principles of success in rehab is becoming an "expert" on two or three neighborhoods that contain the characteristics for resale that we will detail later.

STEP 4—ASK AND ANSWER BASIC BUSINESS START-UP QUESTIONS

What is the market for my product? (Rehab homes.) What is my competition? (What else can people buy for the same price? Condos? New construction?) How much capital will I need to start and operate my project until it produces profit? What is the probability that this business will continue to have a market? (This question can be answered only when matched to local real estate cycles and trends.)

Some of you will recognize these questions as the universal ones asked of every new business venture. They are no less relevant for your new rehab business.

It is a rare individual who at some time or another has not thought of real estate as a way out of the "working for wages syndrome." The real estate industry has a history of embracing those who have the courage to want more for themselves than what everyone expects them to achieve. Unfortunately, many ways of participating in this industry show little or no cash flow over the short term, and, consequently many hopefuls never reach their goals. Rehabbing homes for profit has the potential to overcome this problem, along with the added lures of variety, scheduling freedom, creativity, and independence.

There is no shortage of fast and easy money ideas in the real estate field. The reality is that these ideas are not nearly as fast nor as easy as they claim to be. In this book, you will find refined methods used by thousands of individuals who have independently shown them to be effective. These concepts have been integrated into a system. There may be no secret tricks to make the process fast and easy, but the use of this system and the education you gain will enable you to follow an effective path to realistic profits. The classic "fixer" property is only one vehicle. Our focus is on *problem solving* rather than just fix and repair.

"WINNING TECHNIQUES"

- Putting together your team
- Finding the not-so-obvious deals
- Making research and development an integral part of the "action plan"
- Improving vs. repairing
- Putting out a finished product that sells itself
- Understanding the wonderful world of remodeling contractors and subs
- What to attempt to do by your own "sweat equity" and when to call in a "pro"
- Negotiating a contract and staying "in control" of your project budget
- Choosing your lender and financing before you choose your project.

COMMON PITFALLS IN REHAB

In counseling students and working with beginning "rehabbers," I have found that some universal pitfalls must be faced when beginning this business. Even experienced rehabbers must be vigilant, not to fall into these traps. The most vulnerable to these errors, and therefore the most in need of anticipating these issues, is the owner/remodeler. I often suggest taping a list of these pitfalls somewhere on the job site where you see it each day, to be sure you will consider them in your day-to-day decisions during the rehab.

Checklist of Pitfalls

- Have I entered the rehab/resale market or the remodeling project without proper information and research?
- Do I have specific demographic information on the specific neighborhood the project is in? *Note:* Where do the neighborhood boundaries lie in the minds of the residents and prospective buyers, as opposed to maps, real estate professionals, city planners, or wishful thinking by sellers of property in adjacent marginal neighborhoods who hope to sell at the adjacent neighborhood's prices?
- Am I trying to "save" money with inferior or cheap material substitutions?
- Am I attempting to save money by performing rehab jobs that really require a professional? (For example, buying unfinished

kitchen cabinets and staining them yourself.) *Note:* You need to understand that there is a learning curve for anything we try for the first time; it can result in cost and time overruns.

- Do I ask at 7:30 A.M. each morning where are my subcontractors and where am I at in the rehab plan? Where am I supposed to be in the rehab plan today?
- Do I repeat "time is money, and the profit is in the timing" three times each morning?

Remember: *An ounce of prevention is worth a pound of cure,* or *measure twice, cut once.*

CONSUMER'S GUIDE TO DECODING REAL ESTATE ADVERTISING

Fixer-upper.	Tear it down and build new house.
Room for RVs.	Entire yard is paved parking lot.
Cute starter home.	Wood frame, 800 square feet, three-quarter bath, fake tile, next to the interstate off-ramp.
Pride of ownership.	Fruit decals on cupboard doors, built-in aquarium in den, rock garden with cast ceramic elves and deer, drapes from J.C. Penney catalogue.
Hurry! This one won't last.	Real estate broker's 90-day listing is about to expire.
Oldie but goodie.	Worn, green linoleum in kitchen, dark, pink tile edged in black in bath, one central gas wall heater, asphalt sheet roof, yard loaded with "mature" fruit trees (fruit inedible).
Reduced $1,500. Owner anxious.	Wants out before next big rains.
180-degree panoramic view.	Windows on both sides of house.
Easy-care yard.	Entire yard covered with ivy and snails (mostly snails).
Ocean view.	If it's under $200,000, the ocean can be seen only by hanging out of second-floor window while someone else holds your feet.
Owner will carry or owner financing.	No one else will touch it.
Step-saver kitchen.	20 feet long and 3 feet wide. Room for one thin cook.

Step-down den.	Good way to replace termite-eaten area without tearing out entire foundation.
Bachelor's hideaway.	Need a compass to find driveway, surrounded by trees and undergrowth, long, narrow stairway from garage to entrance, fire insurance not available.
Prestigious neighborhood.	Very little graffiti, previous owners' "Neighborhood Watch" membership assumable.
Large converted den.	Plan on parking in the street (no garage).
Circular driveway.	Neighborhood skateboard freeway.
Lovely eucalyptus grove.	Get to know local Roto-Rooter person.
Heavy slab foundation.	Pipes put in place before cement poured. Try drain cleaner.
Fast escrow.	House straddles San Andreas Fault.
Low down.	Also describes house.

GETTING STARTED—MEMBERS OF YOUR "TEAM"

The first person you need will be a *tax accountant*. It has been my experience that a bookkeeper may not have enough expertise to be able to forewarn you of (1) tax consequences in real estate transactions and (2) the paper trails your projects will need, to appear "together" to your lender. A CPA may or may not be needed. Be sure to ask if the CPA you are considering deals with clients that utilize the more sophisticated 1031 tax-deferred exchange method. Somewhere in your future you will likely use this vehicle. If you decide on a less expensive professional accountant, be sure that you feel he or she can "grow" with you in sophistication. No matter how much you make in real estate rehab, the plan for how best to shelter that income will need to be in place before you begin.

The next person you need to talk to is a *real estate attorney*. You will need a specialist in real estate, and, depending on whether you are working in a mortgage state or a trust deed state (see Appendix), you will need help only occasionally or "at each step of the way" in your transactions.

In mortgage states, attorneys are an integral part of real estate transactions and should be chosen on the basis of personal rapport as well as their real estate specialty, because you will work closely with this person in problem solving.

In trust deed states, an attorney is not usually called into a transaction until there is a major dispute to be resolved or the legality of a transaction is at question. In fact, it is a common adage in real estate circles in those states that, if you want to "kill" a deal, bring an attorney into it. However, you may at some point want to try to buy real estate without any real estate professionals involved. If you are a "lay person" buyer, purchasing from a seller directly, this might be the time for you to consult an attorney to review all the purchase agreement documents for compliance with the complex real estate laws in effect in your state.

For your finance plan, you will need *a mortgage broker.* I recognize that, in some states, especially on the East Coast, the use of mortgage brokers has been limited; however, this is changing. For those not familiar with who this team player is, a mortgage broker is a person who has been accepted by banks, insurance companies, and pension funds that lend money, to act as a marketing arm for them. The mortgage broker operates in relation to direct money lenders the same way a travel agent operates in marketing airline tickets for all airlines. You pay the same price for the ticket from the agent as you do purchasing it at the airport from the air carrier. Mortgage brokers work on a percentage that is already built into the cost of the loan, so the price is the same, whether from them or from the bank. This is a very simple explanation of a very complex industry. The other advantage of a mortgage broker for you is that you will be seeking very specialized financing, that is, acquisition and rehabilitation loans or creative seller financing combined with conventional loans. The broker can access information for you on these loans, and this will cost you less in time and application fees than applying individually to each lender. We will discuss this in more detail in later chapters. The bank that you utilize for your checking and savings accounts will more than likely not be the place you will find rehab loan money.

Whether you think you will or not, you will need a *general contractor.* In many states, the skill level and degree of knowledge required to be a professional contractor vary greatly. In some states, contractors are strictly held to exam and licensing requirements; in others, they can take out a business license at city hall and hang up their shingle. No matter what the case, you will need a person who knows the local construction codes and pool of subcontractors, for at least your first job. We will discuss in much more detail how and why we use this professional. Because we are entering a whole new profession—the building industry—we need a mentor to help us through the mazes and teach us the language of the new business.

Another person we may not think we need but do is *the real estate agent.* This is another profession where the skill level and experience of someone who has a license vary greatly. When you select the right real estate agent for your business venture, he or she will be invaluable to your success, even though you may see yourself as able to do many of the things that the agent does.

1

Real Estate Basics

In this chapter, you will find the real estate terminology and processes that you will need to know. You will learn what the anatomy of a real estate transaction looks like and become familiar with the terminology of the real estate rehab field. This chapter is a primer that can be used as a reference as you get into your own first rehab project.

THE BUYING PROCEDURE

Because most individuals purchase homes only a few times in their lives, the process can be intimidating. However, the more times you go down that road, the easier it is to find your way, and the faster you move along. That first house purchase seems like a huge risk and is usually the largest dollar amount you have ever spent on one item. It is both an exciting and a frightening time. You experience anticipation, anxiety, disappointment, joy, and greed from one minute to the next.

When you are purchasing a house for your living quarters and as your family's point of stability, the transaction is surrounded by a variety of personal feelings as well as financial considerations. As an entrepreneur, you are not burdened by as many of these complications. The process requires a more analytical approach, one that is unemotional. The logistics of the process are similar, but the techniques and strategies for acquiring homes for resale are quite different.

This chapter reviews the documents and procedures that are generic to all locations and necessary for any purchase regardless of the motive. Chapter 2 will cover the details of seeking and obtaining a property specifically for rehab purposes.

Steps in the Buying Procedure

1. Determine your price range.
2. Select the neighborhood(s) you intend to focus on.
3. Find an agent whose talent and experience match your needs.
4. Conduct a cooperative search with your agent, to find prospective purchases.
5. View, inspect, and evaluate any properties that match your requirements.
6. Once a choice is made, prepare a purchase contract and negotiate a deal.
7. Arrange financing and closing.
8. Make the final inspection and take possession.

USING AN AGENT

The single most often asked question is, should I use an agent? The answer is almost always yes. The reason is simply that it is the most efficient way to conduct your search. There are very few locations where multiple listing (the cooperative effort and sharing of commissions among competing agencies) does not dominate the market. Under this system, any house that is listed or registered and being marketed by a real estate firm is placed in the pool of houses that can be sold by any other practicing firm. This means that the commission will be split, but the theory is that half of something is better than nothing. The advantage to you is that you can work with one agent and that agent has instant access to the details of sales and physical properties of any multiple listed property. The agent can provide you with information and can show you any house listed in the system. The system has many advantages for both the buyer and the seller; however, there are some things you should know about how real estate agents work.

Real estate agents work with both buyers and sellers but they have a fiduciary relationship to the seller. Their goal is to bring buyer and seller together.

Agents are commissioned salespeople who want a commission ASAP (as soon as possible). Some may not care if the house suits your needs or if it is the best option for you. (These agents should be avoided.) They do want your future business, so they will generally try to serve you.

In general, the role of an agent is to:

- Find homes for buyers.
- Market homes (listings) for sellers.

- Do research for buyers and sellers.
- Guide buyers and sellers through the purchase/sale procedures.
- Follow through the transaction with the coordination of required services.
- Assist with the search for financing.

THE BUYER'S BROKER—AN ALTERNATIVE TO TRADITIONAL AGENCY RELATIONSHIPS

A buyer who is using a listing or co-operative agent to help locate and purchase a property is not being legally represented by that agent. As stated, the agent has a fiduciary (legal) duty to the seller and a moral duty to honesty in the transaction to the buyer. The agent is representing the seller, or is a sub-agent (in some multiple listing cases) of a broker from another firm. If you, as a buyer, want your best interest protected by a real estate professional, you do have an alternative. Relatively new compared to the traditional agent, and much less common, is the *buyer's broker*.

The buyer's broker generally has the same credentials as other real estate agents, but chooses to work for the buyer instead of the seller. This means that the buyer pays a fee to obtain the broker's fiduciary or binding representation exclusively.

The up-front fee is negotiable and can take the form of a retainer, a percentage of the sale price, or any arrangement mutually agreed on in a contract between the agent and the client. The seller of the property is still obligated to pay the commission to the listing agent if the property is listed.

What are some of the advantages of using a buyer's broker?

- You know that your interests are being protected.
- The broker's time is not being divided between buying and selling. (Some may still function as both. You should check.)
- You have more control and can expect better negotiation on the price of the property. Your broker has a contract to perform with you (e.g., broker to obtain accepted offer on single-family house at least 10% below fair market value in the Fallbrook neighborhood by March 199__).
- Agents will be more willing to pursue nonlisted properties (for sale by owners, tax sales, and so on).
- Agents will be negotiating for you and you alone when presenting offers.

The buyer's broker concept has been utilized for years in commercial real estate but only recently has begun to appear as an option in residential transactions. For this reason, you may have to hunt to locate a buyer's broker in your area, or you can call your local Board of Realtors for information on buyer's agents in your area.

BASIC LOAN QUALIFYING INFORMATION

Today's society functions on credit and monthly payments. The high cost of goods and services has made lump-sum cash payments of high-ticket items a rarity. As a result, the average consumer owns a portfolio of monthly payments for items ranging from car payments to financed appliances. The first big-ticket item to adopt the concept of payment over time was the home mortgage. The idea was to make payment of a large sum affordable to the buyer by keeping the monthly payment the same over the full term of the loan. The lender is compensated for the use of the money by including interest fees in that monthly payment. This is accomplished by creating an *amortization* schedule. Amortization schedules arrange the distribution of interest versus payment toward the amount of the loan (principal) on a sliding scale. As a result, if the loan is paid off in the early years, the original amount is only slightly reduced. The term *negative amortization* in real estate loans means that not all interest is paid out monthly in a payment and thus can be added to the remaining balance.

The ability to calculate what the monthly payment will be on a specific loan amount is necessary for any investor. The next section describes how to calculate monthly payments on any loan amount. It is a simple procedure that is necessary in determining a project's potential. Work through the example provided, then practice with other loan amounts, interest rates, and terms.

Determining What *You* Can Afford

There is a house for every buyer and a buyer for every house. All buyers do not have the financial resources to purchase the house they really want and are forced to settle for one within the price range they can afford. If it were left up to individual buyers, the estimate of what they can afford would most likely be far greater than industry norms suggest. For the most part, lending institutions decide how much the buyer can afford to borrow. The amount they are willing to lend is based on the ability of the borrower to pay it back. This ability is calculated by using ratios applied to the borrower's annual income and long-term debt. The formula for calculating how much the lenders will lend you is used in Table 1.1. As investors, we need to become very comfortable with what lenders do and do not count into the *qualifying ratios*.

Table 1.1   Calculating the Mortgage You Can Afford

Income Ratio

1. Gross monthly income $_____
2. Multiply line 1 by .28 (Ratios vary with various loans.
   This is for fixed rate loans.) $_____
3. Monthly payment for principal and interest $_____
4. Annual property taxes divided by 12 $_____
5. Annual homeowner's insurance divided by 12 $_____
6. Subtract the total of lines 3 + 4 + 5 from line 2 $_____

Debt Ratio

7. Gross monthly income $_____
8. Multiply line 6 by .36 $_____
9. Write the total monthly payment needed to cover all
   long-term consumer debts (car payments, charge cards,
   child support payments, etc.) $_____
10. Write the sum of lines 3 + 4 + 5 $_____
11. Subtract the total of lines 9 and 10 from line 8 $_____

Read through Table 1.1 to become familiar with the process, then calculate your own status by substituting the actual dollar amounts that apply to your current situation. If you know how to use this formula, you can quickly determine your potential for obtaining the loan amount you need for any property that you are interested in. If it turns out that the loan amount is too large for you to obtain, you should not immediately abandon the project. You may be able to reduce the loan amount by raising the down payment, or, if that is not possible, you may be able to obtain unconventional financing alternatives. (See Chapter 4.)

HOW TO CALCULATE MORTGAGE PAYMENTS

The typical mortgage payment includes repayment of the *principal*, the *interest* on the loan, the real estate property *taxes*, and the monthly cost of homeowner's *insurance*. These factors are sometimes referred to as P.I.T.I.

Calculate the principal and interest due on a loan using the amortization schedule in Table 1.2.

Locate the interest rate in the first column, follow it across to the term in years, and use the number given as a multiplier times the loan amount in thousands.

Table 1.2 P & I Factors

Interest Rate	15 Years	20 Years	30 Years
9.000	10.1427	8.9973	8.0462
9.125	10.2172	9.0778	8.1363
9.250	10.2919	9.1587	8.2268
9.375	10.3670	9.2398	8.3175
9.500	10.4422	9.3213	8.4085
9.625	10.5178	9.4031	8.4999
9.750	10.5936	9.4852	8.5915
9.875	10.6697	9.5675	8.6835
10.000	10.7461	9.6502	8.7757
10.125	10.8227	9.7332	8.8682
10.250	10.8995	9.8164	8.9610
10.375	10.9766	9.9000	9.0541
10.500	11.0540	9.9838	9.1474
10.625	11.1316	10.0679	9.2410
10.750	11.2095	10.1523	9.3348
10.875	11.2876	10.2370	9.4289
11.000	11.3660	10.3219	9.5232
11.125	11.4446	10.4071	9.6178
11.250	11.5234	10.4926	9.7126
11.375	11.6026	10.5783	9.8077
11.500	11.6819	10.6643	9.9029
11.625	11.7615	10.7506	9.9984
11.750	11.8413	10.8371	10.0941
11.875	11.9214	10.9238	10.1900
12.000	12.0017	11.0109	10.2861
12.125	12.0822	11.0981	10.3824
12.250	12.1630	11.1856	10.4790
12.375	12.2440	11.2734	10.5757
12.500	12.3252	11.3614	10.6726
12.625	12.4067	11.4496	10.7697
12.750	12.4884	11.5381	10.8669
12.875	12.5703	11.6268	10.9644
13.000	12.6527	11.7159	11.0621
12.125	12.7352	11.8052	11.1599
13.250	12.8176	11.8944	11.2578
13.375	12.9004	11.9841	11.3559
13.500	12.9836	12.0740	11.4542
13.625	13.0668	12.1640	11.5526
13.750	13.1504	12.2543	11.6512
13.875	13.2337	12.3446	11.7499

EXAMPLE

Calculate the P.I.T.I. payments on a $75,000 loan at 10% for a term of 30 years.

$$
\begin{array}{rl}
75 & \text{the amount of the loan in thousands} \\
\times\ 8.78 & \text{multiplier from table} \\
\hline
\$685.50 & \text{principal and interest (P.I.)}
\end{array}
$$

The annual property taxes and hazard insurance divided by 12 would then be added to the $658.80:

$$
\begin{array}{rl}
\$658.50 & \text{P.I.} \\
+\ 200.00 & {}^{1}\!/_{12}\ \text{hypothetical taxes} \\
+\ \ 50.00 & {}^{1}\!/_{12}\ \text{hypothetical insurance costs} \\
\hline
\$905.50 & \text{P.I.T.I.}
\end{array}
$$

Analysis of Table 1.1

If line 11 and line 6 are both greater than zero, the borrower qualifies for the loan amount. If line 10 or line 6 is a negative number, he or she must either be able to show an increase in income or a decrease in consumer debt. If neither is possible, the only alternative is to seek a smaller loan amount.

EXAMPLE

A borrower wishes to obtain a loan of $60,000 at 10% with a 30-year term. Her total gross income is $36,000 per year. She has a car payment of $150 per month, a school loan of $50 a month, and a credit card balance requiring $45 a month. The taxes on the property she wishes to purchase are $3,000 per year. Table 1.3 is a completed version of Table 1.1.

Analysis of Table 1.3

Lines 11 and 6 are both greater than zero, so the borrower qualifies for the loan amount. Neither lines 10 nor 6 is a negative number.

EXAMPLE

Mr. and Mrs. Wanabuy are interested in obtaining a $150,000 home with a $30,000 down payment. They are seeking an 11.5% fixed rate loan for a term of 30 years. Mr. Wanabuy makes $45,000 per year and Mrs.

Table 1.3   Example: Calculating the Mortgage You can Afford

Income Ratio

1. Gross monthly income	$	3,000
2. Multiply line 1 by .28 (Ratios vary with various loans. This is for fixed rate loans.)	$	840
3. Monthly payment for principal and interest	$	526.80
4. Annual property taxes divided by 12	$	250
5. Annual home owners insurance ($450) divided by 12	$	37.50
6. Subtract the total of lines 3 + 4 + 5 from line 2	$	25.70

Debt Ratio

7. Gross monthly income	$	3,000
8. Multiply line 6 by .36	$	1,080
9. Write the total monthly payment needed to cover all long-term consumer debts (car payments, charge cards, child support payments, etc.)	$	245
10. Write the sum of lines 3 + 4 + 5	$	814.30
11. Subtract the total of lines 9 and 10 from line 8	$	20.70

*Did you note that utility costs are *not* counted in ratios?

Wanabuy makes $30,000. Their credit card payment averages $75 per month, they have a car payment of $165 per month, the taxes on the new house will be $3,400 per year, they are paying a total of $90 per month on a school loan, the cost of heat and other utilities for the new home will be approximately $140 per month, and the insurance on the new home will be $550 per year.

Using the information given, determine whether these people will be qualified to receive the amount of the loan they are seeking. (Use a copy of Table 1.1.)

APPLYING FOR A REAL ESTATE LOAN

To fully understand the process of applying for a loan, you must first understand why lenders function as they do. In the early years of mortgages, the vast majority of loans were made by lending institutions. The funds for the loan were generated by the bank's deposits and the bank personnel calculated the interest due, sent out the statements, and recorded payments. Then, investors such as insurance companies began to purchase the mortgages from the banks and what we now call the "secondary mortgage market" was born. Beginning in the 1960s, banks would hold a percentage of their own loans and sell off the remainder to this secondary market. The bank was still in a position to dictate the qualifying ratios and could (and would) make loans based on factors such as previous relationships and performance at that bank. In recent years, banks have found high-interest, short-term money more profitable and less of a risk. This has resulted in almost all of the mortgage loans being quickly sold off to the secondary market. The impact on the consumer or borrower is that banks or mortgage companies are forced to adhere to a set of qualifying standards that are universally acceptable to the secondary market investors purchasing the loans. In order to keep their loan portfolio salable, banks are forced to be much more strict with their loan applicants. Lenders can no longer ignore items such as work history; they now insist on verification of all application information. In dealing with rehab properties, it is important that we seek a lender that keeps its own loan portfolio and does not sell it on the secondary market, because most "fixer" properties do not qualify as saleable to the secondary market. (See Chapter 4 for exceptions.)

The bank or mortgage company to which you make your application is most likely making its profit on the up-front points or application fees you pay at the time of application and will often service the loan for six months or less before selling it. The terms of the loan are fixed, so the only impact on the borrower, if the loan is sold, is that payment is sent to a different address. It should be noted, however, that any time there is a change in the loan holder, there is the potential for mistakes to be made in escrowed amounts for insurance payments and taxes.

Examples of items that you can expect to supply at the time of loan application follow. The company or institution doing the application will be crossing all the Ts and dotting all the Is, so you should be diligent in making sure you have all the information needed and that it is correct. Failure to do so will usually result in a delay in loan approval.

CHECKLIST OF INFORMATION NEEDED AT TIME OF LOAN APPLICATION

Personal Data

- Names and addresses of your employers for the past two years and your income data. If you are self-employed or work on commission, bring IRS 1040s with all schedules, W-2s for past two years, and profit and loss statement prepared by your accountant.

- If alimony or child support income is to be considered, provide a copy of the divorce decree or separation agreement.
- Documentation of income from any other source.

Assets

- Banking data—names and branch offices' addresses, account numbers, and balances.
- Credit union that you belong to. Provide names, addresses, and account number(s).
- Stocks and bonds that you own.
- Real estate that you own.
- Make, year, and approximate resale value of all motorized vehicles, boats, and so on, that you own.
- Life insurance—face amount (include employer's) and approximate cash value.
- Vested interest in any retirement plan—approximate amount.
- "Gift letter" if a relative is providing a gift of funds to the applicant.

Liabilities and Established Credit

- Current debts—names, addresses, account numbers, current balances, monthly payments.
- Former liabilities—names, addresses, account numbers, and dates paid off—only if there is not current credit.
- Explanation of any recently incurred debts.
- Present or former mortgage—same information as above, plus loan type.
- Documentation on *all* required payments for alimony/child support (decrees, etc.).

Other Items

- Check/money order for appraisal fee, credit report, and so on.
- Veterans Administration loans only:
  Name, address, and phone number of veteran's nearest living relative.
  Certificate of eligibility called a DD 214 form (separation papers).
- Previous two months' bank statements.
- Discharge of bankruptcy if applicable.
- Tax bills on property purchased or refinanced.

Despite what you may have heard, lenders do have a sense of humor. A loan underwriter I once worked with kept this sign hanging on the wall:

In God we trust, all else, document.

WHAT WILL MAKE THE LENDER SAY "YES"

The following list includes many of the items that a lender considers when reviewing your loan(s) application.

- Employment must be verified for the past two full years.
- Borrowers with questionable employment histories *must* have offsetting financial strengths to be considered for maximum financing.
- Borrower must explain any employment gaps that extend beyond one month.
- Fewer than two years' commission income will be acceptable *only* if there are significant compensating factors.
- Overtime pay and bonuses can be used as income if the borrower has received it for the past two years and his employer indicates that this income will, in all probability, continue.
- Part-time or second-job income may be used if you can verify that it has been uninterrupted for the past two years and is claimed on tax returns.
- Alimony or child support can be used if it is to continue for at least three years longer.

The following items will not increase your chance of being approved for a loan; they are *not* considered sources of income:

- Automobile allowances.
- Expense account payments.
- Veterans Administration educational benefits.
- Retained earnings in a company.
- Rent from boarders in a single-family property that is also the borrower's residence or second home, unless signed leases can be produced.
- Any sources of income that cannot be verified. The rule in the lending industry is that if you don't report it on your taxes, the income doesn't exist.

Note: This checklist cannot be considered all-inclusive because lenders differ in their individual guidelines.

A STEP-BY-STEP GUIDE TO HOME LOANS

What the Typical Home Buyer Goes Through to Obtain Financing

Prequalification

Lenders are encouraging buyers to get prequalified for a mortgage even before they begin looking for a house. By doing so, buyers know how much money they can spend or how much house they can afford. Lenders caution, however, that prequalification is only as good as the information supplied by a borrower. Neglecting to mention an outstanding car loan or a previous credit problem, for instance, could nullify the prequalification.

When you are ready to resell your property, use a technique that both you and your buyers will find helpful: Shop for a lender who will *preapprove*—not just prequalify the buyer—within 5 days of acceptance of the offer. You save the time your house is off the market, and the buyer saves sleepless nights, hoping, 48 days later, that he or she can still qualify for the loan. Time is money, and your profit is in the timing; this technique keeps you (the seller) in control of your sale.

Loan Search

Although buyers often use a lender recommended by their real estate agent, some prefer to make their own comparisons. In the current real estate market, buyers who plan to do their own homework might want to begin *before* they find a house. Borrowers may choose to contact a mortgage broker who has access to a wide variety of loans or a direct lender, such as a savings and loan, commercial bank, or mortgage broker.

Escrow Company or Attorney Search

Buyers who decide to "shop" for an attorney or escrow company need to do so ahead of time. It is common for a real estate agent to recommend an escrow company after your offer has been accepted.

Loan Application

It's crucial to supply the lender with as much information as possible, as accurately as possible. All outstanding debts as well as assets and income should be included. The application may have an optional check-off for ethnic background. The information is intended for research purposes and is not meant to be used in evaluating the loan application.

Because it is optional, you need not respond. A loan representative is the borrower's main contact through the process.

Documentation

Paperwork supporting the application also must be submitted. See list of documents earlier in this chapter.

Verification

The lender verifies the borrower's employment, income, and down-payment deposit. The down payment cannot be borrowed, although it can be a gift or a secured loan (lender takes collateral for the loan). A credit report is ordered and verified. The verification process may be waived on certain loans, depending on the loan amount and down payment. When this happens, the loan is called a low documentation loan.

Appraisal

Lenders require an appraisal on all home sales. This step could kill a deal if a big discrepancy were to exist between the loan amount and the appraised value of the house. Some lenders use their own staff appraisers and some hire a "Fee for Service" appraiser.

Title Search

This is the time when any liens against the property are discovered. A lien may have been placed against a property by the Internal Revenue Service, court approved judgments, or to secure loans by the seller. All liens must be cleared by the seller before a transaction can be completed.

Pest Inspection

Most loans require an inspection for pest and water damage. Some problems, such as pest infestation, may need to be repaired *before* finalizing the sale.

Processor's Review

Based on the information put together by both the loan representative and the processor, the underwriter makes the final decision on whether or not a loan is granted. Lenders are looking for borrowers who will make their payments on time and for property that will cover the loan amount borrowed, in the event a buyer defaults.

Approval, Denial, or Counter

To approve a loan, the lender may ask the borrowers to put more money down to improve the debt-to-income ratio. The borrower may also need a bigger down payment if the property appraises for less than the loan amount. In some cases, repairs or improvements to the property may be required before the lender will fund (see escrow holdbacks in Chapter 4).

Signing

Final loan documents are signed.

Funding

The lender sends the loan documents to the settlement agent or escrow company. Buyer and seller sign that all conditions have been met and the transaction closes.

Final recording at the county records office completes the sale.

TYPES OF MORTGAGES

Before the deregulation of mortgage banking in the early 1980s, the choice of mortgages was limited to conventional, FHA, VA, and whether you wanted a 15- or 30-year term. Today's market has so many possibilities that the mortgage salespeople have trouble keeping current with the ever changing options.

The one significant change in options is the adjustable rate mortgage or ARM. The interest varies over the term of the mortgage. This is the basis for many other forms of mortgages available today. It is not the purpose of this book to describe the many types of variable or adjustable rate mortgages, but you should be aware of the choices; the advantages or disadvantages of each depends on the application of a particular mortgage to the specific deal or set of circumstances. We in the rehab field will choose adjustable rate mortgages over fixed rate, because ARMs offer assumable financing to our new buyer (see Chapter 4 for exceptions) and offer us the lowest starting interest rates.

If you plan to sell your rehab project in a year or less, the out-of-pocket costs may be the most significant terms of a mortgage. If you plan to hold a property for cash flow over several years, a lower average monthly payment may be the benefit you seek in a mortgage. Develop a general knowledge of the basic types of mortgages and seek the one that best applies to your current project. You will soon discover that the market changes from month to month and that new mortgage products are continually emerging.

Alternative to Bank Financing

In spite of the wide variety of available types of mortgages, there are many occasions, particularly in rehab properties, where bank financing is not available. The reason for lack of financing may lie in the condition of the property or the condition of your financial position. Should you find yourself unable to secure a mortgage by traditional means, and you feel the project is worth pursuing, there are several alternatives. Owner financing, lease options, shared equity, and partnerships are some solutions to consider. Each of these is covered in detail in Chapter 4.

PURCHASE OFFERS

The purchase of real property often involves a large number of payments and transfers. The parties involved in the transfer of title (buyer and seller) must agree on the conditions and terms of each item in advance. In order to ensure a smooth process, a contract known as a *purchase offer* or *contract of sale* is created. It is the most important document involved in the sale; it defines the terms and contents of all the other documents in the transaction.

Your city or town will have a preprinted form that has been drawn up by the local real estate board and/or bar association. The form specifies all the standard items according to local custom and provides spaces for selections of items that relate specifically to your transaction.

Once the offer is signed by both parties, the document becomes a legally binding contract and the terms are fixed from this point on. Both parties should therefore make sure that all the conditions stated in the offer meet individual needs.

The importance of this purchase contract cannot be overstated. Courts will consider this document legally binding should a dispute arise later on. In some states, real estate contracts now contain an arbitration clause to avoid costly litigation over purchase contract disputes. The document utilized in this arbitration process is the purchase contract.

Since this document should be what *you* would like the terms to be in this business transaction, you should not allow the real estate agent to write the document without your specific input. You may also want to add some special agreements, known as *contingencies*, to your offer, to protect your deposit or earnest money.

The contingencies are written into the offer as "subject to" clauses, including:

- Subject to a termite report and repair estimate provided by the seller within xx number of days of acceptance of the offer.

- Subject to very specific financing that you have researched as appropriate to the profitability of this project. Please be as specific as possible, for example, "Subject to buyer obtaining an FHA 203(k) loan at 10.5% interest with discount points not to exceed 2.25%." This statement means that if the specific loan you need for the rehab, the interest rate on that loan, or the discount points change, it is your option to remain in the transaction or withdraw with your deposit monies intact.

- Subject to an appraisal value by the lender equal to the sales price you are agreeing on. Not all purchase offer forms commonly utilized by the real estate community have this buyer protection clause. What if the appraisal comes in $3,000 less than the sales price you have agreed upon? Do not assume that you are then out of the contract. You should never *assume* anything in real estate transactions. The old adage that an ounce of prevention is worth a pound of cure is a very true one.

- Subject to a property inspection report with a repair estimate not to exceed xx amount of dollars. You will need to have this estimate prepared and the property inspected within the time period you specify in the contract. It needs to be done by a neutral third party, so that the seller will see the objectivity of this request and accept this contingency. Property inspections, as we will cover in more detail in the next section, are a cost borne by the buyer and are a cost of doing business. You may be requesting the repair estimate as an added service of the property inspector and should allow for this additional expense. Average fees vary in different parts of the country, but a range of $125 to $300 fee is reasonable. An obvious question that might arise is, "If contractors provide bids without charge, then why request one as an added service of the property inspector?" The answer is that you will need realistic rehab estimates from professionals who are "arm's length from the job." It is considered a conflict of interest for property inspectors who are members of the American Society of Home Inspection to inspect and then bid on a job.

- Just as an appraiser offers the fair market value to the lender, the impartial repair estimate sets the fair market value of the rehab work needed.

HOME INSPECTION REPORTS

It is becoming more and more common for purchasers of homes to request an inspection of the property by a professional home inspection service. In dealing with properties that are in need of rehab work, it makes sense to include this as a contingency in the purchase offer. There are levels of expertise in those that do inspections. It has become popular for inspection companies to use computer software to produce a well-organized, professional looking report. However, the value of the report is not in its appearance, but in the knowledge and experience of its preparer. Some franchised inspection companies do not have inspectors with backgrounds that match the level of sophistication necessary to evaluate rehab properties. It is a good idea to check the individual credentials of the inspector who will be evaluating your property. If you suspect any structural problems, you would certainly want a person with an engineering background. When using this service, there is no saving gained by shopping for bargain rates.

In addition to the points shown in the detailed home evaluation report on page 200, inspection services will also check and evaluate appliances, mechanicals, paint conditions, and floor coverings. Keep in mind that the report will not comment on quality. Inspectors will judge the conditions and possibly the remaining useful life of items.

An inspection will usually take about an hour. It is a good idea for you to be at the site at the time of the inspection and to accompany the inspector room-by-room. Ask questions about things you see; many inspectors will give you tips on maintenance if you ask. A written report will follow the inspection, usually within a few days. Inspectors know they must be prompt in filing their report since a delay or bad report can kill a deal.

Requesting a realistic rehab plan as an additional service of the inspection will include completing the description of materials and cost breakdown (see Chapter 6 for model documents) for the supplemental fee. This plan will give you the set of standards and scope of work to use when obtaining your bids. You thus ensure your contractor bids will be "apples to apples." We will discuss more about this in Chapter 2.

RECAP OF PURCHASE PROCESS

Purchase Contract

The purchase offer does the following:

1. Binds two or more parties to a set of terms (contract)
2. Defines and specifies the terms:
   a. Description of the property
   b. Price
   c. Finances
   d. Inclusions (physical parts)

3. Itemizes responsibilities of both parties, that is, clear title, **deed,** survey, deposits, insurance, and proration of tax bill
4. Specifies timing of conditions of sale (contingencies)
5. Sets final dates for:
   a. Life of the offer
   b. Financing commitments
   c. Sale of contingent properties
   d. Inspection reports
   e. Possession by new owner

Prior to presenting the sellers with a purchase offer, consider the following questions:

1. Is it a fair offer?
2. Are the buyers willing to pay more? Are they prepared for a counter offer?
3. Have offers been made by other buyers?
4. How long has the house been on the market?
5. How much activity has the market experienced?
6. Why are the sellers interested in selling?
7. Why might sellers reject an offer? (Anticipate seller rejection.)

TRADITIONALLY NEGOTIABLE ITEMS

Although everything in an offer to purchase is technically negotiable, there are only certain categories of items that present opportunities for negotiation. In other words, you *can* offer a camel valued at $23,000 as a down payment on the seller's house, but for all practical purposes, a reduced amount of U.S. currency has a greater probability for success.

In the offer to purchase, the buyer can reasonably be expected to request:

- *Amount of deposit money.* The amount of earnest money (deposit) that accompanies the offer.

The choice of services varies from area to area of the country, but a buyer will usually choose the:

- *Title insurance company.* If one has been helping you or your agent in researching properties, you may wish to request that company. The service from one company to another and the price differential are very small. If the listing agent balks at your request to use a particular company, let it go. It is not worth the bad feelings that might ensue should the listing agent feel it is a "professional prerogative" to name the company for this service.

- *Escrow companies or settlement agents in mortgage states.* There can be an advantage to allowing the listing agent to recommend this neutral party to the transaction, although you can request a particular one if you wish. The standard statement in the industry is that an escrow company only gets one chance to screw up an agent's transaction, and never gets another; therefore, agents will steer you to one that has a good performance record. Their income (commission check) depends on it.

- *Financing.* This is always the buyer's choice; however, we will discuss in later chapters how you as the seller of your rehab projects will want to put performance deadlines on the buyer's choice of lender as a way of keeping control of your project's profit.

- *Personal property and fixtures.* For a clear definition of the distinction between these two, ask your real estate agent. Specify, clearly and in writing, the exact item you are requesting and the sales price. More transactions have failed over the status of who owned the chandelier in the hall than any real estate agent would care to recall. An equally important rehab issue that often gets overlooked is specifying what you wish removed from the property prior to the close of the transaction. In one case, recently, there was a dispute over a seller's unwanted storage items in the garage. It came up as an eleventh-hour potential deal killer because the new owner wanted to rent out the garage immediately as a source of supplemental income. The seller said he was unaware he was to have removed the "trash" in the garage.

- *Length of the escrow.* As you become more and more successful and have more projects running concurrently, you'll be getting advice from your accountant with respect to the timing for property exchanges and closings. At the end of the year, from Thanksgiving to January 1st, the escrow, title, insurance, and settlement agents are flooded with those needing to sell or purchase before year-end deadlines change the tax liability of their projects. Timing is profit and you need to specify the time needed to obtain complex rehab loans, and your own cash flow projections, so that funds are available to close on the date you have specified. Build in the delays that occur when at least 18 hands and three to four professions are involved, as is the case in the typical real estate transaction.

- *Real estate disclosure information.* This area is changing rapidly. In California, the requirements for disclosure of what the seller knows to be defects in the property, along with about a dozen other areas of agent disclosure to the buyer, pretty much take care of this issue for you. In other states, there are varying degrees of the policy of "as is" property. This ties in closely with your need to know if "let the buyer beware" is the operating phrase in your real estate market. Request as much information from the seller as you can in the offer to purchase. Rumor has it that the wave of the future is in consumer protection legislation requiring more seller disclosure to the buyer, and new laws are wending their way through various state legislatures.

But aren't you going to be a future seller also? Yes, and that is another reason to think through the corrections needed on a project. Remember that you will have to disclose how you corrected those problems later. The seller who tells you there is a "hairline crack" in the poured slab foundation, which they have repaired with Mastik (thick, white caulking), is telling you that your liability is heightened if you innocently repeat the "crack is repaired" story to your new buyer.

COUNTER OFFERS

Some people in rehab have this business philosophy: they make their first offer at a "steal this house" price, knowing that unless lightning has just impaired the facilities of the seller, they will get a counter offer. Then they will raise their hand a little, and the seller will come down a little, and finally, when their agent has run through the tread on a set of tires, they will get the house at somewhere near the price they wanted. My recommendation to clients who insist that playing "low ball" is the only way they want to play the offer/counter offer game, is to consider instead a career in import/export with third world countries, where the bartering game has been raised to an art form. How can I make any money if I don't get the house at a price significantly lower than they are asking? There is no doubt that "buying low and selling high" is a great way to make money in real estate. But it is best applied to real estate market cycles rather than individual profitability of rehab projects. My suggestion is that we stop here and step for a moment into the seller's mindset. Let's look at what the barriers to be overcome are, and what approach we can take that helps a seller say yes to us the first (or at least the second) time we make an offer.

There are distressed sellers and distressed properties, and our best chance to create the "win-win" of a quick yes to our offer is to find the combination of both.

Typical distressed seller situations are divorce, illness or death of a family member, loss of a job, or business failure. These sellers need very quick transactions and may or may not want to "barter" on the price. The circumstances of the sale is information you should have before you make your first offer; use it to guide you on how much counter offering these sellers are open to. If the real estate market is very active, they may refuse your offer and wait for the next without even countering. In a soft real estate market, they may tend to take a reasonable reduction in price to accommodate their need for a quick sale.

Typical situations that have created distressed property include long-time rental properties that have been abused by tenants, elderly owners who have not had the resources or strength to keep up the maintenance, homeowners who have created a distressed property while attempting to improve it themselves, and those that just do not value their home and so allow it to deteriorate. The reason the property has deteriorated will tell you a lot about the seller's motivation and flexibility. For example, if the seller just wants to be out of the landlord business, this is an anxious and motivated seller who can't move another renter into the "trashed" property and has to keep up the mortgage payments while it is for sale. Elderly owners may have accumulated more in equity build-up than they imagined and feel they are getting adequate compensation when you offer them less than full price. They also are usually motivated to sell because they are planning a major life change and wish to get on with that move.

Each situation calls for evaluation, and a straight formula of always offering 20% less than the asking price may or may not work. In a "seller's market," this approach can actually mean that you lose good deals. Multiple offers on good projects within the first week a property is on the market are not unusual in an active market.

When you become the seller of your project, it will also help to think through the bottom-line price you need to make your profit, and price the property very close to it. This is known as "wholesaling" the project, and is a very effective sales technique.

An example of this may be:

$100,000 average asking price for property similar to yours (within the same neighborhood).

To make $15,000 you need a sales price of $85,000.

Price property at $85,000. Advertise with *firm price, need fast sale.*

You'll get more offers and sell more quickly than the $100,000 property that eventually gets a lower offer, with multiple counter offers, and sells at $92,500. You have saved money that would have been eaten up in monthly mortgage payments on a vacant house (carrying charges) and eliminated the time-consuming counter offer process. Profits in flipping depend on a quick sale of the finished project. The profit is in the timing!

Acceptance of a Counter Offer

The counter offer should specify a time period during which the other party must accept, reject, or again counter the counter offer. Unless one of these actions is taken during that time, the counter offer terminates by expiration of the time period.

The counter offer usually calls for acceptance only by personal delivery of the signed form to the offering party (the sellers in a counter offer) or to the party's agent. After initiating the counter offer, the sellers retain the right to accept other offers (or to otherwise revoke the counter offer) at any time before the personal return of the signed form. This process of formal acceptance may vary slightly, but you need to understand that there is still a window period during counter offers in which the property could be lost to another buyer.

Once the buyers sign and deliver the counter offer form to the sellers or the listing agent in the specified manner, a binding contract is created. The sellers do not have the right to reconsider the offer's terms and you have now "tied the property up."

THE CLOSING PROCEDURE

When there is a neutral third party whose responsibility is to coordinate the activities of the transaction, the process is called *closing*. That third party typically takes the form of an escrow company who specializes in the process. In mortgage states (generally those on the East Coast), attorneys are retained by buyer and seller. Each attorney represents his or her client in completing their respective obligations to the offer.

The final procedure in a real estate transaction is the closing or settlement. The two terms represent the same procedure but differ in the manner in which the process is completed. Typically, states that employ trust deeds close via escrow or title companies. Mortgage states use attorneys or settlement agents and call the procedure settlement. In either case, the purpose is to disburse the funds and to execute all the documents called for in the purchase offer under the terms of the contract to purchase.

Procedures and Steps in Closing the Transaction

Although the escrow customs practiced in various states differ in some ways, the essential purpose of the services is the same: to assist all parties in carrying out the provisions of the contract efficiently, safely, and confidentially. Some procedures that must be completed before closing include:

1. Ordering the title search and preliminary title report on the property. (Generally, a report should be received within one week of acceptance of the offer.)

2. Requesting demands and/or beneficiary statements from the lenders in conjunction with any current loans.
3. Collecting and holding structural & pest control reports required in the transaction.
4. Accepting new loan instructions and documents.
5. Accepting fire insurance policies and settlement calculations.
6. Requesting closing funds.
7. Ordering recording of ownership change and financial instruments.
8. Auditing file to determine that each side is in position to close.
9. Preparing settlement statements for buyers and sellers and disbursing funds.

Signing the Listing Agreement (Sellers)

A real estate sales transaction generally begins at the time a seller signs a listing agreement with a real estate agent.

Intended as a legally binding contract, the agreement specifies the terms of sale and grants the broker authorization to publish the information with the multiple listing service (MLS). The listing form also covers obligations such as the broker's compensation, the acquisition of title insurance in trust deed states, requirements for furnishing a "Structural Pest Control Report," and the seller's and agent's respective disclosure obligations.

Listing Agent's Disclosure Duty

The following applies in *some states only,* at this time. New legislation in this area is pending in several states. The listing agent has two main areas requiring disclosure:

In general, the law requires one who acts as a real estate licensee in applicable transactions to provide written disclosures to both the buyers and sellers of the nature of the agency relationship.

Agency relationships define who is representing whom in that transaction. The listing agent must provide this disclosure form to the sellers before entering into a sales contract. There has been confusion on the part of consumers as to who is representing whom; this is meant to clarify that concern.

The primary purpose of this disclosure process is to help consumers and licensees avoid undisclosed dual agency problems that sometimes occur when an agent represents more than one party (known as the principal) in dealings with third persons in selling, buying, exchanging, or leasing real estate. Therefore, this disclosure should be made early in the transaction.

Documents the Seller Needs to Provide

1. The latest available tax and assessment bills and any other statements or bills that are to be prorated through escrow.
2. Seller's loan payment books and records. (The seller should let the escrow officer know if the mortgage is an existing FHA or VA loan.)
3. Seller's fire, liability, and other insurance policies, if they are to be assigned to the buyer.
4. As required by escrow instructions, a beneficiary statement, demand, certificate, or offset statement from the holder of any mortgage or trust deed of record on the property. (This statement includes the balance due on any existing liens against the particular property being purchased.)
5. List of names of any tenants and the units they occupy, together with the amount of rent paid and unpaid, the dates rents are due, and, if required, an assignment to buyer of any unpaid rent, and details on advance security deposits, if any.
6. An executed bill of sale covering any personal property to be conveyed to the buyer, together with an inventory for buyer's approval.
7. The deed by which seller acquired title to the property and seller's policy of title insurance.
8. Any unrecorded instruments affecting the title, including any extension agreements.
9. Any other documents or instruments which the seller is to prepare or deliver.
10. Any approvals required for documents the seller is to receive at closing.

Documents Requiring Review and Approval by the Buyer

1. Review the preliminary title report for the subject real property to ensure that items of record related to the property have been approved by the buyer.
2. Review any covenants, conditions, and restrictions affecting the property, whether of record or not.
3. Confirm terms of any mortgages or deeds of trust to be assumed by buyer or remaining as an encumbrance on the property.
4. Examine any beneficiary statements, fire insurance, or liability policies assigned to the buyer. (If the buyer must obtain new fire insurance, he or she should act immediately. Late ordering and/or deposit to escrow of fire insurance policies are among the most common causes for delayed closing.)
5. Examine offset (balance) statements on loans to be assumed or under whose terms the buyer is taking title to the property.

6. Review and approve structural pest control and other reports to be delivered through escrow or settlement agents.

7. Carefully review all new loan documents before signing them. (Most people skip this important step.)

8. Compare the terms of the purchase contract, escrow instructions, title report, and deed to make sure transaction documents contain no discrepancies.

9. Examine the bill of sale and inventory covering the items of personal property to be conveyed to the purchaser.

10. Review copies of any bills to be prorated in the closing statement.

11. Verify all amounts and prorations on the estimated escrow settlement sheet.

12. Reinspect the property to determine that it is in the same condition as when previously viewed by the buyer at the time the offer to purchase was made; recheck property for any undisclosed items that might affect the use of the property.

13. Deposit sufficient cash or clear funds to cover any balance owing on the purchase contract plus any buyer's closing costs and expenses, and approvals as required.

These tasks are not all-inclusive, and buyers and sellers may have other lists of their own. Constant checking on steps in the closing process is the key to a smooth transaction.

Under the Real Estate Settlement Procedures Act (RESPA), in transactions involving federally related first-mortgage loans for one to four family dwellings, both the buyers and sellers must be furnished with a "uniform settlement statement." This disclosure provides a financial accounting of all the costs incurred during escrow, including those charges that must be paid in cash. Therefore, preparation of accurate settlement statements is one of the major tasks of escrow companies and settlement agents.

Although some costs may be negotiable between the buyers and sellers, the division of items for which the principals are responsible is often as follows:

- *Sellers' charges.* Sellers are usually responsible for payments related to: drawing the deed, obtaining the reconveyance deed, payment of the owner's title policy, escrow services, notary fees, recording reconveyance, documenting transfer taxes, and other agreed-on charges. Adjustments between sellers and buyers may include: tax debts, improvement assessment debts, liens or judgments to clear title, broker's commission, prepaid rents, deposits, taxes, insurance, and interest. Also, unless agreed on in advance, interest-bearing debts are accrued up to the date of settlement and constitute a charge against the sellers.

- *Buyers' charges.* Buyers are usually responsible for payments related to: standard or lender's title policy in some areas, and inspection fees, drawing second mortgage (if ordered), escrow services, notary fees, inspection fees, interest on new loan (from date of closing to first monthly payment due), appraisal and credit check fees, assumption fees, and fire insurance premium, one-year prepaid, if applicable.

Adjustments between buyers and sellers may include reimbursements for prepaid taxes, insurance, improvement assessment, and prepaid impounds (if buyers assume a loan), and possible occupancy adjustments.

"Hidden costs" may appear on the lender's "truth in lending" statement. Lenders are also obliged to disclose to borrowers the annual percentage rate on the cost of financing the purchase of residential property.

The calculation of APR, or annual percentage rate, will show up about 5 days after you apply for a loan. The APR interest rate will NOT BE the same rate quoted by the loan representative or mortgage broker. That is because lenders' charges, such as application fees, origination fees, private mortgage insurance costs, document drawing fees, and so on, all get folded into the loan amount borrowed and then that total is divided by 360 payments (for a 30-year mortgage) and will equal out to a higher annual percentage rate.

INSURANCE

Insurance is one of the more confusing areas. Even the seasoned buyer may not fully understand what these policies cover and do not cover. In all of the policy types listed below, the buyer and sometimes the seller are paying the cost of the insurance.

Type of Policy: Private Mortgage Insurance
Party Covered: Lender
Who Pays: Buyer

Private mortgage insurance (PMI), very simplistically explained, buys down the lender's exposure or risk to about 78% of the value of the property, in cases where the buyer has put down 10% or less in down payment. The buyer pays for 16 months of premiums in cash at closing. This usually can add up to a larger up-front cash expense and should be reviewed to see if application of that same money to the down payment accumulated can avoid the need for PMI. When an FHA loan is used, this is the same role FHA plays in enabling the borrower to get in with less than a 5% (estimated) down payment. This insurance in FHA loans is called mutual mortgage insurance, or MMIP.

Type of Policy: Hazard Insurance
Party Covered: Lender and Buyer
Who Pays: Buyer

Fire, damage to the structure from natural disasters, and other types of destruction protection, are covered in this policy. These are issued by most major insurance companies to the buyer, with the lender as the "loss-payee." I think the term is self-explanatory; the lender and buyer will be reimbursed should the security for the loan, that is, the house, be destroyed. Buyers should understand what types of coverage best protect their interest and the lenders', before purchasing this coverage.

Type of Policy: Credit Life Insurance
Party Covered: Buyer and Heirs
Who Pays: Buyer

This totally optional life insurance policy on the life of the buyer or buyers of the property pays off the mortgage in the event of the early death of one of them. It will be offered to the buyer customarily sometime in the first month after the transaction has closed and payments have begun. It is an option that the buyer can elect or not, depending on personal financial planning philosophy.

Type of Policy: Title Insurance
Party Covered: Lender or Lender and Buyer
Who Pays: Seller or Seller and Buyer

The use of title insurance in real estate is to protect or ensure that the title to the property that the seller is offering is "clear." Basic title insurance is customarily purchased by the seller for the buyer's protection and, indirectly, for the lender's. However, this is not quite as simple as it would seem. Various types of coverage are available that cover the lender's interest in the property, or the lender's and the buyer's equity (down payment and costs) in the property. Within these two categories of coverage, the list of what problems are being insured against varies significantly. (Get a pamphlet from your local real estate agent to familiarize yourself with these options; they differ from one part of the country to another.) As an about-to-be-professional real estate investor, you'll want to be sure to avoid the trap of "assuming" you are covered, which, unfortunately, many first-time buyers fall into. Title insurance is purchased in a lump-sum premium and is in effect until you resell the property to a new buyer. As a professional "flipping" properties or re-selling them within 5 years, look into the significant cost reductions available to you by purchasing short-term binders or discounts on title insurance when purchased from the same company during a 3- to 5-year period (short-term policy). One such policy is the American Land Title Association–Residential (ALTA–R). A list of title defects that it covers follows; use it to compare coverage of these issues in the policies available to you.

Common title defects you need to be protected from include:

- Someone else owns an undisclosed interest in your property.
- A document in the transfer process was not properly signed.
- Signatures on documents of transfer were obtained by fraud, duress, or forgery.
- Any of the legal documents were recorded incorrectly.
- The property has restrictive covenants that were not revealed to you when you purchased the property.
- Liens, judgments, special assessments, or charges by a homeowners' association are unresolved.
- Mechanic's liens that you may become responsible for as the new owner are outstanding.
- Unrecorded lease or lease option rights to the property affect your title.
- There are unrecorded easements on the property.
- Buildings on the land are found to be encroaching on an adjoining parcel. Replacement or removal may be required to correct.
- There are violations of current zoning laws (happens often when previous owner has turned a single-family into a duplex when zoning allows single family only).
- Policy coverage available to investors should cover all matters not disclosed in a survey, and should pay rent when substitute facilities or land are needed during resolution of any of the above issues.
- There are complications such as hidden marriages, chain of title errors due to similarity of names, previous invalid court proceedings, and errors in wills.

How often do any of these things appear in the transfers? More often than you can imagine which is why title insurance is a must.

CLOSING COSTS

As a seller or a buyer, there are a number of costs associated with the items we have described in the closing process. Table 1.4 will assist you in estimating your transaction costs. Table 1.5 is a filled-out version of Table 1.4.

Table 1.4   Buyer's Approximate Estimated Closing Costs

Application Fee	_____
Loan Orignination Fee _____%	_____
Commitment Fee _____%	_____
Mortgage Insurance Initial Premium (if lender requires)	_____ (1%) (PMI)
(MIP) = .038	_____
Homeowner's Insurance (1 year)	_____ $5/$1000
Interest from closing to 1st of month	_____
Attorney's Fee (Bank)	_____
Title Insurance	_____
Recording Fees (deed, mortgage, transfer, riders)	_____
Mortgage Tax	_____
Subtotal	_____
Estimated tax escrow (12 months)	_____
Attorney (yours)	_____
Total	_____

Approximate Monthly Payments

Principal and Interest	_____
Taxes ($^1/_{12}$)	_____
Insurance ($^1/_{12}$)	_____
PMI (.0025) × mortgage amount (if required)	_____
Total	_____

As a rehab/resale investor, please remember that you will have buyer costs and resale (seller's) closing costs, so it is recommended that you ask for as many closing costs as possible to be paid by the person you are initially purchasing from, to lower your overall closing costs.

A sample of typical buyer (cash) closing cost items is shown in Table 1.5.

OWNERSHIP OPTIONS

Real estate ownership has many forms. The particular form of vesting of title chosen will have several legal implications. The rights of the owner that are influenced by the type of title have to do with his or her ability to

**Table 1.5   Example: Buyer's Approximate Estimated Closing Costs
(For a $100,000 House with 10% Down)**

Application Fee	$200–$300
Loan Origination Fee _____%	Points quoted by lender
Commitment Fee _____%	Varies—pd to bank if required
Mortgage Insurance Initial Premium (if lender requires)	$900 _____ (1%) (PMI)
(MIP) = .038 of mortgage	$3,420
Homeowner's Insurance (1 year)	$450 _____ $5/$1000
Interest from closing to 1st of month	Varies
Attorney's Fee (Bank)	$500–$700
Title Insurance	$350 approximately
Recording Fees (deed, mortgage, transfer, riders)	$50 approximately
Mortgage Tax	Varies
Subtotal	
Estimated tax escrow (12 months)	May or may not be required
Attorney (yours)	$450–$700
Total	

Approximate Monthly Payments

Principal and Interest	
Taxes ($1/12$)	
Insurance ($1/12$)	
PMI (.0025) × mortgage amount (if required)	
Total	

sell in relation to others who may also be on the deed, or to whom the ownership passes in the event of the death of an owner.

Lenders, especially rehab lenders, are set up to make loans to individual borrowers. You certainly should ask your accountant and attorney about all the advantages of partnership agreements and forming Subchapter S corporations. However, starting out, you will have more choices of loan programs if you are an individual borrower or co-borrower with another individual.

Table 1.6 is a chart detailing the rights of each party for most of the available choices in ownership types. In order to be sure you have chosen the form that best suits your needs, you should consult an attorney who can advise you on the full implications of each choice.

Table 1.6 Concurrent Co-Ownership Interests*

	Tenancy in Common	Joint Tenancy	Community Property	Tenancy in Partnership
Parties	Any number of persons (can be husband and wife).	Any number of persons (can be husband and wife).	Only husband and wife.	Only partners (any number).
Division	Ownership can be divided into any number of interests equal or unequal.	Ownership interests must be equal.	Ownership and managerial interest are equal except control of business is solely with managing spouse.	Ownership interest is in relation interest in partnership.
Title	Each co-owner has a separate legal title to his or her undivided interest.	There is only one title to the whole property.	Title is in the "community." Each interest is separate but management is united.	Title is in the "partnership."
Possession	Equal right of possession.	Equal right of possession.	Both co-owners have equal management and control.	Equal right of possession but only for partnership purposes.
Conveyance	Each co-owner's interest may be conveyed separately by its owner.	Conveyance by one co-owner without the others breaks the joint tenancy.	Personal property (except necessaries) may be conveyed for valuable consideration without consent of other spouse, real property requires written consent of other spouse, and separate interest cannot be conveyed except upon death.	Any authorized partner may convey whole partnership property. No partner may sell his or her interest in the partnership without the consent of co-partners.
Purchaser's Status	Purchaser will become a tenant in common with the other co-owners in the property.	Purchaser will become a tenant in common with the other co-owners in the property.	Purchaser can only acquire whole title of community, cannot acquire a part of it.	Purchaser can only acquire the whole title.

38

Death	On co-owner's death, his or her interest passes by will to devisees or heirs. No survivorship right.	On co-owner's death, his or her interest ends and cannot be disposed of by will. Survivor owns the property by survivorship.	On co-owner's death, 1/2 belongs to survivor in severalty. 1/2 goes by will to decedent's devisees or by succession to survivor.	On partner's death, his or her partnership interest passes to the surviving partner pending liquidation of the partnership. Share of deceased partner then goes to his or her estate.
Successor's Status	Devisees or heirs become tenants in common.	Last survivor owns property in severalty.	If passing by will, tenancy in common between devisee and survivor results.	Heirs or devisees have rights in partnership interest but not in specific property.
Creditor's Rights	Co-owner's interest may be sold on execution sale to satisfy a creditor. Creditor becomes a tenant in common.	Co-owner's interest may be sold on execution sale to satisfy creditor. Joint tenancy is broken, creditor becomes tenant in common.	Property of community is liable for contracts of either spouse which are made after marriage prior to or after January 1, 1975. Co-owner's interest can't be sold separately, whole property may be sold on execution to satisfy creditor.	Partner's interest cannot be seized or sold separately by a personal creditor but share of profits may be obtained by a personal creditor. Whole property may be sold on execution sale to satisfy partnership creditor.
Presumption	Favored in doubtful cases except husband and wife case.	Must be expressly stated. Not favored.	Strong presumption that property acquired by husband and wife is community.	Arises only by virtue of partnership status in property placed in partnership title.

*This list is given for informational purposes only. Please check with an attorney in your local area before deciding the method of holding title.

2

Beginning Your Own Game Plan

START TO ASSEMBLE YOUR TEAM

You have now been through the basic steps and met the players involved in the real estate process. Armed with that knowledge, you are now ready to put together your action plan. Implementing step one includes locating a real estate agent for your team. I am often asked:

> How do I find a "good" agent? Do I really need an agent involved? Can't I find properties without one?
>
> Don't I pay more for the property because I'm using an agent? Can't I negotiate a better price without one?

I usually answer questions like these without my real estate hat on and say that, as a smart consumer, you should utilize the resources of the system.

How Do I Find a "Good" Agent?

The same way you find "good" employees. You interview a number of agents and ask for names of clients that they have helped to locate "fixer" properties. Ask if they are familiar with the more sophisticated rehab financing programs (they should show interest in learning, if they do not already know of them), and, most important of all, they should demonstrate, in that first face-to-face session with you, that they can *listen*. Not just give lip service while they are pulling out the Multiple Listing Book, but *listen.* They should ask intelligent questions about your plans and goals, write down information as you are talking to them, and allow you to talk. The skill of "active listening" is the key to building a successful business relationship with anyone, particularly real estate agents. If they want to "throw you in the back of the car" and start driving you to see their listings during that first meeting, they probably have not really heard anything you have said.

Interviewing an Agent—General Questions

To help you compare real estate agents and choose the right one, you'll need to ask about each one's experience and performance level. Whether you're buying or selling, ask at least some of the following questions:

- Are you a licensed broker or agent?
- How long have you been in the business?
- Are you a member of the Multiple Listing Service?
- Have you earned any professional real estate designations?
- What professional courses, seminars, conventions, or training sessions have you recently attended?
- How long have you actively worked in this area or neighborhood?
- How many fixers have you sold?
- How many home sales have you closed in the past 3 months?
- Do you work as a full-time real estate professional?
- What are the names of three reference clients?

It's important to find out more about the real estate company by asking the agent the following questions:

- How long has your company been in business?
- What is the average number of years each agent has been with the company?
- How many agents work for the company?
- Does the company participate in a cooperative listing service, such as the Multiple Listing Service (MLS)?
- Does the company have a relocation division or regularly work with out-of-towners and transferees?
- Will someone be available at all reasonable hours to show my home to prospective buyers? (If you're buying, ask whether the

agent will be available to show you homes at the times most convenient to you.)

Researching Your Area with the Help of an Agent

The research needed to choose your project comes in two forms.

1. The "windshield survey." You drive through a neighborhood you may wish to select, to get your own "gut" feeling of how comfortable you are in that neighborhood. It is very important, even if you

**Table 2.1   An Area Market Survey
Performed by a Real Estate Agent**

Function? AMS (Area Market Survey)
Property Type? 1
Area(s)? 115
List/Sale Price (Range)?
Enter additional search parameters
    ?BR = 2
    ?BA = 1
    ?

Active Listings

List Price Range	No. of Listings	Average Days on Market
$1– $159,999	5	54
$160,000–$199,999	24	66
$200,000–$249,999	13	53
$250,000–$299,999	1	73
$300,000–$349,999		
$350,000–$399,999		
$400,000–$449,999		
$450,000–$499,999		
$500,000–$549,999		
$550,000–$599,999		
$600,000–$649,999		
$650,000–$699,999		
$700,000–$799,999		
$800,000–$899,999		
$900,000–$999,999		
$1,000,000 and over		

The average price for the 43 properties is $152,119.
The HIGHEST price is $219,500.
The LOWEST price is $103,900.
The average market time is 56 DAYS.

Table 2.1 *(Continued)*

Pending Listings

List Price Range	No. of Listings	Average Days on Market
$1– $159,999	1	85
$160,000–$199,999	11	50
$200,000–$249,999	3	21
$250,000–$299,999		
$300,000–$349,999		
$350,000–$399,999		
$400,000–$449,999		
$450,000–$499,999		
$500,000–$549,999		
$550,000–$599,999		
$600,000–$649,999		
$650,000–$699,999		
$700,000–$799,999		
$800,000–$899,999		
$900,000–$999,999		
$1,000,000 and over		

The average price for the 15 properties is $141,613.
The HIGHEST price is $179,000.
The LOWEST price is $115,000.
The average market time is 46 DAYS.

Sold Listings

List Price Range	No. of Listings	Average Days on Market
$1– $159,999	18	42
$160,000–$199,999	86	49
$200,000–$249,999	20	61
$250,000–$299,999	3	30
$300,000–$349,999		
$350,000–$399,999		
$400,000–$449,999		
$450,000–$499,999		
$500,000–$549,999		
$550,000–$599,999		
$600,000–$649,999		
$650,000–$699,999		
$700,000–$799,999		
$800,000–$899,999		
$900,000–$999,999		
$1,000,000 and over		

The average price for the 127 properties is $141,797.
The HIGHEST price is $225,000.
The LOWEST price is $104,000.
The average market time is 50 DAYS.

AREA MARKET STUDY COMPLETE

are going to turn a property over right away, to be comfortable working in the neighborhood.

2. "Hard data" research is provided by your agent in the form of: (a) an area market survey (Table 2.1) and (b) comparable data on recently sold property (within the past 6 months), called a comparable market analysis.

These data are used to establish the highest price point at which you can put your finished rehab on the market and to compare your project with other "like kind" properties in the area, to establish its potential resale price.

This survey information is available only to licensed real estate salespeople through a network of shared information called the Multiple Listing Service (MLS). Your individual agent will compile these data and then review and analyze them with you.

The next area of information agents can provide relates to the "soft data" of buyer perceptions of areas you are considering selecting. In real estate, the perception of a neighborhood can become the self-fulfilling prophecy of what happens in sales activity in that neighborhood. An example of this would be: if most buyers perceive that an area south of the Interstate is high crime, that becomes the negative image you will have to sell against when you market a completed rehab project there.

WHAT KINDS OF PROPERTIES DO YOU WANT?

Before you go out with your new agent to look at properties, you need to establish what you want. The properties you will seek will include one or more of the following set of circumstances:

Priced below market value (or can be obtained at lower than market value)

Has favorable financing available (already has assumable loan or seller may carry financing)

Contains solvable problems

The worst house in the best area you can afford

A distressed or very motivated seller

Although it is unlikely you will find any one property that has all of the above situations, the more it has, the better. On the other hand, some excellent profits have been made on properties that had only one of these qualifiers but to a high degree.

The owners are highly motivated to sell:

    Moving out of state

    Divorce

    Baby on the way

    Overextended financially

    Death in family

    Inheritance

    Promotion

The property is undesirable to buyers (at this time) for acceptable reasons including:

    Floor plan too small for most families

    Outdated facilities

    General or specific worn-out parts

    Poor curb appeal

    Poor decorating choices

    House is just ordinary—has no appeal

    One or more major items need repair

Unacceptable reasons for undesirability:

    Too much road traffic

    Too close to airport noise

    Unacceptable neighbors (talk to people in the area and they will be most accommodating about sharing these problem areas)

    Barking dog(s)

    Unsupervised children

    Deteriorating property values in the area

    Unauthorized use of property (illegal use for its zoning)

    Mixed zoning (commercial and residential in same block)

    Located in an area of pollution

    Location of structure on the site is poor

    Isolation (may be too private in distance from roadway)

    Railroad noise or inconvenience

    Unpublicized or future negative changes (your research should have revealed these)

    Susceptible to natural phenomena:

        Floods

        Mud slides

        Insect infestation

    High crime area

LOCATION ANALYSIS

The single most important aspect of determining real estate value is *location*. Similar properties in different locations often have quite different market values. Positive circumstances such as waterfront locations, views, and good weather can be responsible for differences in market values exceeding 500%. Corresponding lower values can also result from negative factors such as airports or isolation. Within a city or town, the likelihood of such drastic differentials is less common. However, the fact remains that the location of one neighborhood over another or a specific street within the same neighborhood may have more to do with market value than the size and condition of the house itself. Because of this, purchasing, rehabbing, and reselling comprise as much a business of selection as one of upgrading and repairs.

Whichever level of rehab you deal with, there is one location-related aspect you must adhere to: To be consistently successful, you need to seek properties that are at the lower end of the value range in a particular area. The greatest potential for profit exists when you purchase the least expensive house in a desirable neighborhood. Generally, the more difference there is in value between what you buy and the other houses on the street, the better. Go for the *worst* house in the *best* neighborhood. If $50,000 is what you can afford, try to find a neighborhood where $50,000 is the least expensive house. Rehabbing in a large tract of homes that are all similar in size and value can be negative in having little room to move the values up with your rehab, and positive in that you can easily recognize a well-below-market sales price.

A variety of house styles and prices within one area or neighborhood provides the best opportunity for rehabbing. Buyers are willing to pay top dollar for unique properties and those that are in especially good (move in) condition. Locations that have existing variety will more easily accept changes that produce charm. Areas in which existing houses seem to have an individuality yet still fit in with the others are ideal.

In summary, the locations you should look for have the following characteristics:

1. A variety of property styles
2. A small percentage of homes that are currently worth noticeably less than the rest
3. Prices on the rise
4. Topographical or other long-term assets that keep values high.

How Do I Find Out the Neighborhood Information I Need to Know?

There are two kinds of data you are working with:

1. Statistical information
2. Perceptual information.

The real estate agent is providing data using the Comparable Market Analysis and the Area Market Survey function of the MLS. Your local government resources provide more "hard data" in the form of community plans.

The community plans allow you to get information about neighborhoods provided through the local government department responsible for compiling the housing elements for a municipality. In various parts of the country, this will be a city or county department called the Housing and Community Development Department, or the Planning Commission or Department.

Working from the latest available census information, it publishes neighborhood profiles that include the average family size and ages of members, family income levels and sources of income, how long people have owned or rented in the neighborhood, the ratio of owner-occupied units to rental units (very important to ascertain neighborhood stability). Other categories of information include items that will help you determine how marketable this area currently is and projections for improvements that the municipality will be making over the next 5 to 10 years. Some issues addressed will be correction of traffic problems, paving or resurfacing of alleys and streets, acquisition of open space and new parks that are planned, anti-crime programs in place or planned, under-grounding of utilities to enhance the look of the area, current and projected zoning usage, commercial and industrial zoning, and proposed corrective zoning to add to the quality of life in the area. Public transportation and planned tie-in programs to make the area more accessible to people's work and shopping areas, and plans for local issues that schools may be facing are also in this report. Therefore, there isn't much else you need to know that this plan will not give you, in order to understand this neighborhood. The second and equally important research piece is the "windshield survey" that you perform.

In order to really know a neighborhood, you have to get out of the car and see it up close. Walk your dog or ride your bike through the area. Talk to the residents and ask about the past as well as the present conditions. Local merchants will sometimes be good sources as well.

The first thing to find out is where does the area begin and end? Sometimes there are unmapped boundaries that separate the highly prized locations from the "not so greats." You have to make it your business to get the inside info on the good and the bad of any neighborhood you are considering. Remember, you are a pro now, an investor, a speculator of sorts, and you can't leave things to chance. Never forget that you make your money on intelligent, researched choices, not lucky guesses.

In many cases, common sense will tell you if an area is good or bad. Sometimes what you see takes some interpretation.

Questions to Ask About Your Project's Neighborhood

- A boarded-up house or vacant lot is never a good sign. The longer it has been unproductive, the more you should worry about the neighborhood. An owner would not let a property of value remain unproductive very long.

- Badly neglected lawns or sloppy landscaping are usually an indication of problems on the inside too. Several houses on the block with this look indicate poor values.

- Neighborhoods with a mix of people indicate a wide appeal. If you see children as well as the elderly walking the streets, then there is some balance to the population and a larger pool of buyers.

- Too many parked cars in an area can be an indication of rental properties in the area or of single-family homes violating the zoning laws by functioning as multi-units.

- Too many busy streets or speeding traffic frightens buyers. Cul-de-sacs or dead-end streets are generally looked on as safe and desirable.

- Are there neighborhood stores within walking distance? There is a fine line between convenience and annoyance. Are they the right kinds of stores? Boutiques and Mom-and-Pop services are good. Self-serve gas stations are not popular. Generally, operations that bring in lots of outsiders are not welcome.

- Public transportation can be a positive or a negative. If your property will have tenants needing transportation, then access to public transportation is a selling feature. On the other hand, a bus stop outside your door can mean strangers sitting on your front lawn, along with their associated trash, such as cigarette butts, pop bottles, and newspapers. There is also the additional noise generated by diesel engines starting and stopping. The best option is to have the public transportation close enough to be available, but far enough away to be unnoticeable.

Neighborhoods In Transition

There is little chance that you will find the perfect house in the perfect neighborhood. If you insist on finding that set of circumstances, you may never buy a house. The solution is to do the best you can without compromising too much. Many people attempt to enter the rehab business assuming that it is a good idea to purchase in a neighborhood where property is very inexpensive because of the poor condition of the neighborhood. Their hope is that the neighborhood will soon improve and their investment will appreciate dramatically. This is not out of the question, but the risk is higher and the timing is critical. Remember, you must pay the carrying costs for a house for every day you own it until the deed is transferred and the sale is complete. If the area does not improve as anticipated, you may be stuck renting to individuals willing to live in an undesirable area. You may find out that the work you put into the house can be undone very quickly.

If you feel drawn to very distressed properties in down-and-out neighborhoods, one way to determine whether the area is on its way out of trouble is to look for the number of major renovations going on. If 25 to 30 percent of the other houses in the area are being worked on, then there is a good chance that a turnaround is forthcoming. Be a joiner in such activity, not a pioneer. The profits in changing neighborhoods can be high, but the fact that they are changing brings another variable into our equation for success. This variable is not one that you have any control over, and you must be prepared to deal with what time produces. Working with established neighborhoods effectively removes that variable.

Rural property offers another opportunity that may not adhere to the formula of the largest pool of buyers, yet may be a good choice at times. Country properties can be emotionally charged for a select group of buyers who feel they "just have to have this house." This desire to be in the country can offset the convenience factor and make for high profits. This scenario does not have the same risk of possible loss of value that a "down-and-out" city neighborhood has, because there is a smaller buyer pool, but country properties can take more time to turn around.

Ultimately, you will find that you can do business in many different types of areas, and the profit potential and risk level vary accordingly. You must decide whether you are in a position to take on the level of risk associated with each one.

RED FLAGS

Projects that contain the following should be eliminated.

- Freeways in your backyard
- Airports
- Land fills

- Housing projects
- Delivery trucks
- Railroad tracks
- Industrial zoning nearby.

KNOWING YOUR FUTURE BUYER PROFILE

One approach to marketing is to select a product that appeals to the largest pool of buyers. The theory is that the more people you have available to purchase your product, the better chance you have to sell it. This concept can be used with great success in the rehab market as well. If you select a neighborhood that has several attractive features and nothing to offend people, you have created the best opportunity for a quick sale, if only by virtue of the fact that there will be more buyers available.

You need to examine the buyer profiles for whatever neighborhood you select, in order to analyze your competition.

Let's look at this as a graded slope:

> *High end buyers* (price not an object and totally discretionary decision to buy a house).

> *Trade-up market buyers* (they have already owned for a while and wish to use their accumulated equity to now purchase in a prestigious neighborhood. Want more square footage and amenities, comparable to what a new home provides).

First-time home buyers who want to get into the market (they make up the bulk of potential purchasers for your rehab projects. They are looking for basic neighborhood features listed in this chapter, but are buying knowing they will parlay their equity into another house. National average is 1 move every 7 years).

There is a psychological buyer price ceiling that separates each of these categories. You should understand what sales price would put you into these different categories. The slope format illustrates the decreased pool of buyers that are available to you when you determine your buyer profiles.

There is another correlation we should note here: the amount of profit you can reasonably expect from these three categories. The average profit you will need is something that gets costed out each time you do a feasibility analysis on your projects, but actual dollars of profit to reasonably expect may differ greatly.

Bottom of the Slope—First-Time Home Buyers

Note: These are California price examples, so they will be comparable only in high-cost areas of the country.

Purchase price	$135,000
After-rehab sales price	$180,000
Cost to rehab	$ 8,000
Acquisition costs	$ 3,000
Down payment	$ 13,500
Carrying costs and sales commissions	$ 7,500
Net profit	$ 13,000

When I get to this part, I often hear that $13,000 profit is not enough to make it worthwhile. However, this project was done on a part-time basis over a span of 4 months from start to resale. If you start out part-time, as 90 percent of rehabbers do, you can conservatively do at least 2 projects a year (gearing up to 3 next year) to generate at least $26,000 worth of income as a part-timer ($39,000 with 3 projects). Using the standard of earnings of most people working full-time for an employer, this is pretty reasonable compensation. (This project sold very quickly because the average price for a home in the neighborhood was $190,000.)

RESOURCES FOR FINDING REHAB PROJECTS

The "soft data" that a real estate agent can offer you is his or her inside knowledge of the areas you wish to work in. Real estate professionals actually "farm" areas, and by doing so become tapped into information on potential projects before it is generally available.

One example of this is the agent who knows, from years of door-to-door soliciting in an area, not only who the current owners are, but how old they are, the condition of their health, and their plans to go to live with their daughter in Phoenix in two more years. This is the kind of inside knowledge that will allow an agent to get that listing and to quickly give you the information on that property.

It is a common misconception that the agent is often competing with clients in finding "good deals." The agent who is acting as a principal in buying properties is not usually the same type of agent you will find behind the desk of a real estate office, taking on clients. It is also unlikely that, as your relationship and trust grow, you will not know whether you have found the very rare agent/principal who is purchasing in quantity for his or her own portfolio. Residential real estate agents make their money primarily from repeat sales and customers, which will make you a client they will want to cultivate and not compete with. Your main competition for good projects will come from other nonprofessionals who demonstrate perseverance in scouting the market.

The real estate agent you work with should be tapped into the trading sessions of the local Board of Realtors and/or Multiple Listing Service, when that is a separate organization. I have found more good "hot" information at these traditional breakfast meetings than any other source for projects.

Some other ideas that are good sources of possible projects:

- Print business cards that let people you meet in appropriate business settings know what you are doing and how to reach you if they hear of a distressed property or sale.
- Understand the value of offering a finder's fee to anyone you network with to locate projects.
- Be sure to call your agent with any information you are given so that he or she can perform the function of getting the details and so that you do not mistakenly circumvent each other. I have had clients call me and tell me that they went to an Open House and found the perfect project. They then request that I call the listing agent who wrote up the contract for them over the weekend, and explain all those rehab financing programs they learned about in my class!

Investigate all *For Sale by Owner* (FSBO) properties that are advertised as fixer, need T.L.C., and so on. This investigation should include your real estate agent if you are working with one. There is a fallacy that if you deal directly with a seller who does not have a property listed with an agent, you will get a better price. There are very few FSBOs who are not willing to give an agent bringing them a qualified buyer a discounted commission. There are also very few FSBOs who will reduce their asking price by that commission, to sell to you directly. The other problems direct sales between two nonprofessionals present are:

- How will you establish "fair market value" for that property without comparable sale information? In some states, you can use a title insurance company to provide you with a property profile, which lists sales around the property. This is a rough-cut estimate method only. Dates of the sales and whether nearby property is still really within the neighborhood boundaries will need to be investigated further. A physical look at actual properties sold as comparables will also be required. For those of you who are computer information buffs, in some areas of the country you can obtain this information "on-line" to your own computer from a private information provider company for a monthly fee.

- What forms will you use for the offer and counter offer? Real estate professionals use forms approved by the legal department of their State Realtor's association, which contain "boiler plate" clauses that address current real estate law requirements and are updated frequently. The office supply store forms you may be tempted to use, or hand-drawn documents, can leave out important current changes in requirements for the transfer of real property.
- Who is going to problem-solve for you during the transaction, should problems arise? When you are dealing with an FSBO, the "team" attorney we spoke about earlier will most likely be needed.

Another issue that will come up for you as you get into the process of making real estate offers is the investor version of buyer's remorse. I call this "buyer's lag." Anyone you talk to in the real estate profession will agree that tying up a potential profit-making piece of real estate requires quick decision making. So, if a basic principle of making money is to tie the property up, why have I seen so many clients lose out on viable projects? Because it takes a certain amount of trust in your own decision making and risking the uncomfortable feelings of making quick decisions. You as an investor will need to go past these feelings and learn to operate quickly on a property, with the confidence that your contingency (see Chapter 1) clauses are your safety net. When you expand to purchasing a multifamily, you will be asked in many cases to write an offer that is acceptable to the seller, before you are even able to walk inside the tenant-occupied property. Again, this takes faith in your offer, your agent, and yourself. When you are able to write an offer immediately and it "feels" like just another business offering, you have graduated to a full-fledged real estate investor.

The Principles of Profit

- Know your project areas like the back of your hand.
- Build a trusting and respectful business relationship with your agent.
- Be creative in marketing your interest in buying rehabs.
- Be ready and able to play when you are called to perform and tie up a property.
- Location choice and knowing the buyer profile of the person to whom you will sell; ensure success.

We will continue to add to this list as we go into the next chapters. You may have noticed that our process steps take us on an inverted path, because we first need to know the overview of the real estate market in our area. Next, we must conduct research activities that narrow our choice of neighborhood areas to about three. We can then begin to discuss techniques for finding projects within those areas and to narrow the search down to analysis of specific houses or units we locate in these areas.

Gathering Specific Information on the Project

- Obtain as much information on the motivation for the sale as is legally within your right to discover.

- Have the agent provide the "ceiling" price your finished project could command in that neighborhood (provide CMA and AMS data, see Chapter 1).

- If possible, walk the property inside and out, and drive around the surrounding blocks to look for any negative or positive elements that might impact your getting that upper ceiling price.

- You will then, utilizing the walk-through checklist, average cost estimators, and "red flag" checklist in this book, be able to feel out the feasibility of the project in a broad brush manner.

Until you get comfortable with your own decisions on the rehab portion, you may want your general contractor "team" member to walk the project with you. They should understand you are not asking them to bid the job at this time but rather they are there to answer questions (how else will you learn) and analyze only. Ask them to be sure the "ball park" estimate contains a generous offset for the unknowns that rehabs always contain.

At this point, you are seeking a quick assessment, as close to accurate as possible, of cost and of the problems of the property. You will then need to answer the question of whether you can correct the problems.

You will be tempted at this juncture to overanalyze and over-research rehab issues and will need to push past this temptation and get an accepted offer. You should do a thorough analysis during your contingency time frame after your offer has been accepted, and then back out if the rehab figure puts the project out of the ball park.

The following checklists can be used for this initial walk-through to obtain both "hard data" and "soft data."

"Hard data" will include any items appearing on the "red flags" checklist. Estimate from sample costs of repair items (see the example), which you will need to verify for your locality. You may want to purchase the *Home Improvement Cost Guide* by R. S. Mean Company or the *Remodel Cost Guide* published by Marshall and Swift as price reference materials. You should seek to answer the question, how bad is the damage?

"Soft data" are what I refer to as "listening to your own gut feelings" about the property. With the caution that you do not need to love this house personally in order to profit from its rehab, you do need to feel comfortable and see positives in it. When you begin to actually walk into older houses in disrepair, you may not see anything but the dirt, and you may only feel overwhelmed by the amount of work it needs. Clients sometimes have told me that there is no way they could ever touch things that were as filthy as parts of that house were. I have to say that everyone has a different tolerance level to this aspect of rehab, but if you have a low threshold in this area, recognize that professional cleaning teams are an inexpensive cost item when you stand to make a healthy profit. If you are dressed in the same clothes you would wear to wash the dog, your comfort level in a "trashed" house may rise. You might try this technique to help your focus be the "could be" condition of the house and not the "as is" condition.

"TO BE FOREWARNED IS TO BE FOREARMED"

The following is a list of the items that are considered problems that will most commonly need correction from the lender's or appraiser's view. You will use this as a checklist to answer the "How Bad is the Damage" question.

1. No access to unfinished spaces
2. Wet or overly damp basement floors
3. Cracked foundations
4. Crawl spaces less than 18 inches in depth
5. Dry rot and water-damaged areas that are obvious to the eye
6. "Kicker boxes" next to the electrical panel. One may be OK, any more will require a new circuit-breaker panel
7. Gutters and downspouts missing
8. Torn kitchen or bath vinyl flooring
9. Pressure relief valve on hot water tank broken or missing
10. Improper venting of hot water tank or not raised to 8 inches above the floor
11. Earth-to-wood contact in any area of the house; posts, stairs, foundation, and so on
12. Too much moss build-up on the roof
13. Poor roof ventilation. Sign: curling of the bottom edge of composition shingles
14. Stained plaster or ceiling tiles.

The last consideration of this process of elimination is to match the property to problems that may be incurable. If your project contains any one of these, look closely at whether you should eliminate this project.

Cracked Foundations or, in Some Areas, Poured Slab Problems

Unless you are a concrete specialist, the problem here is that, to get an accurate cost of repair, it will cost anywhere from $200 to $750 for the engineer's report, telling you if the problem can even be corrected. Foundation repairs can be sink holes for rehab dollars. Every new buyer will expect a solid foundation and therefore the costs incurred in this repair will never mean you can ask more for the house in its future sale. It may be that "swimming upstream" and solving very complex problems is your challenge, and if so, this repair is for you. As for the rest of us, my recommendation is to pass on the house.

Floor Plan Is Obsolete

If you have to walk through one bedroom to get to another; if, as is prevalent in floor plans of the 1920s, a bathroom opens onto a kitchen area; if the house was added onto by a previous owner to now be a 4 bedroom/1 bathroom home, you have major challenges. You are going to have to address these problems in your rehab and they can be costly. You'll probably need an architect's evaluation. From this report, you may only find that the cost of correction again eliminates this rehab project. There is one area that may be worth a plumber's evaluation, and that is the 4 bedroom/1 bathroom problem. If he can identify a "wet wall," or a way that a bath can be added utilizing the existing plumbing lines, you may be able to correct this problem at a reasonable cost. If the new master suite that is needed means a new bath at the other end of the house from the existing bath, the costs will be significantly higher.

Roof Issues

If the ridge line of the roof resembles a sway-back horse; if there are already three roofs on the property and the visible one looks shot; or if the roof has what I call "end-stage illness," you may want to eliminate this project. The primary reason for this is that your new buyers may love it that you have provided them with a new 20-year roof, but I have not found many who will pay more money for a house just because it has a new roof. Again, you need a specialist to evaluate for you. A roof inspection, you'll be happy to know, is less expensive than most of the other professional evaluations we have discussed, usually about $150 to $400. The cost will vary if you are only asking how salvageable it is or for an actual professional evaluation of how much life is left in the roof. If you think you may want the project and are concerned about this one aspect, a roofing certification can assist you in two ways. When you go to your lender for financing and you want to sell again, it is a great way to overcome any buyer or lender anxiety about the reliability of the present roof.

Garage or Basement Conversions

Here we will find the whole spectrum of what the handyman home-owner can do to decrease value in the name of adding space. We have all seen and can think of examples of what people have done to a property, in the name of improving it. Our concern here relates to how much the owners took on or "improved" themselves without professionals and/or city building permits involved. There are some common sense principles that operate here. If the work was done without permits, you have a "white elephant" in the eyes of most lenders. If work such as electrical, plumbing, or moving of gas lines (unbelievable as it may seem, I have personally viewed the results of gas lines that were re-done by a home-owner) has been done, then the question becomes one of health and safety. West of the Mississippi, I was shocked to learn, health and safety code enforcement is not as commonplace as in the East and Midwest. Depending on the part of the country you are in, you may or may not have city inspections that are preventative, therefore you need to know if the homeowner's or his brother-in-law's work contains dangerous wiring or plumbing defects. Your building inspector team member will be needed to physically inspect and check to see if permits were pulled for the prior work with the proper building department authority. We spoke earlier of the trend toward full disclosure of problems to new buyers. You may be incurring liability if you resell a property in which the previous owner created defects.

Nonconformity to the Neighborhood

These properties would include those that are the only residential use in a commercially zoned block. Even if the block is still primarily single family residences, the resale of this property as a residence will be nonconforming with zoning and the new buyer will have very few lender choices. Let me repeat, there will be *very few* who will lend on your project.

Another example of this would be the only house on a block that is primarily multi-family or apartments. You will find very few new buyers looking for a single-family home who will want to be surrounded by multi-family homes.

What Characteristics Comprise the Ideal Rehab?

In an ideal world, all your projects would contain *all* of the following. Since the world is not ideal, at least three or four of these characteristics should be present to optimize your success:

- Does the house, beneath the disrepair, have a "warmth," or what real estate professionals refer to as curb appeal? This is a subjective feeling, but a valid one. If you drive up to the property and looking beyond its current condition can see a house that will give off the feeling of a home when reconditioned, that's a good potential project.

- When you walk the inside, you are looking for sources of natural light or good potential for light sources if you open the rooms up. This may be the single biggest challenge to the row house, as you only have front, back, and top of the structure options.

- Does the style of the house have any charm or appeal to capitalize on? The 1950s box-style house means you must add that style and charm. This is not an insurmountable problem, but you must ask yourself if you naturally have the ability to add the architectural detail needed, or will this mean a line item in the budget for an architect or designer?

- The floor plan of the house needs to flow well as you walk through or you need to see how it can be opened up with the removal of a wall or closing off a room's present entry.

- When you look out the front windows, is the view pleasant? If not, then is it at least not a detriment? Can your adding mature trees (not 4 to to 5 feet high, but a few mature trees) offset the negative view from the front windows? Mature trees can also be a focal point to an otherwise drab-appearing front lawn and they are not as expensive as you might think.

- Does the backyard afford privacy? Even if you can't really see the backyard for the overgrown weeds, can you see a way to create the privacy your new buyer will want?

- Is the house positioned well on the lot? Does it already have a garage or carport? If not, can "off-street" parking be accommodated on the lot?

- Are there well-maintained and "pride of ownership" properties on either side of the one you are considering?

The rule of thumb here is that the "cuteness factor" of the house when you have completed it will be what sells it, so the more of these building blocks to achieve that end you have, the better your chances for success.

WALK-THROUGH CHECKLIST

Rating: 1 is the least desirable, 4 is the best rating

General Impressions
Decorations   1 2 3 4   _____
Size of Rooms   1 2 3 4   _____
Traffic Flow   1 2 3 4   _____
Personality   1 2 3 4   _____
Other   1 2 3 4   _____

Living Room/Entry
Foyer   1 2 3 4   _____
Coat Closet   1 2 3 4   _____
Size of Room   1 2 3 4   _____
Electrical Outlets   1 2 3 4   _____
Fireplace   1 2 3 4   _____
Other   1 2 3 4   _____

Dining Room
Size of Room   1 2 3 4   _____
Circulation   1 2 3 4   _____
Separation   1 2 3 4   _____
Convenience   1 2 3 4   _____
Other   1 2 3 4   _____

Kitchen
Size of Room   1 2 3 4   _____
Location   1 2 3 4   _____
Appliances   1 2 3 4   _____
Cabinets, Storage   1 2 3 4   _____
Ventilation   1 2 3 4   _____
Personality   1 2 3 4   _____
Other   1 2 3 4   _____

Bedrooms
How Many   1 2 3 4   _____
Location   1 2 3 4   _____
Bathroom   1 2 3 4   _____
Windows   1 2 3 4   _____
Special Features   1 2 3 4   _____
Electrical Outlets   1 2 3 4   _____
Closets   1 2 3 4   _____
Other   1 2 3 4   _____

Bathrooms

Number	1 2 3 4	_____
Size	1 2 3 4	_____
Location	1 2 3 4	_____
Windows	1 2 3 4	_____
Water Conditions	1 2 3 4	_____
Door Locks	1 2 3 4	_____
General Conditions	1 2 3 4	_____
Other	1 2 3 4	_____

Basement

Water Problems	1 2 3 4	_____
Storage	1 2 3 4	_____
Floor Joists	1 2 3 4	_____
Outside Access	1 2 3 4	_____
Other	1 2 3 4	_____

Laundry

Location	1 2 3 4	_____
Cabinet Space	1 2 3 4	_____
Electrical	1 2 3 4	_____
Water	1 2 3 4	_____
Ventilation	1 2 3 4	_____
Other	1 2 3 4	_____

Garage

Size	1 2 3 4	_____
Convenience	1 2 3 4	_____
Problems/Storage	1 2 3 4	_____
Other	1 2 3 4	_____

Attic

Entry	1 2 3 4	_____
Storage	1 2 3 4	_____
Ventilation	1 2 3 4	_____
Insulation	1 2 3 4	_____
Problems		
Other	1 2 3 4	_____

Plumbing

Water Supply	1 2 3 4	_____
Sewage Disposal	1 2 3 4	_____
Quality of Pipes	1 2 3 4	_____
General Condition	1 2 3 4	_____
Noises or Warning Signs	1 2 3 4	_____
Hot Water System	1 2 3 4	_____
Other	1 2 3 4	_____

Heating

General Conditions	1 2 3 4	_____
Turn It On	1 2 3 4	_____
Noises or Warning Signs	1 2 3 4	_____
Service Arrangements	1 2 3 4	_____
Other	1 2 3 4	_____

Air Conditioning

General Condition	1 2 3 4	_____
Turn It On	1 2 3 4	_____
Noises or Warning Signs	1 2 3 4	_____
Service Arrangements	1 2 3 4	_____
Other	1 2 3 4	_____

Electrical System

Capacity	1 2 3 4	_____
Add-ons	1 2 3 4	_____
Age	1 2 3 4	_____
Other	1 2 3 4	_____
Totals	=======	$_____

(Bring a Polaroid® camera and take shots of all notable positives and negatives of the house. After a while, the projects you inspect may get mixed up in your mind.)

COSTS OF TYPICAL REMODELING OR REPAIR

Check your local pricing; these are general estimates.

Remodel Kitchen	$5,200–$7,800
Remodel Bath	$3,250–$5,850
Add Powder Room	$2,000–$3,250
Add Full Bath	$3,000–$5,500
Increase Electrical Service to 200 Amps	$500–$700
Run Separate Electric Line for Dryer	$125–$200
Run Separate Electric Line for Air Conditioner	$125–$200
Install New Warm Air Furnace	$1,200–$1,400
Install Central Air Conditioning, Electric	$1,500–$2,000
Install Central Air Conditioning, Gas	$2,000–$3,000
Install Humidifier	$225–$300
Install Electrostatic Air Cleaner	$500–$650
Install New 40-Gallon Hot Water Heater	$350–$500

Install New 30-Gallon Hot Water Heater	$250–$400
Install Attic Ventilation Fan	$300–$400
Install Storm Windows, Each	$40–$60
Install Replacement Windows, Each	$200–$300
Install New Gutters and Downspouts	$2.90 Linear Foot
Install New Asphalt Shingle Roof	$1,600–$2,800
Dig and Install New Well	$1,800–$3,000
Install New Septic System	$2,500–$3,500
Sand and Finish Floors	$.70 Square Foot
Install New Drywall Ceiling Over Plaster, Per Room	$250–$400
Install New Sump Pump	$350–$400
Install French Drain and Sump Pump	$1,800–$2,500
Enclose Porch	$2,500–$4,500
Install New Copper Horizontal Water Pipes in Basement	$800–$1,500
Insulate Attic	$.75 Square Foot
Remove Interior Non-load-bearing Wall	$500–$700
Remove Exterior Wall and Install Sliding Doors	$1,000–$1,400
New Single Garage	$6,500–$8,000
New Double Garage	$8,000–$12,000
Masonry Fireplace	$1,900–$3,000
Pre-fab Fireplace	$1,200–$1,800
New Kitchen Floor, Solarian	$2.50 Square Foot
Replace Disposal	$175–$250
Install New Disposal Drop Waste	$250–$350
Replace Dishwasher	$400–$700
Replace Refrigerator	$500–$800
Replace Cooking Equipment	$600–$1,200
Install Bath Vanity	$300–$500
Replace Laundry Tub, Single Fiberglass	$150–$200
Install Plumbing for Laundry, Within 5 Feet of Plumbing	$350–$600
Vent Dryer, Easy Access	$50–$80
Pour Concrete Patio	$2.50–$3.50 Square Foot
Install Overhead Garage Door, Single	$250–$400
Install Overhead Garage Door, Double	$350–$600
Install Garage Door Opener	$300–$350
Install Storm Door	$125–$200
Reline Fireplace with Terra Cotta	$1,200–$1,800
Install Skylight	$800–$1,000
Install Ceramic Tile in Tub Area, Mastic	$350–$500
Install Aluminum Siding	$2.00–$2.75 Square Foot
Paint Interior—Small	$1,300–$2,350
Paint Interior—Medium	$2,000–$3,250

Paint Interior—Large	$2,800–$6,000
Replace Slate Roof	$4.50 Square Foot
Replace Shake Roof	$3.00 Square Foot
Install Disappearing Stairway to Attic	$175–$300
Build Redwood Deck	$12–$16 Square Foot
Run New Water Line to Street	$1,300–$1,800
Replace Front Door	$300–$700
Build Closet	$500–$600

COMMON PROBLEMS FOUND IN OLDER HOUSES

Water Problems A very common problem in older homes. Often it is a result of poor gutter alignment, poor downspout direction, and/or poor surface grading. Water can be detected by discoloration of floor tile, stained paneling at floor level, dark spots on cinderblock, and other signs in basement.

Plumbing In older homes, pressure tends to drop substantially because of rusty galvanized pipes. Considered a major expense in older homes. Test for leaks and water pressure. A leak in lead waste piping cannot be patched. If bathroom is remodeled, lead pipe must be replaced.

Termite Activity Combination of wood, dirt, darkness, and dampness will bring termites. Particularly acute if there is crawl space with dirt very close to wood floor joists.

Roofs Older homes may have roofs that have water leaks. Check metal roofs for rust; tile roofs for cracking on sides; slate roofs for rusty nails and tar coming off ridge; tin roofs for rusting; and built-up roof with gravel for spongy spaces and bubbles.

Retaining Walls Large cracks sometimes form; this usually indicates that the surface water is collecting behind the wall, freezing and causing pressure. Can be demonstrative of poor structure work.

Interior Walls Most older homes have plaster on wood lath. Over the years, wood lath strips lose resilience and pull away from joists and studs, causing waves in walls and ceilings. Wood lath is very sensitive to moisture.

Electrical Wiring Most older homes have inadequate wiring, often only one or two outlets per room, which does not meet many codes. Most newer homes have outlets installed every 12 feet from any doorway to avoid the need for extension cords.

Insulation Older homes are not as well insulated as newer ones. There may be lack of insulation between masonry walls and interior walls.

Appliances   Older homes have neither the variety nor the quality of appliances that newer ones do. Technological changes are such that newer and better appliances are available to consumers.

Windows   Older homes usually have windows that readily conduct cold air into the house. Replacement can be expensive. This problem will need correction by adding storm windows.

3

The Rehab Process

IDENTIFYING YOUR REHAB LEVEL

There is a generally prevalent idea that the largest profit can be gleaned from the "cosmetic" fixer. For the sake of clarification, the term cosmetic rehab includes the following list of improvements:

- Removal of overgrown landscaping and replacement with "mature" bushes and flowering shrubs, or better yet, one very tall mature tree, as a focal point for the house.

- Removal of all out-of-date (by color, style, or texture) carpet. (Remember full shag rugs? So will your buyer.) Replace or redye.

- Stripping of exterior paint and repainting with at least two coats. There is nothing worse than skimping on the quality of this improvement.

- Correction of window problems with new sashes and panes. Do *not* replace wooden windows with aluminum. It cheapens the overall look of the project. Invest in quality storm windows if energy efficiency is an issue in your area. Replace what is there with "like kind" quality and materials.

- Haul away all debris and trash from the inside and outside of the property.

- In some areas of the country, aluminum awnings and wrought iron grille-work appear on older properties. Removal of these will do two things automatically. Take away the prison look of the window bars, which says this must be an unsafe neighborhood to live in (but keep them; they may be on the wish list of a particular buyer). Aluminum awnings, no matter how expensive they were, date the look of the house. How about good quality canvas awnings on just the front windows, if your climate dictates this need for shade.

- Old television antennas, especially ones that are so large they dwarf the house, should be removed. If the new buyers won't have cable service, I can guarantee you they will want a more modern and proportionate antenna.
- Remove all dark paneling. If there is quality wainscoting, you should thank your lucky stars and rework it to accentuate and offer detail to the room.
- Clean the entire house thoroughly. Just as you have an aversion to someone else's dirt, so will your new buyer. There are certain items that you may have to replace, as they can never be cleaned thoroughly. Porcelain sinks in kitchens and baths may have lost the ability to appear shiny even after cleaning. Commodes may require replacement for the same reason. The rule here is that if it is an item for personal toileting and cleaning, or cooking, and it doesn't look as if it is brand new, then cleaning it is not enough.

The best rehab dollars I have spent have been to hire professional cleaning teams with proper equipment to establish what items in the house still meet the above test, and what fixtures need replacement.

The reason that replacement or repair dollars spent on cosmetic corrections have the highest yield of return dollars is that they are all *visible improvements.* (See Table 3.1.)

Moderate Rehab—All the Above Items, Plus . . .

- Addition of an item to bring the house up-to-date, such as a kitchen island, dishwasher, and so on.
- Removal of a wall to open the floor plan up to a more modern one. The most common of these is changing a formal dining room and

Table 3.1 Remodeling Cost versus Value

Remodeling Project	Job Cost	Resale Cost	Percent of Cost Recouped
Major kitchen	$23,631	$35,000	148
Minor kitchen	$ 9,995	$17,250	173
Family room addition	$40,117	$47,500	110
Bath	$10,641	$14,750	139
Bath addition	$18,079	$20,000	111
Master suite*	$29,875	$25,000	84
Sunroom addition	$18,610	$16,250	87
Replace windows	$ 8,080	$ 6,500	80
Replace siding	$ 9,744	$10,000	103
Deck addition	$ 6,510	$ 4,500	69

*Combining two existing bedrooms and bath.

living room to an open, combined space used for an eat-in kitchen/ family room use.

- Addition of outdoor living space with a deck or patio (no aluminum patio covers, please). Decks do not need to be large, they just need to add outside area to the living space.
- Rehab of kitchen cabinets. Refacing cabinets is the least costly and highest dollar return you can have. Never replace the entire cabinet if you can avoid it. The quality ones are expensive, and the inexpensive ones always appear inexpensive and devalue the other quality improvements you may have made.
- Replace kitchen and bathroom flooring to update the look of these rooms.

This level of rehab may also provide good overall cost pay-back for your budget in the resale, if that budget does not price the house above the "price ceiling" we spoke about earlier.

Major Rehab

Most of previous items, as well as room additions such as:

- Creating master suites within the original house or as an addition
- Building garages or carports
- Completely redoing the floor plan
- Rewiring, replumbing, and/or new roofing.

The following basic principles are encompassed in the above list:

- *Know thyself.* Understand the level you wish to take on. Your first projects will need to be matched to your experience level and the amount of "sweat equity" you have time to put into a project. A homeowner living in the property can probably accommodate moderate to major rehab without the risks, as he or she will have the time to shop for materials and labor, and evaluate as work proceeds what jobs can be comfortably attempted. The "flipper," who must be highly skilled as a craftsman or hire out all the work due to the time constraint of getting the property back on the market, will be taking more risks as he or she attempts moderate to major rehab. When he or she has three projects completed or has become a full-time rehabber, moving up to these levels has less risk.
- *Attention to details.* The small imperfections of a house stand out like a sore thumb. I recently had occasion to walk a completed rehab that had been done quite well; however, the 20-year-old

original sink and stainless steel fixtures in the middle of a custom laid ceramic tile counter top ruined the feeling of quality. We will talk later about the Ohs and Ahs that attract buyers, and one of these is that there is nothing like a $1.59 cracked switchplate to attract the buyer's eye first.

- *Producing a finished project.* Those of you who "flip" properties may be tempted to rush the resale by listing or showing the house before it is completed. Unlike new construction, buyers do not want a "hard hat" tour of the house. Neither do they commit to buying a property before they see the exact way the carpeting you have on order will look when it is down. When you first market your property, many people will come to see it because it is new on the market. Take advantage of this by having it shown like the decorator model in a new-home tract. *You bought a house, but now you are selling a home.*

- *There are alternative ways to achieve the same results.* We spoke about refacing kitchen and bathroom cabinets; a very light sanding or scrubbing with steel wool to remove layers of dirt and grease build-up, combined with tung oil or Liquid Gold® and hard polishing might bring back older cabinets that were thought to be beyond their life. Vinyl flooring that is not torn or that does not show specific worn spots can respond very well to steel wool, restoring polish from a hardware store, and then elbow grease. I myself understood for the very first time the meaning of "housemaid's knees" when I utilized this method, but I saved over $400 in new flooring costs.

- *Keep up on buyer trends.* There has been a renaissance in hardwood floors. Refinishing hardwood floors is an area that you need professional guidance on, even when you are going to do it yourself. All refinished hardwood floors are not the same. Evaluation of what you have to work with, guidance on the sanding steps, and rental of the equipment are the first and easiest steps. Salespeople you rely on to recommend products at hardware and discount building products stores are usually not studying for architecture degrees at night. Do not take their recommendation as your only source of information. Go see what a quality finished job looks like and ask what was used to accomplish it. A last but important point on hardwood floors: they are supposed to have a soft glow when finished, yet many amateur refinishers turn out high-gloss, polyurethaned floors that resemble basketball courts. Avoid this look at all costs.

REMOVING WALLS

The removal of a wall may be the single most dramatic change you can make to a living space without high costs or complex structural considerations. The difficulties you may encounter in removing a wall depend

Figure 3.1

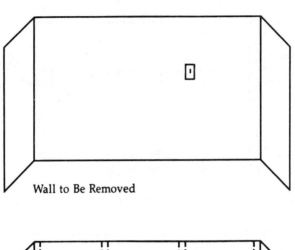

Wall to Be Removed

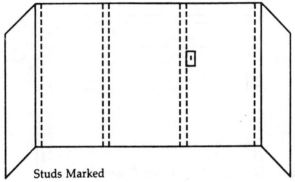

Studs Marked

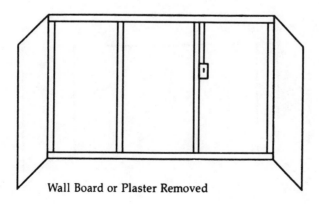

Wall Board or Plaster Removed

Figure 3.2

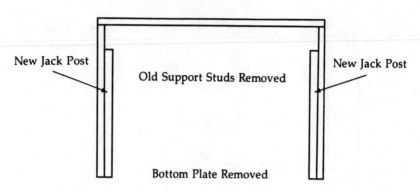

New Jack Post — Old Support Studs Removed — New Jack Post

Bottom Plate Removed

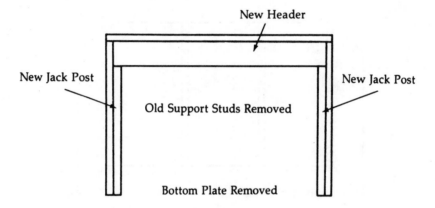

New Header

New Jack Post — Old Support Studs Removed — New Jack Post

Bottom Plate Removed

New Support Beams Covered with Wall Board

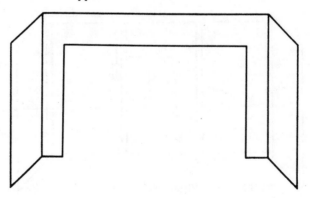

largely on whether it is load bearing or not (for the most part, load bearing walls are those that are perpendicular to the support beams above or below them, as shown in Figure 3.1). Those that are load bearing require support beams installed to replace the function of the removed wall. Figure 3.2 describes the basic process of removal of a wall. This is not intended as a "how to" description, but will provide you with an overview of the process and let you know what to expect.

The actual process, although not difficult, does require some experience in order to obtain quality results. The degree of difficulty and range of experience required depend on the size of the wall and what is housed within the wall. Electrical wiring, heat ducts, plumbing, and furnace chimneys are all possible complications. The first step is to determine which of these are or may be within the wall. Once that is established, if alternate routes for those items can be worked out, then the final decision to go ahead or not can be made. You should not be intimidated by the prospect of wall removal. It is neither very expensive nor difficult and it is one of the most dramatic differences you can accomplish in a home. It can be one of the highest payback changes you can make.

STEPS IN THE PROCESS

We are now well into the steps of the process; we have done an initial evaluation; written and obtained an accepted offer and are beginning to operate on the timelines we specified in our contingencies. We will discuss later in depth how we arrived at the purchase price we offered in Chapter 1. What becomes critical again are timing and quickly getting a "real dollars" budget for staying in or getting out of this transaction. We stated earlier that you should obtain a property inspection report from a professional, and as quickly as possible put this step into action. You should be present during the property inspection and review all matters the inspector feels may be problems. You should then, as pre-arranged, ask him or her to prepare a "line item" cost for the repairs noted and the improvement list you wish to make to this property. This added item is called "preparing a set of specifications." This set of specifications needs to be based on fair-market pricing for the improvements and repairs you need (if the inspector has a computer estimating program, he or she will give you the standard pricing). The "real" dollars that will be needed to complete this project will be the result of the inspector's set of specifications and repair estimate.

This method is analogous to how larger construction projects are set up. When governments need a new bridge, they do not go out and get three bids or estimates on what various contractors think a bridge might cost. They prepare a set of specs and cost breakdown for themselves, showing what the project should cost, and then provide that set of specifications for contractors to bid against. You are going to be professional and use this system to avoid the multitude of problems discussed next.

Avoiding Rehab Construction Pitfalls

I thought about naming this section "Games People Play," because the following problem areas are the reasons that rehab has had such a bad name. Many true-life horror stories can be told about the rehab process by homeowners and contractors alike.

There are as many good people who are contractors and who have prematurely aged due to these games as there are homeowners. The current system does not work very well for either side.

Typical Scenario Between the Homeowner and Rehab Contractor

The owner, or prospective owner, calls out three or more contractors to walk a project with him or her and provide an estimate. Each time the homeowner verbally describes what he or she wants or needs, the scope of work or type of improvements varies slightly. The contractors come to walk the job, thinking that they will only get the work if they are the lowest bidder. The exact quality of the materials to be used is not spelled out in writing in this scenario. The homeowner has relied totally on what he or she has said being explicitly understood by each of the contractors. Each contractor comes back with an estimate, usually just a total dollar figure of the bid (known as a bottom-line bid), which tells the owner nothing about how much each item will cost or what quality of materials that bottom-line figure represents (the communications are now getting even more fuzzy). The contractor will usually state that this is the absolute minimum that the job can be done for. Unfortunately for everyone involved, it usually is. Not *all*, but some contractors have actually put a dollar amount down that is impossible for the job to be completed at. Remember when we asked for the lowest bid? Something that low-bid contractor may be counting on is that when you say yes to this lowest bid, and he gets the work, he will:

1. Substitute brands that are lower in cost or substitute less expensive materials on the job
2. Use subcontractors who have played the "lowest bid to get the job" game with him also
3. Hope or know that there will be changes that will add cost along the way and will be able to make up a decent profit margin on the job this way (called change orders)

4. Hope sincerely that he will get the job to keep his crew working and his cash flow going.

We will avoid this whole scenario by use of the specifications model discussed previously.

HOW TO SELECT A CONTRACTOR

Have a candid first meeting and evaluate your chemistry and communication together. It will not serve you to have an excellent craftsman who has a Gary Cooper "Yep" and "Nope" vocabulary. You need the mentor that we spoke about who will allow you to learn about the language and business of rehab.

Be candid about not wanting to play out the typical homeowner/ contractor scenario that you just read about. Establish yourself as a businessperson by stating that (1) you are not looking for the lowest bid and (2) you have a set of specifications for the project. You need to also let the contractor know you plan to be an on-site presence during the job (you're actually going to be his shadow, but don't reveal that yet). Describe the fact that you have your ducks lined up with your financing and will be using a third-party escrow of fund control for fund dispersement. If the contractor balks at this, say it is to protect yourself from mechanic's liens, or that your accountant insists on a paper trail for each project. This is to dispel the idea you are using the fund control or escrow because you want a third party to protect yourself against the business practice of requesting money as needed or in advance of work performed.

In some areas of the country, this complete list will not be available, but go through each step you can on this list:

- Get addresses and names of rehab projects the contractor has recently completed, and visit or call those previous clients. Be sure they are comparable jobs in size and complexity; a new shower and vanity installation is not equal to a room addition in showing the level of expertise you are seeking.
- Ask for the contractor's license number or obtain it from stationery. Call the state or municipality responsible for issuing that license and ask if there are any formal complaints against it. Get the name of the insurance carrier and agent on file. Usually, this will be directly given only after the contractor feels that you are "for real," so wait until a second or third meeting, if the licensing agency can't directly provide you with this insurance information.
- Be sure the license number is issued to the person with whom you are dealing.

- If the rehab will be moderate to major and the dollars involved are over $15,000 (check your local ceiling on this), request the contractor to obtain a completion bond (see next section). This will be an added cost, which you will pay for. The bond usually runs about 3 percent of the rehab amount ($15,000 × 3% = $450). If the contractor balks at the idea of you having a completion bond, it may be (1) valid feedback that you are being overly protective of yourself, or (2) it may also be that he is unable to go to a bonding company and reveal the financial data on his company that are required in order to obtain the bond. To check this out, call other contractors or subcontractor you trust, and ask if they feel your rehab job is too small to need a completion bond. If they feel it might warrant it, then drop the contractor who was resisting your request. Smaller contractors may protest that this is not fair to them, as they just don't have the kind of volume or time in the business, or whatever, to qualify for a bond and should not be shut out from being your contractor because of this. However, on your first few rehabs, you cannot afford to take chances that the job may not be completed in a timely and professional manner. As you get to personally know contractors, you may drop this "problem prevention" technique.

- You will show the contractor the line item bid forms that you would like them to use (see examples in Chapter 5). They can use their own forms in lieu of these if they wish, as long as they provide the same line-item cost breakdown so that you can follow expenses of the job as they occur and thus stay in control of your project. If the bid is normally presented on the back of an envelope, go on to the next contractor. Assure your contractor that unlike an "amateur" contracting for services, the revealing of a profit and overhead percentage is not the reason you are asking for this line-item bid. In fact, go to great lengths to tell him that you don't care about his profit margin. If he performs well and on time, then he deserves whatever he has allotted for compensation. You do care very much, however, about performance, and that he stay within the rehab budget you have allowed, as that will make or break your profit in this business.

- Be sure that the written contract between you and the contractor includes a clause on change orders, and that both you and the contractor are bound by that clause. Language should state that all changes requested must be in writing. Changes are to include the cost of change before any changes can officially become addendums to the contract. Both you and the contractor need to sign off on them. You are going to be as tempted to change and upgrade as the contractor may be to substitute items during the process. If you read this and nothing else in this book, and incorporate it into your way of doing business, you will recapture the cost of this book and more in future dollars. *All* change orders must be *pre-approved* by both parties.

Changes to the actual plans must be initialed by both parties and estimated cost of each change revealed before it is implemented (see sample in Chapter 5).

- In some cases, you can negotiate for contractors to work for time and materials only.

Another very sticky area is what part of the rehab plan can you do as the owner. Some contractors will not want any owner "sweat equity," others will agree to it, but will not make you specify what part will now be covered by you and what they are still responsible for. Again, in the written contract, subcontract yourself out formally to perform certain line items that you both agree you are able to do, and what dollar value those items are worth. Some good rules of thumb include:

1. Never promise to perform anything of a technical nature, no matter how tempted you might be to want to try a certain repair yourself.

2. The first time you work with a contractor, contain your participation to the tear-out and clean-up items of the bid. You may be surprised to learn that up to 12 percent of the cost is for the manual labor involved in tearing out and disposing of those old items.

3. Do not do trade-outs, reductions in the cost of the job, or any other exotic way you may think of to not pay the contractor money for this part of the budget. Simply have them pay you as they would any other subcontractor for the work and value of that work as in the original plan. Most of you who are avid "sweat equity" participants will resist this, and all I can say is that the purpose of this book is to give you methods to prevent problems and misunderstandings that commonly occur in this area, and hope that you will err on the side of caution.

4. Be sure you have a worker's compensation rider on your homeowner's insurance policy throughout the entire job. You need to be protected because the contractor's insurance alone is not enough should a worker be injured.

What Kind of Contractor Do You Need?

There are many types of contractors, each of whom requires a separate specialty contractor's license. For example, if you want roofing, electrical, plumbing, or painting work, you will need a contractor licensed in each particular specialty. A good rule is that if the work you want done requires *three* or more types of specialists, then the work should be supervised by a licensed general building contractor. For example, if your kitchen remodeling will involve plumbing, electrical, and carpentry work, a licensed general building contractor should be hired.

Licensing

Each state and local government has differing requirements and should be checked before shopping for your contractor. In California, any contractor performing a job in which the total cost of the project, including labor and materials, is more than $200 must be licensed by the Contractors State License Board. Licensed contractors are subject to laws designed to protect the consumer. Unlicensed contractors are a danger to your financial health because they expose you to significant financial harm in the event of injury or property damage. Unlicensed contractors usually do not have bonding or insurance.

Although an unlicensed contractor may give you a lower bid, because of the severe financial and legal consequences you may face, it simply *is not worth the risk.*

To get started, find your first general contractor by referral from a trusted subcontractor/tradesperson. This is a method I have always found useful. Tradepersons are in the business and know who is reliable and who has a good reputation.

Ask the contractor for the address of his or her business location and business telephone number, and verify them. You may also wish to check the contractor out with your local trade association or union, consumer protection agency, and the Better Business Bureau.

BIDS

A bid is an offer to do work. It is advisable to get at least three written bids, using identical plans and specifications as we have discussed. Use these to compare prices and contractors. Beware of any bid substantially lower than the others. It probably indicates that the contractor has made a mistake or is not including all the work quoted by his competitors.

Make Sure *Everything* Is in Writing, *Assume Nothing*

Any bid you sign may become the contract. Do not sign anything until you completely understand what you are signing and agree to all the terms. Be sure to ask questions until you fully understand the contract and what the work will look like. Before signing anything, you may wish to discuss the proposed contract, plans, and specifications with an attorney.

Use of Bond or Control Companies

Don't be confused about bonding. Each licensed contractor should have a license bond posted with the contractor's State License Board or supervising municipality, if required. You can ask your contractor to obtain a payment and completion bond in the amount of the contract price. That way, if the contractor is unable to complete the job or the job goes sour, bonding company funds will be available to complete the job properly and to pay the bills for another contractor to be brought in. Be sure you understand what bond covers what eventuality. It *can* be confusing.

FUND CONTROL

You will want to use a fund control company to disburse contract payments. This is not a substitute for a payment and completion bond. A fund control company is basically a licensed escrow company that specializes in construction. Instead of giving the money to your contractor, you give it to the fund control company. That company then makes payments to the contractor, subcontractors, or companies that supplied labor or materials for your project. Most large lumber companies function also as fund control companies.

Caution: Although many types of checks and balances are used by fund control companies prior to making payments, they are not required to inspect your job to see that work has been completed or materials supplied that is for you, the owner, to verify.

For additional protection, you should make certain that the fund control company you hire uses an *Addendum to Control Agreement/Escrow Instructions* which has been approved for use by the Registrar of Contractors.

This addendum is in writing and must be signed by you, your contractor, and a representative of the fund control company. In the addendum, the control company agrees to a method of making payments on your project which is designed to best protect your money and property. The company also warranties that any work or materials it pays for have been provided.

In looking for a fund control company, check with your lender or your contractor for recommendations. For a small percentage of the contract price, a reputable control company will eliminate or reduce many of the possible problems that could arise on your construction project. If you want a completion bond or fund control company, or both, make sure your desires are clearly set forth in the original contract with the contractor.

Schedule of Payments

Always keep the payment schedule based on the contractor's performance. Never let your payments get ahead of the contractor's work. Make sure the contract provides for a "retention." A "retention" is a percentage of each payment or of the total job, ordinarily 10 percent, which you retain until the job is completed. It may be advisable on rehab jobs to use a 15 percent holdback for the unforeseen problems inherent in older structures.

DURING CONSTRUCTION

Permits, Plans, and Specifications

Make sure that you have copies of the signed contract and plans and specifications for your project with you when you visit the site. Have blank change order forms available for use if needed (see samples in Chapter 5).

The building permit for your job, along with the project plans and specifications, must be posted on the job prior to work beginning. Check to make sure that they are.

Keep a Job File

You should keep a file of all papers relating to your project. It should include:

1. The contract and any change orders
2. Plans and specifications
3. Bills and invoices
4. Cancelled checks
5. Lien releases from subcontractors and material suppliers
6. Letters, notes, and correspondence with your contractor.

It is also a good idea to keep a record of each subcontractor who works on your project, what part of the work he did, and how long he was on the job. When material suppliers make a delivery, write down the name of the company, the date, and a general description of what they delivered. When you receive lien releases from subcontractors or material suppliers, check them against your list. That way you will have a record of who has and has not been paid.

Inspections

As your job progresses, your local building department will make inspections to ensure that completed work meets building codes. These inspections are not made to determine good work quality, only if it has been done to code. You should, if at all possible, be present when inspections are made, ask questions, and make frequent inspections yourself.

When a project is completed, the building department will make a final inspection. Make sure that you also make a final inspection, or "walk-through," with your contractor to be certain there is nothing you or the contractor have overlooked. A notice of completion or certificate of occupancy, issued by the Building Inspector for the city or county your job is in, signals the satisfactory (on their part) completion of the work.

Your final sign-off to fund control that all work is complete to your satisfaction, combined with the Building Inspector's clearance, will trigger the 10 percent (or 15 percent) hold-back funds being released to the contractor.

PRELIMINARY LIEN NOTICES

Shortly after your job commences, you will probably receive preliminary lien notices from subcontractors and material suppliers. Don't panic; this does not mean that a lien has been filed against your property. The law requires you to be furnished with these notices to alert you that those persons who have worked on or have supplied materials for your job may have lien rights.

The law provides that those who furnish labor or materials to your home can record a "Claim of Lien" or "Mechanic's Lien" against your home if they are not paid. This means you could lose your home. Even if you have paid your general contractor in accordance with the contract, if he or she fails to pay any subcontractor or materials supplier who performed work or supplied materials in connection with your project, you still run the risk of having a Mechanic's Lien filed against your home and foreclosure. This could result in your paying a bill twice.

This risk is greatly reduced by protecting yourself with a payment and completion bond and/or use of a fund control company, but it is never entirely eliminated. It is therefore good practice to specify in the contract that the contractor is responsible for obtaining lien releases from each of the subcontractors and material suppliers as work progresses and as each phase of the job is completed.

An "unconditional" lien release from anyone who has worked on or supplied materials to your job protects your property and relieves you of the obligation for payment of any claim filed for the period of time and/or the amount of money covered by the release.

WHEN YOU NEED PROFESSIONAL HELP WITH ASBESTOS

If you want to have your house checked for asbestos, or suspect asbestos-containing materials are present, you need professional help.

Industrial Hygienists, Asbestos Consultants

Industrial hygienists and asbestos consultants can inspect your house, take samples for testing, suggest contractors, assist in drawing up a removal plan, monitor the job, and inspect after the work has been completed.

Check the Yellow Pages under Industrial Hygienists or Industrial Consultants. Asbestos consultants are listed under Asbestos Removal and Abatement. Not all industrial hygienists are trained in asbestos work—be sure to ask. And not all will inspect residences; you may have to call several. Asbestos consultants usually charge less, but you should check their backgrounds and training (EPA certification in asbestos as a management planner, inspector, or project designer is one qualification to look for).

Avoid anyone who uses scare tactics, or suggests removal without taking suspect material to a lab for testing. Ask for references.

Although using one of these professionals adds to your cost, he or she can provide advice and assistance, generally without conflict of interest. Just make sure the one you choose doesn't have a close financial link with any one contractor.

Asbestos Abatement Contractors

Asbestos abatement contractors remove and dispose of asbestos-containing material. Their degree of training and competence varies widely, so select one carefully. Some unscrupulous firms have taken advantage of fears and do unnecessary work at high prices. Also, work done improperly creates a health risk, and can be expensive to correct. Call several industrial hygienists or asbestos consultants for recommendations (note if the same contractor is suggested by several sources).

Legal requirements vary. For example, until recently in California, only minimal certification was required; now, contractors must go through a more stringent state registration process.

To find out about the legal requirements for asbestos contractors in your area, check with your state contractors licensing board, area OSHA (Occupational Health and Safety Administration), or the state health department.

Look into the contractor's record. Ask about citations or violations (for example, permit problems may indicate safety violations); get answers in writing. You may want to verify this by checking with your local air pollution control agency, your state's department of labor, OSHA, and the Better Business Bureau. Check references. How long has this firm been in the asbestos abatement business? (The longer the better.) Are the employees well trained? Will the daily monitoring of your job be done by a supervisor with advanced training? Also check on insurance; the firm should have general liability and asbestos liability insurance.

BOOKS AND RECORDS

Every business needs a means of keeping track of what has happened in order to assist in completing its transactions and to verify what has been done. Equally important is the use of records in planning for the future. Once a project has been completed, knowing its costs, its return on investment, and time factors is very valuable for increasing efficiency in the next similar project. The value of accurate and complete records is critical to the rehab business because of its repetitive nature.

Do you need a computer to keep records in the rehab business? No, the nature and complexity of the records and books is not such that you will be at a disadvantage in not being computerized. There are, in fact, many ways a computer could be utilized, but it is not an item you should run out to purchase if you do not already have one.

What you do need is a system of some sort. No matter how simple or complex a system you use, it must be one you are willing to consistently use. Be disciplined about your entries. The rehab business has a tendency to involve a large number of purchases from a variety of sources. Many of these sources may be individuals or small operations whose paper trail is limited and may not inherently supply you with what you need in terms of documentation. Consequently, you may have to produce your own form of documentation, and, when you are busy, there is a tendency to put that sort of thing off to a more convenient time. The key to accomplishing this is to make your system as simple and easy to use as possible.

A 9" × 12" heavy-duty envelope with a clasp is one way to make things easy. It serves as a holding pen for anything that you are not immediately willing or prepared to enter into its permanent place in the record. The many small receipts, paint colors, and various samples you need to keep can all be tossed into the "holding pen" until you have more time or are in the mood to deal with them. It is important that anything that goes into the "holding pen" is labeled in some way to allow you to remember what it is. If not detailed on the receipt, itemize what was purchased (nails, hinges, glass, and so on). Be sure to label which part of or room in the house it was purchased for.

Figure 3.3 Sample Ledger Sheet

Date	Receipt No.	Details	Amount	Purchaser
6/8/90	1	nails, hinges, glass (kitchen)	$ 23.55	fjs
6/9/90	2	paint, plumbing parts, caulk, stain (kitchen)	$ 37.98	fjs
6/11/90	3	shelf lumber, closet door paint, (bedroom #1 closet)	$145.00	fjs
6/12/90	4	interior door + lock set (br#1)	$ 47.00	kv/pd
6/14/90	5	toilet (master bath)	$122.00	fjs
6/19/90	6	sink and faucet (kitchen)	$256.00	fjs
		total as of 6/19	$631.53	
6/22/90	7	range hood and msc. hdw.	$ 88.76	fjs
6/24/90	8	JS labor	$ 60.00	fjs

Ultimately, each receipt should be numbered and recorded on a ledger sheet with the date of purchase, who paid for it, what part of the house it was for, and any other special information necessary. (See Figure 3.3.)

It is a good idea to total the amount column every 10 days or so and label it as "total as of xx/xx/xx" (date). This gives you a running total of how much you have spent (actually how much you have paid for) as you go. The reason for numbering the receipts is to make them easy to find. Trying to find a receipt by the amount can be difficult and there may be more than one of the same dollar amount. You can include everything from every category on this ledger, then later group items into categories by room. Room grouping tends to be the most useful since you will most likely be evaluating future projects on a room-by-room basis. (See Figure 3.4.) Knowing what you did to a similar room and how much it cost previously makes estimating new projects much easier.

Figure 3.4 Room Grouping Ledger

Room	Date of Purchase	Item	Amount
Kitchen	6/8/90	glass, misc. hdw.	$ 23.55
	6/9/90	paint supl. + plmg.	$ 37.98
	6/13/90	lumber	$ 22.56
	6/17/90	countertop	$166.98
	6/19/90	sink + faucet	$256.00
	6/22/90	range hood + msc. hdw.	$ 88.76
	6/24/90	JS labor	$ 60.00
	6/24/90	garbage dsp. + trap assm.	$ 62.55
	6/27/90	recess lights (3)	$ 74.87
	6/20/90	vinyl floor (instd.)	$192.08
			$985.33

Keep in mind also that this is not simply a materials list. Any expense associated with the project can be listed here or put in the "holding pen." Personal expenses such as gasoline, tools, phone bills, and so on, should eventually be separated out or kept separately from the start because they are considered a business expense as opposed to a cost of rehabbing any one particular house.

HOW TO CREATE THE "OHS" AND "AHS" THAT SELL A HOUSE

Adding Curb Appeal

The attraction that a buyer sees or feels when driving by a property is called "curb appeal." This feeling of attraction can be generated by the style or shape of a house, the way it sits on the lot, its neat and tidy nature, or its wonderful trees and landscaping. Real estate agents refer to this in their ads as charm, quality, desirability, and other general terms. The concept of curb appeal is very important since a high percentage of buyers form their opinion of a property or set their mind, so to speak, before they ever go inside. In fact, many will decide whether to even take the time to go inside based solely on what they see from the road. There is a theory that says job applicants are hired or not based on the interviewer's impression during the first three seconds they are seen. Thus the expression, "you only get one chance to make a first impression." This may also be true for properties.

Since the initial impression of properties is so important to potential buyers, we as sellers must know and understand specifically what produces curb appeal. We must also know what is cost-effective and is likely to make a significant difference in the sale price.

A New Paint Job

Exterior paint may be the most widely cited improvement for adding curb appeal. It is the most noticeable in many cases. Whether or not it is a good decision in all cases is a good question. The deciding factor is, simply, how much difference will it make? If the cost to paint is $3,000, will the new look produce at least that much more at resale time? You should consider painting the exterior if:

- The existing paint is so bad due to color or condition that buyers will not get past the drive-by stage.
- By painting, you can effectively bring out currently hidden architectural details.

- The existing color scheme is drawing attention to parts of the house that are not attractive and producing a significant negative factor.
- The existing siding is of a nature that is typically natural (brick, cedar siding, stone) but it has either weathered badly or was originally a poor choice for the house.

If all you accomplish by painting is to change the color or freshen it up, you may not see a direct profit for your effort. However, if you rectify one of the above items, it is likely you will raise the value significantly and recover your cost as well as a profit. A less expensive alternative to painting is power washing. Very often it will remove enough dirt to make a substantial improvement for 10 percent or less of the cost of a total paint job. Another alternative to a full paint job is to repaint the trim only. Many times the trim is the only portion in need of paint. The body of the house is an acceptable color, but the trim is not. Sometimes you can create a better look by adding a third color to carefully selected trim pieces. The key word here is carefully. If you get carried away, you can do more harm than good. Another alternative is to repaint only the portion of the house that needs it. Most likely, the side that gets the most sun will weather first. If you can find the old paint can around the house, you may get away with doing just one side. Be sure to do a full side; stopping in the middle of one side will leave an obvious line.

Choosing colors can be a difficult task. Generally, you should limit the total number of colors on a house to three. Dark colors make small houses look smaller, and light colors tend to enlarge a house. You must keep in mind the color of your roof. Houses with green or brown roofs give you a more limited range of paint choices. Drive around the area and see if there are other houses similar to yours and what colors look good on them. Also, keep in mind the neighbor's house and its color. Failure to do so could lower the value of both houses. The current trend in colors varies from one part of the country to the next. Houses with Victorian architectural features tend to look best painted with multiple tones of one color. The books in the *Painted Lady Series* graphically illustrate these colors. The books can be found in most bookstores and are worth looking at for color combination ideas. Many paint stores will have charts with recommended combinations for trim and body.

A Roof over Your Head

The roof of a house can be as much as two thirds of the visible exterior. If the roof looks sound and doesn't leak, leave it. However, if it gives the impression that it is unsound by looking at it, you may have to repair or replace it. This is a difficult area to produce a payback on and should be avoided if possible. When selecting a rehab project, be sure your offer reflects the costs of this expense if warranted.

Architectural Details

You will soon find that houses are a lot like automobiles in one sense. Some come loaded with all the extras, and others are stripped down models. Doors and windows come in a wide variety of quality and shapes. Add-ons consist of porches, decks, shutters, extra trim, window boxes, and awnings (canvas only, please). As with cars, you can transform a stripped down model to a "deluxe" with changes or additions. What is critical is that the finished product results in a balanced style and not a collection of random tack-ons. If you want to make exterior improvements, be sure to stay within the bounds of good taste and work toward a goal or style. The most common mistake made is to mix styles, such as brick or wrought iron pillars on wood porches; sliding aluminum contemporary windows among traditional wooden double-hung, leaded glass windows on colonial houses; wrought iron railings on wood-sided houses; too many textures on the exterior, and so on. You should be on the lookout for these mistakes and can profit by correcting them, but take care not to become a creator of them. Other curb appeal add-ons include:

- Wooden fences
- Stone retaining walls
- Dormers
- Exterior light posts
- Upgraded front door
- Shutters
- New walk way or steps
- Sealed blacktop driveway
- Repair anything that looks broken.

Landscaping

The way a house blends with the lot is another strong curb appeal feature. There should be a subtle functional purpose to all the plants or trees. Some add color, some shade, some hide undesirable features, such as foundation plantings. Some trees are used as wind screens, others are used to lend their shape to a blank spot. The trick is to get the right plant for the job. Any bush or tree that obliterates a feature of the house is wrong. Evergreens that grow over windows need to be trimmed back or removed. Bushes that extend onto walkways require the same treatment. Huge trees that effectively block out the corner or other parts of a house are detracting from the look of the house. Trees that dwarf a house do the same thing.

Landscaping also makes a house seem like a home—a place that accommodates the people who live there. If the landscaping is neglected or missing, the house seems to lose its appeal as a home. Buyers relate to houses on a personal level, so it is important to develop that feature. Well-chosen flowers in bloom do a great deal to make a house look prosperous and healthy. If you don't want to pay for a professional design, look at flower beds created by professionals. You can get ideas by looking at plantings around commercial buildings. Whatever you plant, pick fairly mature plants. You'll get better results from a few medium sized plants than a bunch of little ones. Using mulch in flower beds is a good idea. It helps the plants, gives a good look, and cuts maintenance. Flowers planted in pots and placed on steps, porches, and decks add an extra touch that pays high dividends.

The Entrance Foyer

The first part of a house that is actually touched by prospective buyers is the front door handle. That first touch makes an important initial impression. If a worn, loose, or inoperative handle is the first thing that is contacted, the chances are the buyers will be oriented to looking for more of the same. If, on the other hand, they are impressed with a quality, heavy feeling door and handle, they have been set up to have the positive approach of looking for more high-quality items and they may tend to overlook some of the house's weak points. The entrance foyer is often rushed through by many buyers in order to see the more important parts of the house. The fact remains that it is the first and last part of the house that they see. If it is exceptional, it will be remembered; if it is ordinary, it will be forgotten. If it is inadequate or has obvious negatives, it can be a subtle but strong deterrent to buyers.

Do's and Don'ts in Foyers

If there is no actual foyer and you enter directly into a room, create a foyer area by adding a 4 foot by 4 foot area of ceramic tile, brick, or other paver apart from the carpet at the entrance. If there is hardwood in the room, add a small oriental or area rug for guests to stand on as they enter.

Hang a quality mirror (at least 2 feet by 3 feet). This serves several purposes.

1. A foyer should have a mirror so that when you leave the house you can check your appearance.
2. If the foyer is small and somewhat confining, a mirror relieves that to some degree.

3. The buyers will see their image in the setting of the house and symbolically place themselves as part of the house package.

If there is no closet for coats available, look for a place in the room to create one. Sometimes there is a 'dead' corner that can easily be converted to a coat closet.

A small ceiling light fixture over the area should be added if not already there. A brightly lit foyer creates a positive feeling upon entering the house.

A floor plant or decorative umbrella stand can add charm and warmth to this part of the house, which is supposed to say "welcome."

Avoid overdoing the walls with busy wallpaper or colors that don't ease you into the rest of the house. If there is a large dynamic entrance, you can be more expressive in design, but if it is small or not separated from the rest of the house, it should be kept light and simple.

Fresh flowers are a nice touch, but must be watered frequently. Dead or wilting flowers are worse than none at all. Avoid fake flower arrangements. This tends to look commercial and can make a house feel cold and impersonal. Plants or quality silk flower arrangements should appear in various areas of the house.

THE 3 MOST IMPORTANT INTERIOR CHANGES

Refer to Table 3.2 and the discussions that follow for the main points to consider in these interior changes.

Kitchen Cabinets

If you are lucky, you or your contractor knows a talented, hungry, custom cabinet maker. This is always the first choice to again tailor your "finished product" and appeal to all strata of buyer. If you aren't so lucky, the next best is prestained, manufactured cabinets. Go to the next "Home Show" in your area for more ideas and choices than you'll ever need.

Tip: Do not try to cut rehab dollars by buying unfinished cabinets and hanging them and staining them yourself. This is one of the most difficult projects for a do-it-yourself rehab and often the most costly. When you see what they look like, you'll be calling in a cabinet maker to tear them out and redo them.

Good Choices

- For low- to mid-range: Natural oak color is accepted by most people and matches well with most floors and countertops.

Table 3.2   The Kitchen's Update

Problem	Correction
Out-of-date color and appliances	
Pink and grey—1950s	Pink and grey? If you can create an art deco backdrop only! Otherwise plan to update the colors.
Harvest gold and chocolate brown appliances	Use a neutral monochromatic color scheme to enlarge appearance and update it.
Floor plan is closed off by wall between dining area and kitchen	Needs open 1990s lifestyle of a combination kitchen/eating area. If possible, remove wall.
No natural light comes into kitchen. Usually has a solid door to outside	Replace with glass-paned French door. Add skylight or make windows.
No window large enough for light to reach whole room	Put in a skylight or a greenhouse window. Use track lighting to get light to dark areas of kitchen.
Window coverings that mask all the light that a window could bring in	Remove and replace with shutters to have maximum light in daytime and maximum privacy at night.
More light in work areas and eating areas needed	Update with recessed spot lights over work areas, put in track lighting for flexibility in adjusting light to maximum need for your particular kitchen/dining area. A dropped ceiling of light panels can offset many common kitchen lighting defects.
Decorator touches lacking	Put in a traditional style chandelier in dining area and replicate a smaller version in kitchen area. Always add rheostats (dimmers). They are inexpensive and always get an oh and an ah! Only add ceiling fans if they are high quality and the climate dictates them.

Appliances

Choices here can make or break the look of a "finished product" in a kitchen.

Recommended Colors

White or almond	No olive green, harvest gold, copper, brown or red appliances.

Table 3.2 *(Continued)*

Problem	Correction
Pointers on Individual Appliances	
Refrigerators	24 cubic feet for 3- to 4-bedroom home. Never less than 14 cubic feet.
	Ohs and ahs are generated by side-by-sides and, surprisingly, freezer-on-the-bottom models.
Stoves and cooktops	Freestanding ranges if the kitchen is small.
	Double wall ovens with a cooktop surface on a center island, if you want a decorator touch.
	Be sure the oven is self-cleaning!
	A microwave is necessary as a built-in only if you have little kitchen counter space or you again want a decorator quality "finished look."
Sinks	The sink of choice is a double-bowl baked enamel, in white.
	Stainless steel is acceptable if you are on a moderate budget.
	Tip: Never leave the original sink in if you are remodeling a kitchen; a new buyer can always tell it was already there and the feeling of a brand new kitchen is destroyed. If you have the option, go to the top end of the decorator faucets—brass, European, single lever. It adds a lot.
Disposals	A necessary and expected item in today's kitchen. You can install them yourself usually and they are low-budget line items.
Other Kitchen Appliances	
Dishwashers	Also now standard. Buy the low end of the top of the line, without all the added frills of cycle options.
Trash compactors	In large cities, they are now considered standard. Again, ask yourself if your new buyer will expect one or just think it was a nice idea on your part.
Try Adding	A 1930s-type built-in ironing board w/storage for iron and sprays. A great oh and ah getter.

(Plan space for a washer and dryer in your layout, but don't put these appliances in. Most people already have their own.)

- For upper-end rehabs: Use high-quality oak, cherry, or the European-style laminate look.
- Whatever cabinet you select, be sure the drawers slide well (double slide ball bearings are the best). Avoid the wood grain formica look.
- Reline drawers and cabinet shelves.

Kitchen Countertops

Whenever you replace kitchen cabinets, you are almost always obligated to replace countertops as well. The countertops are built or cut to fit the exact size and shape of the base cabinets, and it is almost impossible to fit new cabinets to an existing countertop. It follows then that in most cases the countertops were put in at the same time, are showing their age along with the cabinetry, and therefore need replacing also. If you are going to the expense and trouble of replacing cabinets, it is a mistake to try to retain existing sinks or faucets. They may look fine with the old stuff, but alongside the new installation, they will show their age and diminish the impact of your nice new cabinets.

A possible exception to this situation is when you elect to reface existing cabinets. Counter replacement now becomes an option since the cabinet frames will remain in place. However, you may still face the dilemma of the counters looking worn compared to the new look of the refaced cabinets. When in doubt, replace them. The cost is proportionately not that much and the overall look of the job, in an important area like the kitchen, is critical to the success of the finished product.

Eat-in Kitchens

Eat-in spaces in kitchens are desired, requested, or required by many buyers. At the very least, you should try to incorporate a space at the counter where a couple of stools or chairs could be placed and snacks or quick meals enjoyed. Whether or not eat-in areas are a resale necessity depends on the availability of adjacent rooms for dining.

Kitchen Planning

Whether the kitchen you are dealing with is large or small, it pays to spend the time to plan well. You need to research all the many possibilities for space utilization, choices of cabinet style, functional placement of appliances, and general interior design appeal. The kitchen is usually where the bulk of the rehab dollars are spent and is often the most warranted. Unless you have some training or experience in kitchen design, it pays to deal with a cabinet shop where there is some expert advice available. There are many small to medium shops that fabricate counters on-site and sell prebuilt cabinets at a wide range of prices. You can often do as well price-wise at a specialty shop as at a discount lumber yard. You get the benefit of hands-on knowledge rather than a recently hired salesperson who has had a 3-day quick course in sales and design. There are a wide variety of magazines on the market that feature kitchen decorating and design. They are valuable resources for ideas; however, many projects depicted are done on unlimited budgets and to pick one aspect from them can be dangerous. Sometimes, what looks spectacular as part of a whole design concept can look very out of place when injected into an unrelated kitchen design. This does not mean you should not use magazines. They are valuable for ideas, but they must be used with some reservation. Bookstores are good sources of planning information and instruction. Libraries can also be possibilities, but their books tend to be behind the times in terms of current trends and technology.

No matter which or how many sources you use, and no matter how good they are, you must make your decisions based on your budget and how the design and material selection fits the total package of the house as a whole.

Kitchen Floors

Kitchens are among the highest traffic areas in the house and have more potential for damage from spills and stains than any other interior portion of the house. At the same time, this floor must be attractive and blend well with the highest cost per square foot area of the house. Some options to accomplish this challenge follow.

Ceramic Tile

This material offers more variety in color and texture than all the other choices. It is also the most resistant to traffic and stains (the grout that joins the tile is porous, however, and must be sealed with silicon to avoid darkening and grease stains). Ceramic tile is also the easiest to clean and will maintain its good looks and luster the longest. Because of all these positive features, it is the first choice among many buyers of homes. Its payback is very high since it is universally attractive among buyers and is generally regarded as an upgrade. The cost, as you might expect, is high in relation to other choices, but if the funds are available, and the quality of the rest of the house is good, then tile is an excellent choice. There are a few drawbacks to consider. Tile is essentially a permanent floor and if the color and pattern selected are not in good taste, it may turn some buyers away. Tile is also very hard and anything that falls on it is likely to break.

Note: Installation of ceramic tile is not beyond the abilities of most people. You can generally learn to work with it by assisting an experienced person on one or two jobs. Once you have learned the skills involved, you can save a considerable amount on installation, and, by purchasing tile at wholesale prices, the cost of a tile floor can then be as little as $3.00 per square foot.

Resilient Flooring

Often called "sheet goods" or linoleum, resilient flooring is essentially a one-piece covering glued down over the entire floor. In some cases, it is necessary to have a seam that joins two large pieces. The range of colors and patterns is also quite extensive. Vinyl is probably the most common type of kitchen floor seen in homes. Its life span is between four and eight years, depending on its quality and the traffic it must endure. While it is more forgiving to things that fall on it and easier on legs that must stand on it, its original sheen diminishes with age, and it is susceptible to scratches and cuts. The popular "no wax" varieties do hold their sheen well, but tend to show signs of wear after a year or so. Most buyers are satisfied if they find a good quality vinyl floor in place, but as with wallpaper, they are often not in agreement with the color or pattern chosen for them. Many patterns attempt to simulate tile, but like most imitations, they often fall short of that goal. If you must replace the vinyl floor in a home due to its unacceptable condition, or if its color or pattern is not suitable, try to select a tasteful, neutral look. Avoid patterns that try to simulate stone, tile, or wood, and do not try to install it yourself. Installation is a job for a skilled, experienced mechanic. A poorly installed new floor is noticeable and unacceptable to most buyers. Do not be tempted to buy low-priced goods. The installation costs will be the same and the floor will look worn and cheap in a short period of time. Your best bet is to select a medium-priced material. Once again, remember to keep the quality and overall look in sync with the rest of the house.

Carpet

No, No, No! It looks wrong, it offends buyers, and it doesn't perform well. If it is already in place when you buy the house, tear it out and choose any other floor. I can't think of any reason or situation where carpet is appropriate in a kitchen area.

Bathrooms: The Next Most Valuable Rehab Room

Kitchens may be the most functional room in the house, but bathrooms are the most personal. Some buyers may be willing to think in terms of making minor changes to these areas, that is, paint and wallpaper, but the idea of major work that involves carpentry or plumbing is often enough to turn the majority away. On the positive side, a sparkling clean, well-maintained bath with quality features is often a reassuring sight and can give the buyer a feeling that the entire house is sound and well cared for.

Bathrooms are among the most worked-on areas of a house. This is because they are subject to the most wear and tear. They get used many times per day, are typically a relatively small space, and are subject to exposure to water on a continual basis. The typical homeowner will be willing to make a short-term repair to a water problem, but will usually put any more involved solutions on a list marked "one of these days I should." The result is a large number of houses with baths that are in need of repair and any fixer house most likely will need a major bath renovation. The two questions most people ask are, "Is it difficult to rehab baths?" and "Is it expensive?" The answer to both is "It all depends." In most cases, the work involved in major changes to the tub area are both expensive and somewhat difficult for anyone without previous experience. It can often involve difficult repairs to walls and awkward plumbing problems. The toilet and vanity/sink area are much less likely to be complicated and are more approachable by the average rehabber.

Moving Fixture Locations

When the bath is on the first floor and has a basement beneath it, moving fixtures and plumbing is not too difficult. When located on the second floor or on a slab foundation, the relocating process is much more difficult and expensive. Generally, the decision whether to rearrange fixture locations in a bath can be answered by considering whether the change will be functional as well as aesthetic. If so, most likely the payback on the costs will be worth the expense. If the work will produce only one of the two, the total cost must be kept in line with what is accomplished.

As with all changes, you need to keep them in balance with the rest of the house and consistent with the needs of your potential buyer profile.

Overall Size

For some reason, architects and builders squeeze the bathroom down to the smallest size possible that can accept the necessities of a tub, a toilet, and a sink. They fail to realize that an extra two feet of width in this area can be some of the most appreciated space in the house. The difference between what it takes to make a bath feel luxurious versus cramped is usually less than 20 sq. ft. In a rehab setting, you may or may not have the option to add that space, but if you are adding a bath or making a major change, you should think big in terms of space. No matter what style or quality of fixtures you put into a small bath, the impact they make is restricted by being crowded.

Tubs

There are a large variety of tubs to choose from. Each has advantages and drawbacks. Generally, you get what you pay for. The most expensive is the cast iron tub with the enamel finish. Its colors look the best, the finish is the most resistant to scratches and chips, but the tub is very heavy and difficult to manipulate in tight places.

Steel tubs in contrast are very light, but their finish is thin and apt to chip easily. White steel tubs look much like white cast iron tubs, but are more apt to feel cheap and the color choices are more limited. Their advantages are ease of installation and they cost much less.

Ameri-cast is a new tub on the market. It has the advantage of moderate cost, it is very chip resistant, and it is much lighter than cast iron while having a similar finish.

Fiberglass tubs are still another choice. They are light, but their finish is delicate compared to enamel and they tend to have a muted shine. They cost less than cast iron, but more than steel.

The tub you choose should be suited to the rest of the house. When in doubt, make your decision in favor of the better quality.

Tub Enclosures

The area surrounding the tub must be treated in some way to protect the walls from shower over-spray. Originally, ceramic tile was the only option, but now there are several other choices. The type of tub used will be the determining factor in selecting the enclosure material.

Ceramic tile is definitely the most versatile material in terms of the effect that it can produce. The number of types of tile and colors is enormous. Tile tends to have a glossy surface similar to that of a cast iron tub's enamel finish, and makes for an excellent match to that type of tub. The drawback to ceramic tile is its initial expense and the fact that the grout or filler between the tiles can be a maintenance problem. Of all the choices, other than marble, tile is generally regarded as the top of the line and most desirable.

Fiberglass tub enclosures are a relatively new development (12 years) and are available in several choices of styles, levels of quality, and a few colors. Some units come as a one-piece tub and enclosure system. The advantage of these is that they can be installed very quickly and they eliminate the joint between the tub and the enclosure. Good-quality one-piece units are close in cost to a high-quality iron tub and moderately priced ceramic tile combination. They do, like the fiberglass tubs, tend to be somewhat delicate. Their finish is apt to scratch easily and they are susceptible to breakage during installation. Once installed and fastened to the wall, their tendency to breakage is minimal. The one-piece units will not fit through normal doors or up stairwells, so they must be installed during the initial construction of the house or through an opening created for them. Three-piece units can be purchased, but they have seams and lose some of the aesthetic value and seam-free virtues of their one-piece counterpart. Because of the difference in sheen and texture between fiberglass and enamel finishes, a combination of fiberglass enclosure and metal tub is not a good choice. As a rule of thumb, keep the enclosure and the tub material similar.

Plastic laminate panels are available with special joint pieces to make them impervious to water. If they are installed correctly, they may initially be fine, but over a period of time, they tend to warp and look unsightly. They are sold as tub kits and attempt to imitate the look of marble panels or squares of tile. At best, they are a poor substitute and don't approach either material's looks or functional ability. Their sole virtue is low cost. Their pay back is usually negative and their appeal to buyers nonexistent. Should you find yourself owning a house with this type enclosure, your best choice is to replace it.

Alternatives to tub replacement do exist. There are companies who specialize in resurfacing tubs, sinks, and toilets. They will repair damage and spray paint these fixtures. They have the ability to produce an excellent looking finished product. Their color selection is identical to the original manufacturers' but the durability is not. The cost of resurfacing generally runs about $300 for a tub, which seems like a lot but, depending on the type of replacement tub and potential damage to the walls resulting from tear out, removal, and replacement; that cost could easily reach $1,000. These same companies will also resurface ceramic tile. They are, however, sometimes hesitant to do walls. The scrubbing and the preparation work on the grout is not their favorite task. There are epoxy paints on the market that will do a reasonable job and can be brushed or rolled. Their drawback is that the paint is difficult to work with and very expensive ($30.00 per quart). Being epoxy, they are more apt to adhere and resist chipping, but nothing will be as durable as the original glaze finish of the tile. The use of these products will produce a very good looking result, but a close examination will reveal that the fixtures have been painted. Your decision to use this alternative must be made based on the overall quality of the house and your need to keep a consistent quality in the various areas of the house. In low- to moderately priced rehabs, these options are probably a reasonable choice and can be both money and time savers.

Showers

Most people want a tub and a shower and will judge a house as lacking if it does not contain either one tub and one shower or at least one combination unit. Freestanding shower units made of either fiberglass or metal do little more than lower the overall impression of a house. If a separate shower must be used, it should be of the built-in variety and of high quality. Many deluxe bathrooms have separate tubs and showers. While this is often a convenience, most people do not expect it and are happy with a combination of the two. If you are rehabbing with the intent to rent and hold, choose only high-quality units and be sure they are installed with the maximum attention to waterproofing. Water is the landlord's biggest enemy. Tenants will have no regard for small leaks or water problems and, over time, water damage will eat up your profits.

Vanities and Countertops

Most buyers look upon extra large vanities and counterspace in a bathroom as a sign of luxury and are impressed by this feature. A general rule of thumb is to install the largest vanity possible without crowding. The larger the vanity, the more drawers and the more space available to accommodate today's ever increasing personal care products.

Vanities. Vanity cabinets come in two depths, 18 inches and 21 inches (from front to back), and widths starting at 18 inches and increasing by 3-inch intervals up to 60 inches. Whenever possible, use the 21-inch deep models and nothing less than 24 inches wide. Anything smaller than that and the drawers are either nonexistent or ridiculously small. As far as style goes, your best bet is to keep things simple. The more elaborate or stylized, the more opportunity you have to offend a buyer. In terms of quality and costs, vanity cabinets are much like kitchen cabinets. Drawer slides are important and the structure of the frame should be wood or high density particle board if a plastic laminate type.

Countertops. Tops for vanities are available in pretty much the same varieties as kitchen countertops. If you choose tile, plastic laminate, or Corian®, you will need to purchase a sink separately and install it much like you would a kitchen sink. Some Corian and cultured marble tops are one-piece molded combinations. The cultured marble combinations are less expensive and provide an easy-to-clean surface with no joints. They have their applications, but are not a good choice in a deluxe installation. Solid colors that do not attempt to imitate marble are the best looking, but are often hard to find. They are also hard to find in the larger sizes, perhaps due to the fact that they offer little versatility in installation (a necessity in fitting the wider sizes). Corian is available in either a molded one-piece sink/counter combination or in sheets which can be fitted with a separate sink. There are also wood countertops with waterproof coatings. These are not good choices as they tend to not be as waterproof as they should be, the shine tends to wear off, and many people do not like the look.

Sinks.   As with tubs, the best choice for a sink is the cast-iron enameled type. These are usually self-rimming, meaning they sit directly on the counter and do not require a separate metal strip around their edge. You can also buy self-rimming steel sinks but they are prone to chipping and will rust wherever the thinner enamel cracks or chips. Pedestal sinks are another choice. These may be very attractive for some installations, but lack the countertops and storage provided by drawers and doors in vanities. Developing plumbing for pedestal sinks can be a frustrating experience as well. Wall-hung sinks are institutional looking and do little to impress buyers.

There is more room for color variety in the bath than in the kitchen. It is a good idea to keep the color of the toilet and the tub the same. The sink can be used as an accent color although you will pay a premium for the deeper, more exotic colors. Keep in mind: the darker the color sink, the more water marks show. White is never offensive, always looks good, and blends well with almost any color counter or floor. One thing to keep in mind is that if you are doing white on white, white tiles may not be the same shade as white sinks. Each manufacturer has its own interpretation of what white is and you could be disappointed or even alarmed that the whites do not match. This is not such a problem in fixtures that are not in direct contact with each other, such as the tub and toilet; the difference may not be noticeable. Wherever tile is in direct contact with a fixture, the potential for a mismatch of whites exists.

Faucets.   Once again, the variety of faucets available in this area is huge. The rules to follow are to keep the style simple and the quality medium to high. There are some extremely expensive faucets on the market. Most of them are overkill and can be a little too stylish for some buyers. Chrome is the safest choice in terms of acceptance. Some of the European porcelain/color fixtures are attractive but they can look out of place unless the vanity and sink are high-fashion to match.

Faucets with brass inner workings are the best quality and most people prefer the single-handle type of convenience. You should pay attention to matching styles in the tub and sink, and make sure towel bars are compatible to both. Don't mix gold and silver.

Floors.   The choices are ceramic tile, linoleum, carpet, vinyl tiles, hardwood, or pavers. The best choices are those that are inherently impervious to water. The high-quality self-stick vinyl tiles are fine but require careful installation. If they are not accurately laid, they can detract from the quality of the other materials. Ceramic tile, on the other hand, has the ability to enhance or upgrade other fixtures, but installation is difficult and requires experience and special tools. Hardwood is expensive and is often pictured in magazines, but would probably make most buyers nervous about maintenance. Carpet is the most comfortable, especially when getting out of the shower or early in the morning when barefoot. It should not be fiber-backed or permanently installed over subflooring. High-quality rubber-backed carpet or area rugs over tile is the best option for carpet. Most often the buyer expects to make that purchase. Your best choice is to provide a tile or linoleum floor.

Lighting and Mirrors.   Mirrors and lighting go together and should be planned to function in concert with each other. Both have a dramatic effect on the function and aesthetics of the room. The area above the vanity requires a high-quality mirror. Choose the biggest one you can afford. This is where people spend the most time getting ready or checking their appearance. Men shaving and women applying makeup require lots of light. Theatrical type lights above the mirror are a popular choice. They are both attractive and functional. Recessed lighting and track lighting are both popular for modern or contemporary baths. Ornate fixtures end up costing a lot of money and producing very little light. Be sure light reaches the shower or tub area as well. They are sometimes neglected even though they are the most expensive part of the room. A dark tub or shower area is annoying to the user if only from a comfort point of view. Bathrooms should also have a ventilation fan. If you install one, be sure it is the type that is vented to the outside. If it merely dumps its moisture into the attic, it is not doing its job. If your vent is a combination vent and light fixture, be sure to purchase the type with a separate switch for the fan. Fans tend to be noisy and can be very annoying when they don't need to be on.

Walls.   The bathroom walls are going to get wet! Latex or water-based paints will not hold up as well as oil-based. Semi-gloss should be used for washability. Colors should be mild. Once again, shades of white and off-white keep you out of trouble and consistently keep from offending buyers. Wallpaper is generally not a good idea, but if used, you must be selective as to type. Some of the more elaborate and interesting wallpaper is also very delicate and will not do well in the moist atmosphere of the bathroom.

Closets and Storage

One of the reasons people move from one house to another is because the old house is just too small. The house itself may have an adequate number of rooms and the individual rooms may have been large enough, but the house still seemed small. The reason for this may be too many belongings and not enough room to store them. When a family's belongings overwhelm the living spaces, the house suddenly feels too small. Houses built several years ago were designed to accommodate the needs of people of that time. Now husband and wife are both in the work force, their wardrobes have increased proportionately, and the closet spaces of 20 years ago are inadequate. The scenario goes on to include children's possessions and their life-styles as well. The end result is that our possessions are squeezing us out of our houses. After living in an apartment or an outdated house, people are conscious of just how much space they really need and are willing to pay for the convenience of good storage. This should be a high priority for initial selection of a property. If a house does not have good storage and can be changed by adding space, or adjusting the old space, you can increase resale value.

Foyers

The point at which you enter or leave a house is the natural and most convenient place to store jackets and outerwear. Without a closet in this location, bedroom closets get overloaded with bulky jackets (especially in cold climates), and guests' coats end up being laid over chairs or other awkward places. This is usually a difficult part of a house to add space to, but many buyers will be disappointed if the foyer closet is missing. A light in the closet with a switch on the outside is another plus.

Kitchens

Most kitchens have space allocated for storage of pots, pans, and dishes, but brooms, canned goods, and the vacuum cleaner seem to get squeezed into some space as an afterthought. If you can, incorporate a floor-to-ceiling cabinet for this purpose. You will have produced a winner.

Bathrooms

This room is becoming more and more a focus in the modern home. Bathrooms are getting bigger and bigger to accommodate the larger fixtures and increased functions of the room. Whether the house is low end or high end, a spacious bath is appreciated. Vanities usually provide storage for some items, but a special place for towels and a medicine chest are expected. Almost every bathroom can have a medicine chest recessed in the wall space if necessary. If a pedestal sink is used, the storage usually found in the vanity is lost and must be made up for.

Bedrooms

Today's life-style has generated a new variety and volume of clothing for most people. Most houses have not kept pace with the increase by adding closet space. The concept of a bedroom in older homes was that it was a room to sleep in. Even those homes with exceptionally large bedrooms rarely had large closets. They simply were not needed or demanded. These days, bedrooms often double as office space for home computers, as places to study, and as storage for books, sporting equipment, hobbies, and certainly all the usual clothing, plus any specialized apparel. As a result, most closets are too small. Most people would like at least twice as much closet space as they actually have. There are now companies whose entire business is built around closet improvement. There have been books written on the subject of closets and closet design.

It is not the purpose of this book to teach you how to design closets, but to make you aware of their importance as a marketing item and as a source of profit. This is not to say that you should expect that someone will buy a house for its closets alone, but it is very possible that a house may not sell as a result of poor closets. On the other hand, it is also true that buyers are willing to pay more for a house with exceptional closets. If the floor plan of a house lends itself to increased bedroom closets without diminishing another attribute, and the overall balance of the house fits with the change, an additional or enlarged closet should be considered.

Generally speaking, you get more functional space out of a closet that runs the length of a wall rather than a walk-in type. The walk-in type can, depending on what you are starting with, be less expensive to build, since it has only one small door. A full wall closet with high-quality mirrored sliding doors can get a bit pricey. The advantage is that, although the addition of such a closet may actually make the room smaller, it can give the illusion of making the room larger due to the mirrors. The benefit is then two-fold:

1. You have added a large closet.
2. You have produced a desirable design effect.

There are times when it makes sense to make an entire room into a closet. In houses where the fourth bedroom is very small—8 feet by 9 feet—the impression is one of "what a small bedroom." If that room were converted into a closet, the comment would be "what a huge closet." Taken a step further, an extra bedroom could be converted into a combination new closet and master bath. For around $4,500 you may make your house unique in a neighborhood of older homes, and solve a problem of "what will we do with that little room?" You must always remember that the majority of buyers have little imagination when it comes to visualization of floor plans, or they are intimidated by the prospect of making a change by themselves. This offers you the opportunity to provide a service and make a profit. The only caution here is to again keep your future buyer profile in mind and don't over improve for the neighborhood.

WAYS TO MARKET YOUR "FINISHED PRODUCT"

What Are Your Chances to Sell It Yourself?

What are your chances to sell and save the commission? Not very good. First of all, the pros, who have the tools, who know the tricks, and who work at it full time, have a success rate of only around 40 percent, despite the fact that about 80 percent of the buyers are believed to be working with agents.

Second, a lot of buyers are not eager to deal with a For Sale by Owner (FSBO). Aggressive bargain-hunters shop for FSBOs but most buyers do not do the same. Many people are too unsure of themselves to deal with another amateur.

Third, can you sell and save the commission, and not just sell at a reduced price? National studies have supposedly shown that the average FSBO nets less than a similar listed owner. If this is true, it doesn't have to be: the FSBO should be able to save a majority of the commission, if that seller will take all the steps necessary to get the top dollar for a house. Jerry Bresser, a real estate educator, says,

> . . . a ten-year study showed that owners selling directly to buyers grossed 9.5 percent less than when similar houses were sold by real estate firms . . . anytime [someone] buys directly from the owner (be it a car or house) they expect to pay less.

It's an Auction

Why should FSBOs net less? Perhaps because some don't understand that marketing a house is an auction, in slow motion. But the idea is the same: the bigger the crowd, the higher the price, up to a point. But we hear sellers talking about "the right buyer." "It only takes one," says the seller, who has been waiting for months. Such nonsense. If there is only one buyer for what you are selling, why would that person pay your price, when there is no competition for it? If you have to sell, and there is only one buyer, you have to take whatever that buyer offers.

Don't get mired in the mud of clichés or you may be just one more FSBO that flopped.

If You Decide to Try the FSBO Approach

As long as you don't badly overprice your house, you probably won't lose anything but time. And even if you don't do all the things you should, you may still come out of this with two benefits: (1) the commission you set out to save if you get lucky, and (2) some appreciation of what agents endure.

Try it for a month or so, if you have the time. Just make sure you've priced it right. And don't do it too long. Buyers are very sensitive to "time on the market," or, as agents say, the "shopworn" house.

Using an Agent to Help Market Your Project

- Real estate commissions are negotiable; however, under 4 percent you will lose the advantages of the market penetration or agent exposure of the property you are paying for.
- Estimate you will reach 12 percent of the market when you go FSBO.
- You reach 67 percent plus when you have the realtor's resources working for you.
- Use a "Help-You-Sell" realtor who discounts the commission, usually 3 percent.
- Your time is a major consideration. You must perform some realtor functions, for example, Open Houses, meeting buyers, prequalifying buyers. With a discount, you'll be expected to do these things.

The Charles Schwab Approach

1. It's always possible, when you lease, that you will find the perfect tenant—the one who wants to buy. A beneficial arrangement for you both would be the lease option. Lease options are win/win situations in slow markets. Discuss the possibilities with your tenant, and request a 5 percent nonrefundable deposit in return for a year's option to purchase the property at a set price. At the end of that time, when the lease is up, you may have a live-in buyer on your hands—while the monthly rent payments have covered your carrying costs. If he or she doesn't buy, you keep the deposit and you can remarket the property.

2. Live in the property yourself. The benefit of residing in it before you sell is that it buys you time. If the market is not right, you can simply stay put, enjoying the fruits of your equity in the property, and deducting the mortgage payments until the world of real estate sees brighter days. This means that, regardless of present market

conditions, you're earning money just by staying put. Small builders often use this tactic when they can't sell what they just built right away.

3. Take a smaller profit than the one you expected. You never get hurt taking a profit. When you planned on making $15,000 but find yourself in a position to make $5,000, you're still doing all right. Maybe you should sell and move on. A $5,000 profit may look okay when you have only one more mortgage payment in the bank.

OFFER A BUYER'S PROTECTION PLAN

You may want to purchase a policy for the new owner as an incentive to buy. It has shown to be an effective marketing tool, particularly in rehabs which, by virtue of their price and size, are in competition with new homes. Some real estate companies offer the policy at no charge when you list your property with them. The average one-year warranty policy will cost about $250.

Timing of Coverage

- *Optional seller's coverage* starts 7 days after receipt of application by company and continues until close of escrow or cancelled.
- *Buyer's coverage* starts at close of escrow and continues for 1 year.
- *Renewals* are for a 1-year period.

Payment

- Payment is due at close of escrow and must be received by the company within 10 working days.
- Renewal payment is due prior to expiration date.

Contract Coverage

The following items are usually covered for the buyer and are an option for the seller. Also, we show examples of items "not covered" to assist your understanding of the contract. It is also important to review limits of liability of the particular company's policy you purchase.

- Water heater
- Gas or electric
- Tank leaks
- Control thermostat and thermocouple

- Gas valve
- Temperature and pressure relief valve
- Drain valve
- Heating elements.

Heating

- Gas, electrical, oil furnaces
- Thermostats
- Baseboard convectors
- Radiators
- Pumps and motors
- Combustion chambers
- Heating elements
- Gas valves
- Switches, wiring, and relays
- Burners.

Not covered: Auxiliary space heaters, filters (including electronic air cleaners), registers, oil storage tanks.

Kitchen Appliances

- Range/Oven/Cooktop: Burners, switches, thermostat pilot assemblies, door and hinges, wiring and elements.
- Dishwasher: Motor, pump, timer, seals and gaskets, dispenser, air gap, door liners and latches, heating elements, switches, spray arms. Units rusted beyond repair are not covered for sellers nor for buyers if condition is visible during first 30 days of buyers' coverage.
- Garbage disposal: All parts and components including motor, wiring, blades, switch and casing.
- Microwave oven (built-in only): All parts and components including electronics, door latch, magnetron tube, timer, transformer, and touch tone panels.
- Trash compactor: Parts and components including motor, ram, switches, and wiring.
- Instant hot water dispenser: All parts and components including casing, element, wiring, and valve.

Not covered: Knobs, racks, clock/timer, rotisserie, removable baskets, cosmetic defects, lock/key assembly, refinishing or replacement of cabinets or countertops.

Plumbing

- Leaks and breaks of water, drain, gas, vent, or sewer lines
- Stoppages in drain, vent, and sewer lines
- Valves: shower, tub, diverter, angle stop, and gate valves
- Toilet tanks, bowls, and mechanisms (replaced with builders' standards as necessary)
- Circulating hot water pump
- Permanently installed sump pumps.

Not covered: Sinks and bath tubs, faucets, filter, shower enclosure and base pan, caulking and grouting, septic tank, inadequate or excessive water pressure, water softeners, pressure regulators, sewage ejectors.

Electrical

- Wiring
- Panels and subpanels
- Switches and fuses
- Plugs
- Breakers (including ground fault)
- Junction boxes
- Conduit
- Exhaust fans.

Not covered: Door bells, intercom fixtures, alarms, garage door openers, inadequate wiring capacity.

Optional Coverage for Buyer

The buyer is covered for the following items when additional premium is paid at closing.

Central Air Conditioning (Ducted)

- Refrigeration system (includes heat pump)
- Condensing unit
- Compressor
- Motors
- Coils
- Fuses, breakers, disconnect boxes and wiring

- Thermostats
- Liquid and suction line dryers
- Valves
- Leaks in freon lines.

Not covered: Condenser casings, registers, filters (including electronic air cleaner), gas air conditioners.

Evaporative Cooler

- Pump
- Motor
- Float assembly
- Casing
- Belts and pulleys.

Pool and/or Spa Equipment

- Jacuzzi tubs and whirlpools
- Heating unit
- Motors
- Valves
- Impellers, switches, and relays
- Above-ground plumbing and electrical
- Filter
- Timer
- Seals and gaskets
- Pumps
- Bearings.

Not covered: Cleaning equipment and pool sweeps, liners, lights, structural defects, and solar water heaters, inaccessible components.

4

Rehab Financing
Techniques and Programs

PURCHASING HOMES THROUGH A VARIETY OF METHODS

There is a tendency to want to know all of the possible means of purchasing homes, in hopes that you will eventually come upon one that is significantly easier than the others and has an inherent built-in foolproof profit. If there is such a mechanism, it is a well-guarded secret. The selection of the proper house in the proper neighborhood with carefully selected improvements is the criterion for success. The financing and various avenues for purchasing are, however, often what make the purchase possible. Good terms on a bad house are no bargain, and the wrong terms on a great house can force a sale at an inopportune time or limit options due to up-front expenses.

Choosing a property just because it can be purchased well below market value does not insure success and buying at an auction does not insure a price below market value. As an investor, you need to be aware of several sources for properties and a variety of financing. Knowledge of what is possible makes the likelihood of finding good properties on a regular basis a reality.

This chapter will cover a number of finance areas, from acquisition formulas to using government loan programs for purchase and resale. A synopsis of the material follows:

1. Purchasing:
   a. How to calculate your offer price on a fixer property.
   b. Evaluating the true cost of assuming a seller's existing loan.

   c. Use of seller "carry back" financing.

   d. Other resources to locate fixer projects and financing methods required by each.

   e. Using "real" government loan resources for rehab.

   f. Innovative buying and selling methods that every professional rehabber should consider.

We will start with the way to calculate your purchase offer on a project. It is a universally used formula that has been tailored to the research methods outlined in previous chapters.

Calculation Example

Listed Price for Property $__130,000__

1. Ceiling price for any property in this neighborhood	$ 175,000
2. Real estate commission—6% of item #1	– $ 10,500
3. Ball park rehab estimate	– $ 15,000
4. Profit you want to make	– $ 15,000
5. Less 3% of current asking price	– $ 6,950
6. Estimate 6 months of carrying costs	– $ 6,936
7. Your best offer	$ 120,614
Add back in step 7 (optional, but should be used to calculate at 5% annual appreciation)	$ 6,500
Amount you can offer and make the profit you need	$ 127,114

If You Intend to "Flip" a Property

Step 1.   Establish which is the best house, in the best condition, within the boundaries you know to be the subject property's neighborhood. Ask the agent for comparable market information and the computer area market survey information to verify this "ceiling" value.

Best houses have sold at (in last 3 months; if data not available, go back 6 months)   _____

Step 2.   Begin to subtract marketing expenses and rehab estimated expenses (Steps 2 through 6).

Deduct: Commission percent to sell completed project (see section on negotiating agent commissions)   – _____

Step 3.   Estimated (ballpark this high) cost to rehab (done with walk-through and sample cost of items forms in an earlier chapter, or a trusted contractor).   – _____

Step 4.   Amount of money you feel is a
reasonable profit for the complexity and time you
estimate this particular project will require (I have had
people ask about whether there is a formula of $3 back
for each $1 spent on the rehab, and yes, there are those
who use this). I prefer you ballpark an amount of time
you will be sweat equity participating or supervising
and put a dollars-for-your-time value in this section. If
you don't get a profit equal to what you felt your efforts
were worth, you will have defeated your goal in getting
into this business, so only you can assign this value.   – _____

Step 5.   Costs associated with the purchase and
the resale of the property—ballpark 3 percent of asking
price, as a rough (higher than probable) estimate of this
cost.   – _____

Step 6.   The costs of "carrying the project" for 6
to 8 months. Calculate high on the expense items, so
that the news will only get better when these costs
actually turn out to be lower. Get this figure from your
agent based on the current asking price, less your down
payment, at the interest rate prevalent for the program
you will be choosing for this project. Total principal,
interest, taxes, and insurance, times the number of
months needed from closing on this purchase to closing
the resale transaction. Ideally, and as you get more
experience, this will not exceed 3 to 6 months. Again,
this number will have been calculated high.   – _____

Subtotal

This represents the bottom-line, most conservative
offer price you can give on this project and still make
the profit you wish.   = _____

What about the appreciation that will occur in owning the project for 6
months, even if you did nothing to improve it? I strongly recommend to
students that, in some proportion, they add back in the projected appreciation, to be able to offer more; thus, they can tie the property up
quickly. This may be more important than trying to keep this profit as a
bonus on the other end of the project. You can't make a profit if someone
else has gotten the property. How do you know what appreciation rate to
use? When there is any appreciation occurring in your market, calculate
the very conservative figure of 3 to 5 percent annually, and this will
guide you to a figure. Your agent can give you an accurate estimate.

Step 7. Equals the amount you can either offer
or counter offer with, and have a reasonable degree of
probability for keeping your profit figure.   _____

Blank Calculation Example

Listed Price for Property $_____

1. Ceiling price for any property in this neighborhood	$_____
2. Real estate commission—6% of item #1	− $_____
3. Ball park rehab estimate	− $_____
4. Profit you want to make	− $_____
5. Less 3% of current asking price	− $_____
6. Estimate 6 months of carrying costs	− $_____
7. Your best offer	$_____
Add back in step 7 (optional, but should be used to calculate at 5% annual appreciation)	$_____
Amount you can offer and make the profit you need	$_____

ASSUMING A SELLER'S LOAN

Another whole chapter could be devoted to assumable financing variations, but, for our purposes, a brief summary of the main points on
assumable financing follows:

- Since the mid-1980s, fixed rate conventional (nongovernment) loans
  have not been assumable to a new buyer. These are now what are
  called "due on sale" and must be paid off by the seller when the
  property passes to a new buyer. The government loans, FHA, and VA
  loans that are fixed rate and were originated before 1988 are assumable under certain criteria, with notification to the lender and a
  small transfer fee.

- Government loans that are newer than that time frame need to be
  researched specifically for their assumability. In general, they are
  assumable, with credit qualification by the lender of the new buyer.
  Adjustable rate loans, again as a general rule, are assumable to new
  buyers with the lenders' approval of the buyer (must formally apply) and the right to "bump" the interest rate, along with charging a
  fee for the assumption. This is very general and *each loan* a seller
  offers as assumable must have its terms and specifications cleared
  with the lender.

We noted earlier that you will want to choose adjustable rate mortgages when you use conventional financing so that you have large assumable loans to offer new buyers as a marketing tool for your project.

When you evaluate the cost of assuming financing and adding a new loan in order to purchase, you will use a *blended rate calculation* that shows how much of an effective interest rate you will be paying when you blend the existing loan balance rate with a new supplemental loan at the current interest rate. The formula and an example of this calculation follow.

FORMULA: CALCULATING EFFECTIVE INTEREST RATE

$$\frac{\text{Original loan amount}}{\text{Needed loan amount}} \times \text{Old loan interest rate} = \begin{array}{l}\text{Loan \#1 portion of} \\ \text{rate (old money)}\end{array}$$

+

$$\frac{\text{Added new loan}}{\text{Needed loan amount}} \times \begin{array}{l}\text{New money needing to} \\ \text{be borrowed loan rate}\end{array} = \begin{array}{l}\text{Loan \#2 portion of} \\ \text{rate (new money)}\end{array}$$

+

2 Loans = the Blended Rate

EXAMPLE: CALCULATING THE COST OF ASSUMING SOMEONE'S LOAN

Purchase price	$150,000
Minus down payment	− 15,000
Total financing needed	$135,000
Assume original loan	$ 80,000
Added new loan	55,000
New loan amount	$135,000

EXAMPLE: CALCULATING AN EFFECTIVE INTEREST RATE

$$\frac{\$80,000}{\$135,000} \times 8\% \quad \begin{array}{l}\text{(interest on} \\ \text{original loan)}\end{array} = .0474$$

+

$$\frac{\$55,000}{\$135,000} \times 14\% \quad \begin{array}{l}\text{(interest on new} \\ \text{loan needed)}\end{array} = \underline{.0570}$$

$$.1045$$

Change to a percent = 10.45%
This is the Blended Rate Calculation.

We begin now to review purchase or purchase and resale methods, and what problems these techniques and programs are meant to overcome.

For investor buyers, it has become increasingly more difficult to purchase properties with low down payments. As a flipper of properties, this becomes even more of an obstacle. The traditional investor down payment required by lenders is 20 to 25 percent. Investors would like, and most need, to be more highly leveraged (cash out of pocket in ratio to amount of real estate purchased) in their purchases. Owner occupants can more readily find traditional loans that allow for 10 percent down payments. We will even be discussing 5 percent down in one loan program. Let's look at a brief example of this:

Traditional Financing

Purchase price of a fixer property in "as is" condition:	$100,000
Investor down payment:	$20,000 to $25,000 down (depending on lender chosen)
Owner occupant:	$10,000 to $20,000, depending on the lender

Now we must have the money for the repairs.

Estimate average cosmetic to moderate rehab:	$12,000–$15,000
Investor, total out-of-pocket expense:	$32,000–$40,000
Owner occupant, total out-of-pocket expense:	$32,000–$35,000

If you have $35,000 cash to invest, you need to be looking at multi-units or higher-end property. This is not a very well-leveraged project with the above scenario.

The other side of the coin is that you must recognize the problem faced by most of the potential buyers of your projects—the down payment.

In a recent national survey, participants identified the biggest obstacle to buying a home as:

Down payment:	70%
Prices too high:	47%
Trouble affording the payments:	30%

(Total equals more than 100% because some participants checked 2 categories.)

In examining the purchase/sale methods that follow, you will want to get into the property with as little down as is reasonable. No money down *is not* a reasonable approach! Set up the financing option for new buyers that helps them overcome the down payment hurdle.

THE 80–10–10 MODEL

Recommended for Both Investor and Owner-Occupied

This is the most widely accepted method for getting into property with a 10 percent down payment. Inquire with your lender choices or broker and be sure they do 80–10–10 loans.

   Note: Shop for loans for fixer properties with lenders that are called portfolio lenders, as they have the most relaxed property underwriting and buyer down payment requirements. How do you know if they are portfolio lenders? You ask if they sell their loans after they make them to the secondary market or if they keep them. If they keep them and collect the payments, they are portfolio lenders.

Typical Transaction Using 80–10–10

Purchase price:	$80,000
Down payment:	$8,000
Financing from lender:	$64,000
Seller to carry back a second mortgage or trust deed on the property:	$8,000
Total:	$80,000

Most sellers, especially in slow markets, are willing to take back part of the financing, especially if you are only asking for a short period of time. The recommended time frame is a 5-year balloon payment (or due date) with a 30-year amortization on the note payments or interest-only payments.

   If you are flipping properties and not living in the property, you may not need this much time, so a 1- to 2-year term request will serve your needs and most likely be music to the seller's ears.

   There are occasions when you might try to get the seller to carry more financing, but for most cosmetic or moderate rehab this technique will work. If the house is a major rehab, then you may need to request a higher percentage of seller financing.

   You can then finance the rehab costs with one of the special rehab loan programs from the menu that follows later in this chapter.

OTHER ACQUISITION METHODS TO CONSIDER TO LOCATE POSSIBLE PROJECTS

Tax Sales—Property That Has Gone Back to the County for Taxes

These properties are generally distressed and are sold by public auction. To get on the list to receive notice of these sales (they occur only on an as-needed basis), call the County Recorder's office and ask for whatever they are calling their property disposition department. This is a great way to pick up below-market properties, and you can usually preview them and conduct your research ahead of time so that you know which ones contain all the recommended elements. The caution here is that, as with every auction, you must be prepared to control the heat of the moment and know when to get out of the bidding. I recently attended a property tax auction and again was reminded of this principle, as I watched over 60 people bid a property up to about 125 percent of fair market value. Professionals take a real estate agent with them and give them the top dollar they want to bid. This ensures that they will not get themselves caught in an emotional bidding process. On the other hand, at this same auction, I saw a completely "trashed" fixer property sold at about 25 percent below market, with only one bidder. Check your local jurisdiction bidding rules, but commonly you must present at least 10 percent in cash or cashier's check to seal the offer on the day of the auction and then you have 30 days to close the transaction. If you are smart, you will already have lined up your lender and be preapproved, so that you can accommodate the 30-day requirement without any major effort.

Probate Sales

In each state, there are specific rules about how the properties of a deceased person are sold to glean money for the heirs and estate. This is an under-prospected area for fixers, and for that reason if no other, is a good avenue for you to pursue. Due to the differences from area to area, I can't comment on a uniform approach to financing these sales. Utilize your local agent to help you become a savvy bidder on this rehab opportunity.

Bank-Owned Properties

Most large residential banks and savings and loans have a department they wish they did not need to have, called Real Estate Owned (REO). This avenue has become very confusing in the wake of bank losses that created the need for the government's super agency to liquidate real estate for insolvent savings and loans. The Resolution Trust Corp. is that agency, and it is just now beginning to put the residential parts of its portfolio on the market. You should connect with this resource for possible projects through a real estate agent who has become a recognized broker to handle Resolution Trust properties. There is a national 800 phone number for the Trust that can tell you who in your area is participating. Also watch your local business journal publication, which we spoke about in the beginning of the book, for seminars on how to do business with the Trust.

Not all bank-owned properties are in this pool. Again, locating a real estate agent who has had REO listings is the best way to learn this aspect of acquiring properties. In general, the advantages to you are about a 10 percent down payment, waived fees, and lower interest rates than lenders' "retail" loan rates. You also have built-in financing for the project. A very high percentage of REOs are in need of repair, and some lenders do those repairs and ask "fair market value" for the finished house, while others do no repairs and sell at an "as is" price.

Government Foreclosures

There have been books, and books, and more books written about this subject, so we will add only two pieces of information here that may help you.

In VA foreclosures, you are given different categories of property; some come with financing and others without. The ones with the financing traditionally attract the most bidders, and therefore often are sold at "over bid" or higher prices than the VA wanted. This is not your "window of opportunity"; rather, it is in the ones that are offered with no financing. These properties usually are advertised as "no CRV (the VA's term for appraisal) will be issued." They are the properties the most in need of rehab and without any financing attached. As an investor, you will already know where you can get your financing in 30 days, and how much you qualify for, so these are perfect projects for you. You will find there is not as much competition in the number of sealed bids for these properties, because no financing is offered. Again, the best way to explore this avenue is to utilize an agent who has been through the bid process before and can give you the same computer data to evaluate the profit potential of the property.

A general information outline on the FHA or HUD foreclosure process follows. My one tip here is to remember that HUD is not required to take the highest bid; they must take the bid that yields the *best net proceeds back* to the agency. For example, if you are an all-cash buyer, or do not ask them to participate in any closing expenses, or have used a buyer's broker and are not asking FHA to pay a commission, you could conceivably offer less and still come out the winning bidder.

HUD SALES PROGRAM

Sales Program Description

Here is how their sales program works: Shortly after a property is acquired by HUD, it is programmed for sale. They have two principal sales programs: (1) Properties are either offered for sale all cash, as-is or (2) with FHA mortgage insurance. All cash means that the purchaser must pay cash for the property at closing. While they understand many buyers get conventional financing to buy these properties, they will not refund the earnest deposit if such financing cannot be secured and the buyer can't close. On properties sold with FHA mortgage insurance, HUD is willing to provide mortgage insurance. The lower down payment requirements make these properties easier to sell and the deposit will be refunded if a purchaser does not pass mortgage credit approval.

Closing Time

Properties offered for sale, all cash, as-is, are expected to close escrow within 30 to 45 days of acceptance of the sales offer. Properties sold with FHA mortgage insurance are generally given a little longer time. Extensions may be requested but there is a fee. They are granted on a case-by-case basis. The special FHA 203(k) loan we cover later in this chapter is one of the exceptions. (See Table 4.3.)

How Properties Are Listed

Properties are listed for sale either in local newspapers in the real estate classified section or in a list sent directly to real estate brokers by the local HUD Office. To get a list mailed to you, contact your local HUD Office. If they publish one, you will be asked to sign a nondiscrimination statement and will be given specific bidding requirements used by that Office. You or your realtor will also receive a master key to the HUD properties and a supply of HUD bid forms that must be used when presenting offers.

Bidding Procedures

Each property offered for sale will have a "list" price. This is what HUD considers the fair market value of the property. But just like in conventional real estate transactions, you can submit offers for less than the list price. Each of the offerings will have a specific date and time for a bid opening, generally about 10 days after the properties are first advertised for sale. All offers are submitted in sealed envelopes and opened at the designated time, generally at the local HUD Office. At this public opening, the bids are read aloud. The bidder who offers the highest net price and has an acceptable sales package will be accepted.

An advantage of their bidding system is that bidders can request that HUD pay mortgage and closing costs (even on all-cash sales), but the amounts payable cannot exceed actual costs. In determining the highest net bid, whatever costs the bidder requests that HUD pay, including the sales commission, are subtracted from the purchase offer price. It is the highest net bid that determines who gets the property. Just like conventional real estate, purchaser bid amounts are varied. HUD will consider all offers, but offers below that list price are accepted at their discretion.

All listed properties that do not sell at the bid opening remain available for purchase until sold or relisted. Once an offer has been accepted and the owner/selling agent notified, it is sent to one of their escrow agents for closing. It is still important for you to keep involved to make sure the deal closes. When it does, the real estate agent will get a commission.

Necessary Sales Documents

The sales documents package used to purchase a HUD property consists of a sales contract, several addenda to the contract, a broker tender form, and an earnest money deposit of 5 percent of the list price, but no more than $2,000. All of the necessary forms and specific written instructions can be obtained by contacting your local HUD Office. Each is responsible for managing and selling HUD-owned properties in its area.

EQUITY SHARING MODELS

> The problem is no longer confined to the renter and first time home buyer, it now touches us all. Shared equity is one of the ways we can address the issue of availability and affordability.
>
> *Jim Antt, President 1990*
> *California Association of Realtors*

Even in markets with lower home prices than California, the problem, as we have seen, is the same—"the Down Payment."

As someone looking to invest in more affluent neighborhoods that return better rehab profits, you may also want to examine equity sharing as a way to buy into bigger profits as well as a quick resale tool for your projects.

There are many variations of equity share agreements, and although this means the investor and buyer have many choices to tailor their agreement to a particular situation, it also means the choices can be confusing to the point of overdose.

Table 4.1 shows five of the most common structures and the legal issues common to all equity share agreements. Within these models are two basic structure choices:

1. Co-ownership (each party on title)
2. Lender model (investor is the lender and title is solely in buyer's name).

Both choices have legal, financial, and tax ramifications which should be explored thoroughly with your accountant and attorney prior to choosing which structure you will offer to your new buyers.

Please note, equity sharing is sometimes called by other names, such as:

Equity partners
Equity splitting
Dual owners
Joint venture
Reverse amortization
Shared appreciation
Shared ownership
Venture equity

All are terms for the same basic equity sharing model.

EQUITY SHARING RECOMMENDED MODEL

The simplest, as is often true in life, is the best. The easiest and most equitable model I have found would include:

Model: Co-buyer

Vesting: Title taken as tenants in common in both names

Equity Share Percent: 50 percent each party

Term: Five years (never more than seven years, since your property's value could outstrip the ability to buy a partner out)

Financing: Both apply as individuals for the first trust deed or mortgage. A second mortgage is executed in the amount of the

Table 4.1 Comparison Chart of 5 Equity Share Models*

Co-investment Structure	Remedy on Default	Risk of Sale Without Repayment	Priority over Subsequent Liens	Relationship to First Lender	Homeowner's Income Tax Treatment	Property Tax Consequence	Liability to Third Parties
Second mortgage (lender)	Non-judicial foreclosure	Unlikely	Priority	Subordinate	Not deductible or included in gain	No charge	No liability
First mortgage participation (lender)	Non-judicial foreclosure	Unlikely	Priority	Depends on terms of participation	Not deductible or included in gain	No charge	No liability
Limited partnership (co-owner)	Litigation	Possible	No priority	Subordinate	Not deductible or included in gain	Possible exemption from taxes	Liability, but limited to amount of investment
L.P. secured by deed	Non-judicial foreclosure	Unlikely	No priority				
General partnership (co-owner)	Litigation	Possible	No priority	Subordinate	Not deductible or included in gain	Possible exemption from taxes	Liability
G.P. secured by deed	Non-judicial foreclosure	Unlikely	Priority				
Tenancy in common (co-owner)	Partition litigation	Possible	No priority	Subordinate	Not deductible or included in gain	Likely exemption from taxes	Liability
T.I.C. secured by deed	Non-judicial foreclosure	Unlikely	Priority				

*Default remedy in mortgage states will differ and this chart should be matched to your own state laws regarding these categories.

investor's cash down payment, with an interest rate and term specified. Buyer pays closing costs.

Benefits: Investor obtains current market per year yield on his or her down payment money, at 12 percent or legal interest limit paid as interest only on the second trust deed or mortgage by the buyer. Buyer gets 100 percent of the mortgage interest tax deduction on income taxes.

A private party agreement is executed separately from the lender-required security agreements. In this way the agreement cannot be misconstrued as a partnership formation, which could invalidate the mortgage documents and/or the tax benefits to the new buyer.

A sample of the issues that should be addressed in this agreement follows and would be what you would request your attorney to include in your documents.

CO-BUYER PRIVATE PARTY SHARED EQUITY FINANCING AGREEMENT

Details of Transactions

- Set forth the parties to the agreement: Owner/Occupant and Owner/Investor
- Property description
- Owner/Occupant to occupy property as a principal residence
- Parties will own an "undivided interest"
- Parties will set forth their respective rights and obligations.

Agreements

- Ownership interests (percentage of ownership)
- Acquisition of property
- Restrictions
- Permitted uses: Only as residence by Owner/Occupant
- Prohibited uses
- Waiver of Right of Partition: Parties waive their right to partition under tenancy-in-common
- Maintenance
- Alterations
- Insurance
- Payment of ownership and operation costs

- Entry of Owner/Investor
- Liens
- Utilities
- Eminent domain
- Additional contributions: How are they treated?

Terminations of Events

- Default
- Breach of obligation or provision
- Abandonment
- Death
- Sale of property: Division of proceeds, payment of debts and obligations
- Buy-out options: Rights of First Refusal
- Appraisals.

Other Possible Inclusions

- Agreement to cooperate in IRC Section 1031–Tax Deferred Exchange
- Distribution of cash from Refinance and Insurance
- Notices
- Successors and Assigns
    Waiver to assigns
    Heirs, executors, and administrators bound by this agreement
    Attorney fees, arbitration clause, and separate counsel
    Indemnifications
    Disclaimers.

ADVANTAGES FOR EQUITY SHARING INVESTORS

1. Higher yield on investment money. $__X__ down payment × 12 percent interest plus $__X__ appreciation when 50 percent of 5 years appreciation rate is factored in
2. Ability to access lower owner-occupied interest rate on first trust deed/mortgage money (usually 1 to 2% below investor rates)
3. Elimination of the traditional tenant headaches of property management

4. If structured properly, may be able to still write off depreciation on the property (see your tax accountant about this issue)
5. Reduction in the negative cash flow (all costs borne by buyer/ owner).

The Way This Could Work for the Rehab Buyer

1. **To flip property:** Structure the transaction with agreed-on improvements plan. Share equity with a contractor who will work for time and materials as part of the venture to match your down payment money. Calculate a 50 percent split of profit, after costs.
2. **To sweat equity a rehab:** Equity share model is the same as previously outlined except that the co-owner agrees to match materials cost to your labor charges. Be sure and use an impartial guide for labor costs in your area, such as the *Residential Cost Handbook,* published by Marshall & Swift. Available through local bookstores by special order.

Again, actual increased value of your improvements should greatly exceed actual costs and you split 50 percent of profit with co-owner. Special research on what appraisers consider increase value and a written rehab plan are essential for success.

INVESTOR PROFIT POTENTIAL WORKSHEET

Property Address:	Term: 5 years
Owner/Occupant:	Annual Appreciation Rate: 8 percent

	Owner/Occupant
Purchase price	$ 90,000
Projected value	$132,200
− Mortgage Payoff	− $ 75,557
− Seller's settlement	− $ 10,600 (8%)
= Gross equity	$ 46,043
× Percentage of ownership	× 50%
= Gross profit	$ 23,022
− Initial investment	− $ 9,000
= Net profit	$ 14,022
Average annual yield	31%

Sample of considerations in calculating profitability.

LEASE OPTION MODEL

The lease option to purchase method has been around for many years, although it is most often found in the commercial sector of real estate and only resurfaces in residential in times of a slow market or high interest rates. Its main value is in eliminating the barrier of a large down payment. It is especially valuable to resell your project quickly if the market turns around during your construction phase or to make your project stand out in a sea of other inventory. The advantages and disadvantages of this method are outlined in the next section.

Definition

A lease option is a binding contractual agreement to purchase a parcel of real estate at a specific future date and sales price. The optionee has rights in that property that are less than "fee simple" rights, but greater than "lessee" rights. The holder of an option may sell that option to a third party at any time during the option period, unless barred by the contract language from doing so.

EXAMPLE

January 1990   Sales Price **$225,000**

Buyer offers an option of purchasing in June of 1991.

Sales Price of **$230,000**, with a **$2,500** nonrefundable option fee, and an additional $250 over fair market rent for the 18-month option period; to count as the down payment or be retained by the seller if the option is not exercised. Title is to remain in the seller's name.

A rehab twist to this would be to add a rehab plan with costs and performance deadlines, and get an agreed-on amount as leasehold improvements that also would be credited as a "sweat equity" down payment.

LEASE OPTION ANALYSIS

Advantages

Seller	*Buyer*
Title remains in seller's name.	Gets into property with maximum leverage.

Seller	*Buyer*
Option $$ and monthly credit remain if buyer doesn't exercise the option.	Gets a chance to try out living in the house and area without a lot of risk.
Seller has a secure tenant.	Gets onto a timetable of savings.
Seller has a positive cash flow.	Buys time to get ready for lender scrutiny of finances.
Seller can still hypothecate property to get cash out.	May have the escape clause of selling the option if desired.
Seller can resell the property if option is not taken at higher new market price.	Gets property under real value at option time.

Disadvantages

Seller cannot get all equity liquid at one time.	May lose option monies.
Seller may lose out on the "real" appreciation vs. the "projected" property sales price.	May pay higher price for house at option time than its "fair market value."
Seller may have to go through more than one buyer.	May not be able to find buyer if needed to sell the option.

Special Note: Always record your option with the County Recorder's office as if it were a purchase, so that the rights and agreements of both parties become a matter of public record.

WHEN YOU WANT A PARTNER

How do you get started when you have no real experience? As you can see, there are lots of areas you need to access knowledge in to be a success. I recommend that you do a partner project with a contractor, as a joint venture. Contractors have the "hard skills" knowledge and usually have all their available capital tied up in their business. It makes sense that, if you have (1) the financial resources to be the strongest borrower, (2) the enthusiasm for this business, and (3) the skill and ability, you can create a win/win situation. This needs one caution, however; you first must know the contractor you approach with this model. If you are an unknown, this may be construed as an unequal proposition by the contractor. The contractor's rehab plan will be for time and materials, and you'll be the finance provider.

As with all other business agreements, don't get fancy with the compensation percentages, do trade-outs for expenses, and so on. Keep it at 50 percent profit if you can. Proportion the profit to the actual dollars invested in the project on the front end, and use a fair market dollar value for the rehab budget. It will save you a lot of agony, if the contractor should be hit by a truck mid-way through the project and you need to give the widow his 50 percent profit in the project.

You will need a written partnership agreement drawn up by your attorney, who will no doubt think of more protection clauses than you or I can think of. Figure 4.1 is an example of how a transaction might work out to illustrate the advantages of this method.

Figure 4.1   Joint Venture—Rehab Model

As-is—Sales price of duplex	$150,000
Rehab costs (15K each unit)	$ 30,000
	$180,000

Transaction financed for 18-month term as an 80-10-10
80 percent (bank 1st) 10 percent (owner 2nd) 10 percent (cash down)

Sales price	$150,000
Down payment	$ 15,000 ($7,500 per investor)
Owner carry back	$ 15,000 (2nd)
Bank loan balance	$120,000 (1st)

After Rehab Value $225,000 ($112,500 per unit)

Investor's Hard Costs

Cash closing costs to acquire	$ 2,000
Realtor discounted commission	
deducted from sales price	$ 11,250
Cash closing costs to sell	$ 4,000
	$ 17,250 Total
After rehab sales price	$225,000
Less costs of purchase and resale	$ 17,250
	$207,750 Subtotal
Less mortgages	$135,000
	$ 72,750 (must be split between partners)
Total Profit per Person	$ 36,375
Each investor put up	$ 15,000 for rehab costs
	$ 7,500 for down payment
	$ 3,000 closing costs
	$ 25,500 Total Costs

NET PROFIT PER PARTNER $10,875
Most closing costs on initial purchase were borne by the seller.

USING YOUR CONTRACTOR TO HELP OBTAIN FINANCING

In Figure 4.2, acquisition and rehab money is obtained in one loan for a time period not to exceed one year. Your contractor's lender sources are the best access to these loans. In many cases, the lender will make the loan based on the contractor's track record or relationship strength with that lender, but would not make the loan on your strengths alone. Typically, only certain smaller lenders who specialize in construction have this type of loan, which is called an acquisition and development loan.

GETTING THE SELLER TO PARTICIPATE IN REPAIRS PRIOR TO CLOSE OF ESCROW

Escrow Holdbacks

Escrow holdbacks, as defined by secondary market guidelines, are items that cannot be completed prior to loan closing due to such conditions as inclement weather and do *not materially* affect *the value or habitability* of the property. If held for completion after close of escrow, this is an "escrow holdback." The lender will allow an escrow holdback period of no more than 90 days to complete the work. Holdbacks for *roof* and *termite* inspections are generally *not acceptable*.

To obtain approval for escrow holdbacks, submit a detailed written estimate based on a licensed contractor's/appraiser's inspection.

The amount of the funds to be held back will equal $1^1/_2$ times the amount of the estimated cost of the work to be completed.

The escrow holdback agreement must be executed by all parties, including the settlement agent, prior to closing.

The advantages of this method to you as the buyer are:

1. You don't have to renegotiate the sales price because these repairs would be out-of-pocket expenses for you without this method. (I've never seen a seller pay dollars out of pocket to repair a house being sold if there is any way out of it!)
2. You'll find sellers agreeable to this method and, in effect, the rehab repairs are being paid for out of *their* equity dollars. Your rehab dollars can then all be put into improvements that add value.

Table 4.2 Example of How a Construction Loan Flows

Note amount = $200,000
Amount initially disbursed = $100,000
(pay off existing loan and misc. charges)
Amount construction LIP account = $100,000

Construction Period Information

Rate: Fixed at 12%
Construction period: 5 months
Payment: Interest only (based on disbursed funds)

Amortization Period Information:

Initial Effective Rate: Index Value/Margin
Initial Payment: Full amortization (based on full loan amount), payment due Sept. 1

	Construction Period						Amortization Period		
	March	April	May	June	July	August	September	October	Continued
Rate	12.000%	12.000%	12.000%	12.000%	12.000%	*9.75%	Adj mth Index/Margin	Continued	
Payment	N/A	$ 1,000	$ 1,100	$ 1,500	$ 1,600	$1,750	$1,722.40	Continued for 12 months	
Initial funds/ Cumulative funds advanced	100,000	100,000	110,000	150,000	160,000				
Construction funds advanced during month	0	10,000	40,000	10,000	15,000				
Total outstanding funds	100,000	110,000	150,000	160,000	175,000				

*You will need to have resold the property within the typical 9 months to 1 year term or a new Long Term Mortgage will need to be obtained.

*Amortization period initial interest rate calculated 45 days prior to rollover date:

Index = 7.00
Margin = 2.75
Initial Effective Rate = 9.75

Payment calculated on full loan amount ($200,000) over remaining loan (355 months)

WHEN PROPERTY NEEDS "MAJOR REHAB"

You sometimes just have to quickly tie a property up with interim financing and refinance your way to a better loan.

1. Acquire/Rehab/Refinance
2. Use "hard money" lenders. These are equity lenders who loan strictly on the low percent of loan to value, at higher than average interest rates and discount points. They do, however, usually fund in 21 days or less.

EXAMPLE

Sales price	$100,000
Loan	75,000
Down payment	10,000
Seller carries 2nd mortgage for a 1-year term	15,000
Closing costs	
Estimate	3% of sales price
Approximately	$3,000

After Acquisition

Use a Title I loan to do rehab repairs. (See details in the next section.)

After repairs (currently up to $17,500), property should reappraise at $120,000 or better to make up for the high cost of 2 loans. This amount is scheduled to increase in 1992 to $25,000 per single-family house. You can then refinance to maximum with a 30-year adjustable rate and recover costs of acquiring and rehab. Alternatively, you can sell the property with no financing offered and cash yourself out.

FHA TITLE I LOANS

Title I Advantages

- Fast turnaround—one week for funding—24-hour credit OK, one week more for over four units. It has streamlined processing and documentation which allows prompt funding.
- Six months to complete improvements. Then you must have the HUD verification of completion affidavit signed. Homeowner

can do the work or hire a contractor. Capable homeowners can save a great deal of cash.

- Can submit own rehab plan
- Fixed rate assumable loans
- 15-year term
- No prepayment penalties
- No appraisal costs
- No expensive title or escrow costs.

Situations Where Title I Makes Sense

- If you have a 1st and 2nd mortgage that originated as part of the purchase transaction. For example, when you obtain an 80 percent loan, the owner carries 10 percent or more!! No equity is needed for a Title I loan.
- When it was a 90 or 95 percent purchase loan, and there is no equity to borrow against for the improvements.
- When your first mortgage has a very low interest rate. Calculate a blended rate, and look at the effective interest rate. You'll be surprised to find it usually is compatible with a total refinance in interest rate plus costs.
- When you are a fixer upper investor, and you need cash to rehab a home. You may then refinance or sell property with an assumable Title I loan. When you purchase rental units (up to four), and need to do rehab work, but the condition of the units makes a lender turn loans down, you may borrow a maximum of $8,500 per unit ($43,750 maximum loan amount). (This loan amount is scheduled to increase significantly by 1992 and will be an even more attractive financing option.)

Common Misconceptions on Title I

1. **It's a signature loan**

   No. It is a real estate secured loan. It is a government insured loan designed for rehab.

2. **It's a low interest government loan**

   No. It is a market rate *priced* loan made by a lender that is obtaining FHA mortgage insurance, which protects the lender in the event of default. Because of the insurance premiums, rates are normally a bit above equity loans.

3. **I can use loan proceeds any way I wish**

   No. You must submit what improvements loan proceeds are to be used for. You can legitimately retain some profit and sweat equity, if you are an owner/contractor. But all work submitted must be completed.

4. **There are no points on a Title I loan**

   True. However, fees associated with this loan can average up to $1,000 for $17,500, the upper loan limit.

5. **Nobody inspects to see how I used the proceeds**

   No. There is a property inspection by the lender. A $50 fee for all loans is charged.

6. **Cash flow from the property can be used to qualify for the loan**

   The overall income of the borrower is the most important consideration—41% maximum debt ratio.

7. **Even if I've had credit problems I can qualify for Title I**

   No. Good credit and income are counted heavily, since there is so little equity. Some minor derogatory information with an acceptable explanation is OK. Major derogatory is out.

INELIGIBLE ITEMS

No part of the proceeds of a loan shall be used to finance any of the following items:

- Barbecue pit
- Bathhouses
- Burglar alarms
- Burglar protection bars
- Dumbwaiters
- Fire alarms or fire detecting devices
- Fire extinguishers
- Flower boxes
- Greenhouses (except commercial greenhouses)
- Hangars (airplane)
- Kennels
- Kitchen appliances which are designed and manufactured to be freestanding and are not built in and permanently affixed as an integral part of the kitchen in a residential structure
- Outdoor fireplaces or hearths
- Penthouses
- Photo murals
- Radiator covers or enclosures
- Stands

- Steam cleansing of exterior surfaces
- Swimming pools
- Television antennae
- Tennis courts
- Tree surgery
- Valance or cornice boards
- Waterproofing of a structure by pumping or injecting any substance in the earth adjacent to or beneath the basement or foundation or floors.

Other items may become ineligible as dictated by HUD policy. Please check with lender.

USING THE FHA REHAB PROGRAM

What Is a 203(k) Rehabilitation Loan?

This loan allows you to go to 110 percent of after-rehab value. The 203(k) rehabilitation loan is a FHA loan. It is a 30-year fixed rate mortgage. It is basically a fixed loan with a construction phase. The construction funds allow a borrower to "fix up" or "rehabilitate" a property, creating a value that will be higher than its current value.

This program is designed for remodeling or improving 1- to 4-family dwellings. It allows the closing of a loan prior to making the improvements. An escrow account is established from the loan proceeds to pay for the work as it is done. The program can be utilized by both occupant and nonoccupant borrowers. This and Title I are the only two FHA loans that still allow investor participation, other than buying a HUD repo.

This program is for:

1. The purchase and rehabilitation of a dwelling and the real property on which the dwelling is located.
2. To refinance existing indebtedness and to rehabilitate such a dwelling.

This loan program doesn't allow cash. It is designed specifically to rehabilitate property.

Maximum Loan Amounts

The maximum loan amount is set by the HUD. It is identical with the current loan limit on regular FHA loans. Check your local area for loan limits.

Application Process

- Choose a 1- to 4-unit property to purchase.
- Contact 203(k) lender for application package, including the description of materials form.
- Have contractor and/or rehabilitation agent determine work requirements and complete the description of materials form.
- Ask lender to complete FHA application forms and submit to FHA for firm commitment.
- Wait for lender to receive FHA firm commitment, draw closing documents, and proceed to loan closing.
- Begin rehabilitation work.

Excluded Property

Condominiums, 5 or more living units on a lot, and commercial property are excluded from this program.

Eligible Improvements

This program is designed to rehabilitate property. Single line-item repairs are ineligible (e.g., a heater). The borrower must do two or more improvements and the total of rehabilitation must be at least $5,000, depending on the HUD guidelines for the area. Following is a list of eligible improvements:

1. Structural alterations and reconstruction such as additions to the structure, finished attics, etc.
2. Termite damage repairs and/or termite treatment.
3. Changes for improved functions and modernization such as remodeled kitchens and bathrooms.
4. Changes for aesthetic appeal and elimination of obsolescence such as new exterior siding.
5. Reconditioning and/or replacement of plumbing, heating, air conditioning, and electrical systems.
6. Roofing and sidewall work.
7. Gutters and downspouts.
8. Flooring, tiling, and carpeting.
9. Energy conservation improvements such as insulation, double pane windows, and solar hot water systems.
10. Major landscape work and site improvements such as patios, terraces, and fencing.

11. Improvements for accessibility for the handicapped.

12. When eligible improvements totaling at least $5,000 occur, then general painting, decorating, and built-in fixtures (e.g., dishwashers) are eligible. The conversion of 1-, 2-, or 3-unit dwelling(s) to a 2-, 3-, or 4-unit property using "new construction" or "move-ons" is allowed, provided the minimum $5,000 eligible improvements are made to the original structure.

13. When the property will not be livable during construction, the borrower can request up to 6 months of the loan to be included as a cost of construction. These payments are to be made during the construction phase. Once the property is completed, any additional funds set aside to make the payment will be used toward a principal reduction.

Ineligible Improvements

The following items are classified as "ineligible" under this program:

1. Condominiums.

2. Commercial property (unless being converted to residential and in compliance with zoning ordinances).

3. Structures not completed for at least 1 year.

4. Non-realty items which by established custom are supplied by the occupant and removable when vacating the premises (e.g., refrigerator).

5. Luxury items.

6. Recreational improvements such as swimming pools, hot tubs, and saunas.

7. Additions or alterations to provide for commercial use or to equip or refurbish space for such use.

Always Required

1. Smoke detectors.

2. Minimum energy conservation standards (e.g., weather stripping).

3. Compliance with city building codes and zoning ordinances.

Note: Another advantage of this program is that it does not require the 3.8 up-front mortgage premium payment (on a $100,000 loan this equals $3,800). Properties needing a minimum of $5,000 in improvements in the above categories make this a very attractive loan. Mortgage insurance is collected monthly in this program.

Table 4.3   FHA 203(k) Rehab Loan Worksheet

1. MORTGAGE BASIS CALCULATIONS
   A. Sales price or existing debt $_____
   B. Estimated cost of improvements $_____
   C. 10% of Line B (or ball park rehab estimate) $_____
   D. Total acquisition $_____

2. MAXIMUM LOAN CALCULATIONS (Choose 1 for your situation)
   ☐ Investor purchase (85% of Line 1-D) $_____
   ☐ Owner occupied purchase (95% of Line 1-D) $_____
   Plus costs to apply for the loan (estimated) $_____
   TOTAL $___550.00___
   ☐ Refinance (100% of Line 1-D) $_____

3. ESTIMATED DOWN PAYMENT & TOTAL CASH REQUIREMENTS
   Line 1-D $_____
   Minus Line 2 $_____
   Subtotal $_____
   .05 of Line 2 $_____
   Total D.P. requirements $_____
   Plus up-front costs (single-family residence estimate) $___550.00___
   TOTAL $_____

4. PAYMENT CALCULATIONS
   A. Principal & interest (consult Factor Chart for calculation) $_____
   B. Taxes (est. 1.25 of line 1-D) $_____
   C. Mutual Mortgage Insurance (.03 of 1-D/12 mo × 14 for total) $_____
   D. Homeowners Ins (1 yr premium/12 months) $_____
   E. TOTAL HOUSING PAYMENT $_____

5. QUALIFYING RATIOS
   (Use 75% of gross monthly projected income for rental property)
   A. Total monthly income (gross) $_____
   B. Total all other mo. payments $_____
   C. Divide 4-E by 5-A   = $_____
   D. Add 4-E plus 5-B   = $_____
   E. Divide 5-D by 5-A   = $_____

   HUD Ratios   29%   Line 5-C ____%   41%   Line 5-E ____%

- 30-year fixed rate mortgage
- This loan can be assumed by your new buyer if you are planning to Rehab and Resell.
- Your Agent or Lender Representative can be of assistance in filling this out.

Table 4.4   Example of FHA 203(k) Loan Closing Cost Worksheet

Loan Origination Fee	$_____
MMI (Mutual Mortgage Insurance) (See local HUD chart for calculation)	$_____
Pre-paid Items—Homeowner's Insurance (1 year Premium)	$_____
Interest from closing to 1st payment (estimate 30 days pre-paid interest)	$_____
Tax Impounds (estimate maximum of 6 months taxes)	$_____
Attorney or Escrow fees	$_____
Recording fees	$_____
Discount Points (paid in cash on purchase)	$_____
Miscellaneous charges	$_____
Total Cash Required to Close Transaction	$_____

PLEASE NOTE:

If this is a refinance, then closing costs are folded into the new loan balance.

Closing cost items are calculated identically for either Owner Occupied or Investor rehabber.

These costs will also be addressed in the Good Faith Estimate provided by your Loan Officer.

ESCROW PHASE

   A. Contractor draws:

     1. Contractor and borrower execute request for release of funds.

     2. Inspector reviews completed work. American Funding Corporation (Lender) will release 90 percent of the funds available for that specific draw. This can occur up to 5 times (5 draws). Once all of the work is completed, the 10 percent holdback will be released to the contractor. Remember, only 90 percent of the draw amounts are released during the construction phase.

   B. Final release of funds:

     1. Contractor and borrower execute final release.

     2. Contractor provides final termination clearance.

     3. Notice of completion from contractor is recorded.

     4. Inspector reviews the work completed and signs off.

     5. Contract analyst reviews compliance inspection and authorizes final release.

6. Balance of contract (10 percent holdbacks) is paid when the window period for mechanic's liens expires (30–90 days).

7. If mortgage payments were included in the escrow account, the lender may no longer release payments and you must begin paying them. Any unreleased mortgage payments in escrow will be applied as a principal reduction to the loan.

C. Any unused contingency funds are applied to principal balance of borrower's mortgage.

D. The borrower is paid accrued interest in the escrow funds, closing out the escrow account.

Note: Call your local HUD Office for a free booklet on this rehab program and a list of lenders in your area who offer this loan. If you need further help with finding or using this loan program, please use the coupon at the end of this chapter for more information and specific questions.

FANNIE MAE

Note: There is also a very similar program offered through lenders in various parts of the country by the Federal National Mortgage Association (FNMA) (Fannie Mae), the secondary market lender. Check with your local realtor to obtain a list of participating lenders. The advantage of this program is it allows *much higher purchase prices* for 1 to 4 units. Contact FNMA at 202-752-7000 for the lender nearest you.

BEGINNING INVESTMENT CONCEPTS USED IN PURCHASING 1–4 INCOME UNITS

Traditional Rates of Return

A recurring challenge of investment real estate practice is the search for that "perfect rate of return," the one percentage that will effectively measure all the benefits of a particular investment. However, like the mythological Camelot, the "perfect rate" is nowhere to be found.

What is left is a curious assortment of rates of return dealing with a hybrid of cash flows, accrued benefits, and other elements of the "income stream." Some are simplistic, and therefore short-sighted in their approach; other rates are burdensome and all too futuristic and hypothetical in their projections.

Three Fundamental Questions for Investment Decision Making

1. How much does it cost?
2. How much can it make?
3. When might that happen?

Three Fundamental Rules for Investment Decision Making

1. More is better than less.
2. Sooner is better than later.
3. For sure is better than maybe.

Terms

Gross scheduled income (GSI)—Total possible income received in a year *if* rented all the time.

Gross operating income (GOI)—What's left after subtracting vacancy allowance and adding in any other income from the Gross Scheduled Income.

Net operating income (NOI)—What's left after subtracting operating expenses (not principal or interest payments) from the Gross Operating Income. NOI is important in that this is the income available for payment on a loan to buy the property and/or for the production of cash flow.

Cash flow—What's left after subtracting principal and interest from NOI.

FUNDAMENTAL FORMULAS FOR ALL INVESTMENTS

The most basic formulas in Investment Analysis are the I.R.V. formulas.

A. There are three elements of an investment, measured in I.R.V.:
1. Income, or I.
2. Rate, or R.
3. Value, or V.
B. There are three I.R.V. formulas:
1. $I \div R = V$
2. $I \div V = R$
3. $R \times V = I$

1. If the income from an investment equals $1,000 and the rate of return on the investment equals 10%, then the value of the investment is determined by dividing the income by the rate, or dividing $1,000 by 10%, which equals $10,000. Therefore, the investment has a value of $10,000.

2. If the investment has an income of $1,000 and the value of the investment is $10,000, then the rate of return on the investment is determined by dividing the value into the income or by dividing $10,000 into $1,000, which equals 10%. Therefore, the rate of return on the investment is 10%.

3. If the rate of return on an investment is 10% and the value of the investment is $10,000, then the income from the investment is determined by multiplying the rate times the value, or multiplying 10% times $10,000 which equals $1,000. Therefore, the income from the investment is $1,000.

INVESTMENT FORMULAS FOR REAL ESTATE

1. **Gross rent multipliers**—a factor (number) multiplied, times the gross scheduled income, of an income-producing real estate investment property, to determine the approximate market value
   GRM = Value ÷ GSI

   a. **Example:** A four-unit property has monthly income of $200 per unit, or $800 times 12 months, or a gross scheduled income of $9,600. If the gross rent multiplier factor common to this example is 7, then the approximate market value of the property is determined by multiplying the gross scheduled income times the gross rent multiplier factor or, in this case, $9,600 times 7, which equals $67,200 or the approximate market value of the investment.

   b. The gross rent multiplier is derived through analysis of comparable sales in the market area. Consequently, the gross rent multiplier changes frequently as the market changes.

   c. The gross rent multiplier deals only with the *gross* income from the real estate property rather than the *net* income of the real estate property, after expenses.

2. **Capitalization rates or cap rates**—an application investment real estate analysis of the I.R.V. formulas.

   a. Formulas:

   R = NOI ÷ V

   V = NOI ÷ R

   NOI = R × V

    b. If a real estate investment has a net operating income of $10,000 and an approximate market value of $100,000, the cap rate is determined by dividing $10,000 by $100,000, which equals 10% or a cap rate of 10.

    c. Cap rates are used frequently in various types of real estate investment property analysis, both in the area of purchasing and negotiations and more significantly in the appraisal and financing of real estate investments.

    d. In most cases, cap rates represent the rate of return on a real estate investment *that is owned free and clear, or that is evaluated without financing considerations.*

        NOI = Net operating income

        GSI = Gross scheduled income

3. **Cash-on-cash rate of return**—the amount of cash flow from a real estate investment in any year, usually the first year, compared to the amount of cash down payment made by the investor to purchase the investment (some investors include buyer's transaction costs).

    a. If an investor pays $30,000 as a cash down payment at the time of purchase, and at the end of the first year of operation the property produces a $3,000 positive cash flow, then the cash-on-cash return is the cash flow divided by the down payment, or $3,000 divided by $30,000 which equals 10%, or a 10% cash-on-cash rate of return.

    b. The cash-on-cash rate of return method looks at only one year, usually the first year.

    c. The cash-on-cash method is widely and commonly used by investors in the investment real estate market.

Rule-of-Thumb Comparisons

1. Value per Unit:
    VPU = Sale Price ÷ # of Units
    $100,000 ÷ 1 = $100,000

2. Gross Rent Multiplier:
    GRM = Sale Price ÷ GSI
    100,000 ÷ 9,600 = 10.42

3. Capitalization Rate:
    Cap Rate = NOI ÷ Sale Price
    6,400 ÷ 100,000 = 6.4%

4. Cash-on-Cash Rate of Return:
    COCROR = CFBT ÷ Down Payment
    −3,845 ÷ 17,000 = −22.6%

5. Net Spendable Rate of Return:

$$NSROR = CFAT \div Down\ Payment$$

$$1,755 \div 17,000 = 10.32\%$$

6. Equity Yield Rate of Return:

$$EYROR = CFBT + Tax = Appreciation + Equity\ Build\text{-}up \div Down\ Payment$$

$$-3,845 + 5,600 + 8,000 + 301 \div 17,000 = 59.15\%$$

CONCLUSION

Although this book has been written to give you a wide range of choices for rehab, others you might consider for your area of the country are:

- Condos (ideal cosmetic rehab)
- Land sale contracts (as an acquiring and reselling technique)
- Research local rehab monies available through each municipality's Community Development Block Grant Funds.

If you wish to stay updated on rehab programs and options, you may wish to subscribe to a quarterly rehab newsletter. For information or questions, please complete the no obligation coupon below:

- -

Name: _____

Address: _____ Business Phone: (___)_____

_____ Home Phone: (___)_____

City: _____ State: _____ Zip: _____

Send to: Sandra M. Brassfield
Real Estate Rehab Group, Ltd.
4845 Ronson Court
San Diego, CA 92111-1803
(619) 560-6361

- -

5

Sample Contractor Forms

TYPICAL FORMS USED BY CONTRACTORS

The forms that follow are not all of the forms you will need, and they may not be the best of their kind for your particular needs. They represent typical examples of some forms you may find useful. To enable you to become familiar with the functions and variety of the forms that are available, this chapter includes the following:

Description of Materials (HUD form)
Specification of Repairs (HUD Form)
Change Order
Draw Request (HUD form)
Red Flags Inspection Checklist*
Buyer's Property Inspection Report*
Inspection Addendum*

* Reprinted by permission of the copyright owner, Professional Publishing Corporation, © Copyright PROFESSIONAL PUBLISHING CORPORATION, 122 PAUL DRIVE, SAN RAFAEL, CA 94903 (415) 472-1964.

VETERANS AD   STRATION, U.S.D.A. FARMERS HOME ADMINI: ITION, AND
U.S. DEPARTMENT OF HOUSING AND URBAN DEVELOPMENT
HOUSING - FEDERAL HOUSING COMMISSIONER
For accurate register of carbon copies, form may be separated along above
fold. Staple completed sheets together in original order.

☐ Proposed Construction   **DESCRIPTION OF MATERIALS**   No. _____

☐ Under Construction   *(To be inserted by HUD, VA or FmHA)*

Property address _____   City _____   State _____

Mortgagor or Sponsor _____   _____
                          (Name)   *(Address)*

Contractor or Builder _____   _____
                          (Name)   *(Address)*

INSTRUCTIONS

1. For additional information on how this form is to be submitted, number of copies, etc., see the instructions applicable to the HUD Application for Mortgage Insurance, VA Request for Determination of Reasonable Value, or FmHA Property Information and Appraisal Report, as the case may be.
2. Describe all materials and equipment to be used, whether or not shown on the drawings, by marking an X in each appropriate check-box and entering the information called for each space. If space is inadequate, enter "See misc." and describe under item 27 or on an attached sheet. THE USE OF PAINT CONTAINING MORE THAN THE PERCENTAGE OF LEAD BY WEIGHT PERMITTED BY LAW IS PROHIBITED.
3. Work not specifically described or shown will not be considered unless

required, then the minimum acceptable will be assumed. Work exceeding minimum requirements cannot be considered unless specifically described.
4. Include no alternates, "or equal" phrases, or contradictory items. (Consideration of a request for acceptance of substitute materials or equipment is not thereby precluded.)
5. Include signatures required at the end of this form.
6. The construction shall be completed in compliance with the related drawings and specifications, as amended during processing. The specifications include this Description of Materials and the applicable Minimum Property Standards.

1. EXCAVATION:
Bearing soil, type _____

2. FOUNDATIONS:
Footings: concrete mix _____ ; strength psi _____   Reinforcing _____
Foundation wall: material _____   Reinforcing _____
Interior foundation wall: material _____   Party foundation wall _____
Columns: material and sizes _____   Piers: material and reinforcing _____
Girders: material and sizes _____   Sills: material _____
Basement entrance areaway _____   Window areaways _____
Waterproofing _____   Footing drains _____
Termite protection _____
Basementless space: ground cover _____ ; insulation _____ ; foundation vents _____
Special foundations _____
Additional information: _____

3. CHIMNEYS:
Material _____   Prefabricated *(make and size)* _____
Flue lining: material _____   Heater flue size _____   Fireplace flue size _____
Vents *(material and size)*: gas or oil heater _____ ; water heater _____
Additional information: _____

4. FIREPLACES:
Type: ☐ solid fuel; ☐ gas-burning; ☐ circulator *(make and size)* _____   Ash dump and clean-out _____
Fireplace: facing _____ ; lining _____ ; hearth _____ ; mantel _____
Additional information: _____

5. EXTERIOR WALLS:
Wood frame: wood grade, and species _____   ☐ Corner bracing. Building paper or felt _____
Sheathing _____ ; thickness _____ ; width _____ ; ☐ solid; ☐ spaced _____ " o. c.; ☐ diagonal; _____
Siding _____ ; grade _____ ; type _____ ; size _____ ; exposure _____ "; fastening _____
Shingles _____ ; grade _____ ; type _____ ; size _____ ; exposure _____ "; fastening _____
Stucco _____ ; thickness _____ "; Lath _____ ; weight _____ lb.
Masonry veneer _____   Sills _____   Lintels _____   Base flashing _____
Masonry: ☐ solid ☐ faced ☐ stuccoed; total wall thickness _____ "; facing thickness _____ "; facing material _____
Backup material _____ ; thickness _____ "; bonding _____
Door sills _____   Window sills _____   Lintels _____   Base flashing _____
Interior surfaces: dampproofing, _____ coats of _____ ; furring _____
Additional information: _____
Exterior painting: material _____ ; number of coats _____
Gable wall construction: ☐ same as main walls; ☐ other construction _____

6. FLOOR FRAMING:
Joists: wood, grade, and species _____ ; other _____ ; bridging _____ ; anchors _____
Concrete slab: ☐ basement floor; ☐ first floor; ☐ ground supported; ☐ self-supporting; mix _____ ; thickness _____
reinforcing _____ ; insulation _____ ; membrane _____
Fill under slab: material _____ ; thickness _____ ". Additional information: _____

DESCRIPTION OF MATERIALS

7. SUBFLOORING: *(Describe underflooring for special floors under item 21.)*
Material: grade and species _____ ; size _____ ; type _____
Laid: ☐ first floor; ☐ second floor; ☐ attic _____ sq. ft.; ☐ diagonal; ☐ right angles. Additional information: _____

8. FINISH FLOORING: *(Wood only. Describe other finish flooring under item 21.)*

Location	Rooms	Grade	Species	Thickness	Width	Bldg. Paper	Finish
First floor							
Second floor							
Attic floor _____ sq. ft.							

Additional information: _____

9. PARTITION FRAMING:
Studs: wood, grade, and species _____ size and spacing _____ Other _____
Additional information: _____

10. CEILING FRAMING:
Joists: wood, grade, and species _____ Other _____ Bridging _____
Additional information: _____

11. ROOF FRAMING:
Rafters: wood, grade, and species _____ Roof trusses (see detail): grade and species _____
Additional information: _____

12. ROOFING:
Sheathing: wood, grade, and species _____ ; ☐ solid; ☐ spaced _____ " o.c.
Roofing _____ ; grade _____ ; size _____ ; type _____
Underlay _____ ; weight or thickness _____ ; size _____ ; fastening _____
Built-up roofing _____ ; number of plies _____ ; surfacing material _____
Flashing: material _____ ; gage or weight _____ ; ☐ gravel stops; ☐ snow guards
Additional information: _____

13. GUTTERS AND DOWNSPOUTS:
Gutters: material _____ ; gage or weight _____ ; size _____ ; shape _____
Downspouts: material _____ ; gage or weight _____ ; size _____ ; shape _____ ; number _____
Downspouts connected to: ☐ Storm sewer; ☐ sanitary sewer; ☐ dry-well. ☐ Splash blocks: material and size _____
Additional information: _____

14. LATH AND PLASTER
Lath ☐ walls, ☐ ceilings: material _____ ; weight or thickness _____ Plaster: coats _____ ; finish _____
Dry-wall ☐ walls, ☐ ceilings: material _____ ; thickness _____ ; finish _____ ;
Joint treatment _____

15. DECORATING: *(Paint, wallpaper, etc.)*

Rooms	Wall Finish Material and Application	Ceiling Finish Material and Application
Kitchen		
Bath		
Other		

Additional information: _____

16. INTERIOR DOORS AND TRIM:
Doors: type _____ ; material _____ ; thickness _____
Door trim: type _____ ; material _____ Base: type _____ ; material _____ ; size _____
Finish: doors _____ ; trim _____
Other trim *(item, type and location)* _____
Additional information: _____

17. WINDOWS:
Windows: type _____ ; make _____ ; material _____ ; sash thickness _____
Glass: grade _____ ; ☐ sash weights; ☐ balances, type _____ ; head flashing _____
Trim: type _____ ; material _____ Paint _____ ; number coats _____
Weatherstripping: type _____ ; material _____ Storm sash, number _____
Screens: ☐ full; ☐ half; type _____ ; number _____ ; screen cloth material _____
Basement windows: type _____ ; material _____ ; screens, number _____ ; Storm sash, number _____
Special windows _____
Additional information: _____

18. ENTRANCES AND EXTERIOR DETAIL:
Main entrance door: material _____ ; width _____ ; thickness _____ ". Frame: material _____ , thickness _____ "
Other entrance doors: material _____ ; width _____ ; thickness _____ ". Frame: material _____ ; thickness _____ "
Head flashing _____ Weatherstripping: type _____ ; saddles _____
Screen doors: thickness _____ "; number _____ ; screen cloth material _____ Storm doors: thickness _____ "; number _____
Combination storm and screen doors: thickness _____ "; number _____ ; screen cloth material _____
Shutters: ☐ hinged; ☐ fixed. Railings _____ , Attic louvers _____
Exterior millwork: grade and species _____ Paint _____ ; number coats _____
Additional information: _____

19. CABINETS AND INTERIOR DETAIL:

Kitchen cabinets, wall units: material _____ ; lineal feet of shelves _____ ; shelf width _____

Base units: material _____ ; counter top _____ ; edging _____

Back and end splash _____ Finish of cabinets _____ ; number coats _____

Medicine cabinets: make _____ ; model _____

Other cabinets and built-in furniture _____

Additional information: _____

20. STAIRS:

STAIR	TREADS		RISERS		STRINGS		HANDRAIL		BALUSTERS	
	Material	Thickness	Material	Thickness	Material	Size	Material	Size	Material	Size
Basement _____										
Main _____										
Attic _____										

Disappearing: make and model number _____

Additional information: _____

21. SPECIAL FLOORS AND WAINSCOT: *(Describe Carpet as listed in Certified Products Directory)*

	LOCATION	MATERIAL, COLOR, BORDER, SIZES, GAGE, ETC.	THRESHOLD MATERIAL	WALL BASE MATERIAL	UNDERFLOOR MATERIAL
FLOORS	Kitchen _____				
	Bath _____				

	LOCATION	MATERIAL, COLOR, BORDER, CAP. SIZES, GAGE, ETC.	HEIGHT	HEIGHT OVER TUB	HEIGHT IN SHOWERS (FROM FLOOR)
WAINSCOT	Bath _____				

Bathroom accessories: ☐ Recessed; material _____ ; number _____ ; ☐ Attached; material _____ ; number _____

Additional information: _____

22. PLUMBING:

FIXTURE	NUMBER	LOCATION	MAKE	MFR'S FIXTURE IDENTIFICATION NO.	SIZE	COLOR
Sink _____						
Lavatory _____						
Water closet _____						
Bathtub _____						
Shower over tub △ _____						
Stall shower △ _____						
Laundry trays _____						

△☐ Curtain rod　△☐ Door　☐ Shower pan: material _____

Water supply: ☐ public; ☐ community system; ☐ individual (private) system. ★

Sewage disposal: ☐ public; ☐ community system; ☐ individual (private) system. ★

★*Show and describe individual system in complete detail in separate drawings and specifications according to requirements.*

House drain (inside): ☐ cast iron; ☐ tile; ☐ other _____ House sewer (outside): ☐ cast iron; ☐ tile; ☐ other _____

Water piping: ☐ galvanized steel; ☐ copper tubing; ☐ other _____ Sill cocks, number _____

Domestic water heater: type _____ ; make and model _____ ; heating capacity _____

_____ gph. 100° rise. Storage tank: material _____ ; capacity _____ gallons.

Gas service: ☐ utility company; ☐ liq. pet. gas; ☐ other _____ Gas piping: ☐ cooking; ☐ house heating.

Footing drains connected to: ☐ storm sewer; ☐ sanitary sewer; ☐ dry well. Sump pump; make and model _____

_____ ; capacity _____ ; discharges into _____

23. HEATING:

☐ Hot water. ☐ Steam. ☐ Vapor. ☐ One-pipe system. ☐ Two-pipe system.

☐ Radiators. ☐ Convectors. ☐ Baseboard radiation. Make and model _____

Radiant panel: ☐ floor; ☐ wall; ☐ ceiling. Panel coil: material _____

☐ Circulator. ☐ Return pump. Make and model _____ ; capacity _____ gpm.

Boiler: make and model _____ Output _____ Btuh.; net rating _____ Btuh.

Additional information: _____

Warm air: ☐ Gravity. ☐ Forced. Type of system _____

Duct material: supply _____ ; return _____ Insulation _____ , thickness _____ ☐ Outside air intake.

Furnace: make and model _____ Input _____ Btuh.; output _____ Btuh.

Additional information: _____

DESCRIPTION OF MATERIALS

☐ Space heater; ☐ floor furnace; ☐ wall heater. Input _____ Btuh.; output _____ Btuh.; number units _____

Make, model _____ Additional information: _____

Controls: make and types _____

Additional information: _____

Fuel: ☐ Coal; ☐ oil; ☐ gas; ☐ liq. pet. gas; ☐ electric; ☐ other _____ ; storage capacity _____

Additional information: _____

Firing equipment furnished separately: ☐ Gas burner, conversion type. ☐ Stoker: hopper feed ☐; bin feed ☐

Oil burner: ☐ pressure atomizing; ☐ vaporizing _____

Make and model _____ Control _____

Additional information: _____

Electric heating system: type _____ Input _____ watts; @ _____ volts; output _____ Btuh

Additional information: _____

Ventilating equipment: attic fan, make and model _____ ; capacity _____ cfm

kitchen exhaust fan, make and model _____

Other heating, ventilating. or cooling equipment _____

24. ELECTRIC WIRING:

Service: ☐ overhead; ☐ underground. Panel: ☐ fuse box; ☐ circuit-breaker; make_____ AMP's _____ No. circuits _____

Wiring: ☐ conduit: ☐ armored cable; ☐ nonmetallic cable; ☐ knob and tube; ☐ other _____

Special outlets: ☐ range; ☐ water heater; ☐ other _____

☐ Doorbell. ☐ Chimes. Push-button locations _____ Additional information: _____

25. LIGHTING FIXTURES:

Total number of fixtures _____ Total allowance for fixtures, typical installation, $ _____

Nontypical installation _____

Additional information: _____

26. INSULATION:

LOCATION	THICKNESS	MATERIAL, TYPE, AND METHOD OF INSTALLATION	VAPOR BARRIER
Roof ___			
Ceiling ___			
Wall ___			
Floor ___			

27. MISCELLANEOUS: *(Describe any main dwelling materials, equipment, or construction items not shown elsewhere; or use to provide additional information where the space provided was inadequate. Always reference by item number to correspond to numbering used on this form.)* _____

_____

_____

_____

_____

_____

_____

_____

_____

HARDWARE: *(make, material, and finish.)* _____

_____

SPECIAL EQUIPMENT: *(State material or make, model and quantity. Include only equipment and appliances which are acceptable by local law, custom and applicable FHA standards. Do not include items which, by established custom, are supplied by occupant and removed when he vacates premises or chattles prohibited by law from becoming realty.)* _____

_____

_____

_____

_____

_____

PORCHES:

_____

_____

TERRACES:

_____

_____

_____

DESCRIPTION OF MATERIALS

GARAGES:
_____
_____
_____

WALKS AND DRIVEWAYS:
Driveway: width _____ ; base material _____ ; thickness _____"; surfacing material _____ ; thickness _____ "
Front walk: width _____ ; material _____ ; thickness _____ ". Service walk: width _____ ; material _____ ; thickness _____, "
Steps: material _____ ; treads _____"; risers _____". Cheek walls _____

OTHER ONSITE IMPROVEMENTS:
(Specify all exterior onsite improvements not described elsewhere, including items such as unusual grading, drainage structures, retaining walls, fence, railings, and accessory structures.)
_____
_____
_____

LANDSCAPING, PLANTING, AND FINISH GRADING:
Topsoil _____" thick: ☐ front yard; ☐ side yards; ☐ rear yard to _____ feet behind main building.
Lawns *(seeded, sodded, or sprigged)*: ☐ front yard _____ ; ☐ side yards _____ ; ☐ rear yard_____
Planting: ☐ as specified and shown on drawings; ☐ as follows:
_____ Shade trees, deciduous. _____" caliper.   _____ Evergreen trees. _____' to _____', B & B
_____ Low flowering trees, deciduous,   _____' to _____'   _____ Evergreen shrubs. _____' to _____', B & B
_____ High-growing shrubs, deciduous,   _____' to _____'   _____ Vines, 2-year _____
_____ Medium-growing shrubs, deciduous, _____' to _____'   _____
_____ Low-growing shrubs, deciduous,   _____' to _____'   _____

IDENTIFICATION.—This exhibit shall be identified by the signature of the builder, or sponsor, and/or the proposed mortgagor if the latter known at the time of application.

Date_____   Signature _____

                                                           Signature _____

HUD-92005
VA Form 26-1852
Form FmHA 424-2
(6-79)   ○ U S GOVERNMENT PRINTING OFFICE   1983 - 421-488 - 415/0108

SPECIFICATION OF REPAIRS

Applicant's Name: _____	Contact Name: _____
Property address: _____	Contact Phone No.: _____
City: _____ State: _____ Zip: _____	Best Time to Call: _____

HUD Case No.: _____ .	Contractor's Name:(If applicable)	◆Estimated Number of Months to complete work?
FHA Loan No.: _____	_____	
Name of HUD Assigned Plan Reviewer:	Address: _____ City: _____ Zip: _____	
Telephone No.: _____	Telephone No.: _____ Licence No.: _____	

Date of Final Acceptance:	Name of HUD Assigned Appraiser:	Telephone No.:	Date Assigned:
_____ Signature of HUD Reviewer			

STEP BY STEP PROCEDURE

1. Each item below must be addressed by either filling in the information on the work to be performed with brief explanation or entering "NONE" in the "SUBTOTAL COST" portion if no work is being performed in that particular sub section.

2. The "Description of Materials" (Form #26-1852) does not need to be used IF the materials being used are described, in detail, on this form. For major items, such as; kitchen cabinets, appliances, heating & air conditioning, etc., the manufacturer's brochure can be attached.

3. A copy of any and all proposals from all contractors and sub-contractors must be attached.

4. PRELIMINARY FEASIBILITY ANALYSIS: Two sets of plans should be attached. They must show the property address and the borrower's name, (use either letter or legal paper).
   FIRST SET: These will be existing floor plans.
   SECOND SET: These will be the PROPOSED PLANS. Only floor plans are required, unless there are additions or major structural changes, then cross sections, elevations and plot plans will be required. The proposed plan must show all the work outlined on this format. (Architectural exhibits may be required).

5. In addition to the above plans, detailed kitchen plans, patio plan, air conditioning layout, electric plans, etc. must be furnished if this type of work is planned to be done.

6. "OUTLINE OF WORK PLAN" Letter, briefly detailing the proposed work must be attached. Any format may be used however, estimated quantity and cost of each item must be listed below. (Use check list below, items 1 - 36).

7. Transfer costs to draw request HUD Form #9746-A for each draw required.

8. If this is a purchase and not a refinance, then a sales contract should be attached indicating the Loan is contingent upon HUD approval.

9. If Owner intends to perform any of the proposed work, other than painting, a letter detailing their qualification to perform the work is necessary.

10. Meaning of Abreviations: Linear Feet = LF   Each = EA   Square Feet = SF   Lump Sum = LS
    Square Yard = SY   ◆ = Required Item

1. MASONRY	Unit	$ Cost	Qty	Total
Point brick work	SF			
Stucco	SF			
Build brick wall	SF			
Build masonry, brick, or stone chimney	SF			

Describe the work to be done, and itemize materials to be used.

Draw No.: 1   2   3   4   5
(Circle One)

SUB-TOTAL SECTION NO. 1

This portion of the work will be done by: (check one) ☐ Owner ☐ Contractor ☐ Sub-contractor $ _____

☐ Cost Estimate Attached   ☐ Yes   ☐ No
☐ Photo Furnished   ☐ Yes   ☐ No
☐ Diagram Furnished   ☐ Yes   ☐ No
☐ See description of materials Form #26-1852
    See item Nos.: _____
☐ Other documentation:
☐ Comments:

HUD CASE NUMBER:				PAGE:

---

2. SIDING

	Unit	$ Cost	Qty	Total
Replace defective siding	SF			
Replace defective facia	LF			
Replace defective soffit	SF			

Describe the work to be done, and itemize materials to be used.

Draw No.:　1　　2　　3　　4　　5
(Circle One)

SUB-TOTAL SECTION No. 2

This portion of the work will be done by: (check one)　☐ Owner　☐ Contractor　☐ Sub-contractor　$ _____

☐ Cost Estimate Attached　☐ Yes　☐ No

☐ Photo Furnished　☐ Yes　☐ No

☐ Diagram Furnished　☐ Yes　☐ No

☐ See description of materials Form #26-1852
　　　　　　See Item Nos.: _____

☐ Other documentation:

☐ Comments:

---

3. GUTTERS & DOWNSPOUTS

	Unit	$ Cost	Qty	Total
Replace gutters & downspouts	LF			
Clean gutters & open downspouts	LS			

Describe the work to be done, and itemize materials to be used.

Draw No.:　1　　2　　3　　4　　5
(Circle One)

SUB-TOTAL SECTION No. 3

This portion of the work will be done by: (check one)　☐ Owner　☐ Contractor　☐ Sub-contractor　$ _____

☐ Cost Estimate Attached　☐ Yes　☐ No

☐ Photo Furnished　☐ Yes　☐ No

☐ Diagram Furnished　☐ Yes　☐ No

☐ See description of materials Form #26-1852
　　　　　　See Item Nos.: _____

☐ Other documentation:

☐ Comments:

---

4. ROOF

	Unit	$ Cost	Qty	Total
Install a new builtup roof, with new metal gravel stops.	SF			
Install 240# Sealtab asphalt shingles on all roofs with a 3:12 pitch or greater.	SF			
Remove old roofing	SF			

Describe the work to be done, and itemize materials to be used.

Draw No.:　1　　2　　3　　4　　5
(Circle One)

SUB-TOTAL SECTION No. 4

This portion of the work will be done by: (check one)　☐ Owner　☐ Contractor　☐ Sub-contractor　$ _____

☐ Cost Estimate Attached　☐ Yes　☐ No

☐ Photo Furnished　☐ Yes　☐ No

☐ Diagram Furnished　☐ Yes　☐ No

☐ See description of materials Form #26-1852
　　　　　　See Item Nos.: _____

☐ Other documentation:

☐ Comments:

HUD CASE NUMBER:		PAGE:

---

5. SHUTTERS

	Unit	$Cost	Qty	Total
Install shutters at windows	Pair			

Describe the work to be done, and itemize materials to be used.

Draw No.: 1 2 3 4 5
(Circle One)

SUB-TOTAL SECTION No. 5

This portion of the work will be done by: (check one) ☐ Owner ☐ Contractor ☐ Sub-contractor $ _____

☐ Cost Estimate Attached   ☐ Yes   ☐ No
☐ Photo Furnished   ☐ Yes   ☐ No
☐ Diagram Furnished   ☐ Yes   ☐ No
☐ See description of materials Form #26-1852
   See Item Nos.: _____
☐ Other documentation:
☐ Comments:

---

6. EXTERIORS

	Unit	$ Cost	Qty	Total
Remove defective, buckled wood members	LF			
Provide a structurally sound porch floor, properly finished.	SF			
Replace existing porch with masonry steps and stoops	SF			
Provide ornamental iron or wood railing or parts	LF			

Describe the work to be done, and itemize materials to be used.

Draw No.: 1 2 3 4 5
(Circle One)

SUB-TOTAL SECTION No. 6

This portion of the work will be done by: (check one) ☐ Owner ☐ Contractor ☐ Sub-contractor $ _____

☐ Cost Estimate Attached   ☐ Yes   ☐ No
☐ Photo Furnished   ☐ Yes   ☐ No
☐ Diagram Furnished   ☐ Yes   ☐ No
☐ See description of materials Form #26-1852
   See Item Nos.: _____
☐ Other documentation:
☐ Comments:

---

7. WALKS:

	Unit	$ Cost	Qty	Total
Install new concrete walks	SF			
Install concrete steps	LF			

Describe the work to be done, and itemize materials to be used.

Draw No.: 1 2 3 4 5
(Circle One)

SUB-TOTAL SECTION No. 7

This portion of the work will be done by: (check one) ☐ Owner ☐ Contractor ☐ Sub-contractor $ _____

☐ Cost Estimate Attached   ☐ Yes   ☐ No
☐ Photo Furnished   ☐ Yes   ☐ No
☐ Diagram Furnished   ☐ Yes   ☐ No
☐ See description of materials Form #26-1852
   See Item Nos.: _____
☐ Other documentation:
☐ Comments:

HUD CASE NUMBER:	PAGE:

8. DRIVEWAYS

	Unit	$ Cost	Qty	Total
Remove old driveway and apron	SF			
Install blacktop drive (min. 2") over existing drive and apron	SF			
Install new concrete driveway (min. 4") and apron with wire mesh	SF			

Describe the work to be done, and itemize materials to be used.

Draw No.:   1   2   3   4   5
(Circle One)

SUB-TOTAL SECTION No. 8

This portion of the work will be done by: (check one)   ☐ Owner   ☐ Contractor   ☐ Sub-contractor $ _____

☐ Cost Estimate Attached   ☐ Yes   ☐ No
☐ Photo Furnished   ☐ Yes   ☐ No
☐ Diagram Furnished   ☐ Yes   ☐ No
☐ See description of materials Form #26-1852
                                See Item Nos.: _____
☐ Other documentation:
☐ Comments:

9. PAINTING - EXTERIOR

	Unit	Total
Scrape, sand smooth, and paint a min. 2 coats of good quality paint at all exterior woodwork and metal. *All old defective paint to be removed in accordance with lead paint removal procedures.*	LS	

	Unit	$ Cost	Qty

Describe the work to be done, and itemize materials to be used.

Draw No.:   1   2   3   4   5
(Circle One)

SUB-TOTAL SECTION No. 9

This portion of the work will be done by: (check one)   ☐ Owner   ☐ Contractor   ☐ Sub-contractor $ _____

☐ Cost Estimate Attached   ☐ Yes   ☐ No
☐ Photo Furnished   ☐ Yes   ☐ No
☐ Diagram Furnished   ☐ Yes   ☐ No
☐ See description of materials Form #26-1852
                                See Item Nos.: _____
☐ Other documentation:
☐ Comments:

10. CAULKING

	Unit	$ Cost	Qty	Total
Caulk all windows and door frames.	EA			

Describe the work to be done, and itemize materials to be used.

Draw No.:   1   2   3   4   5
(Circle One)

SUB-TOTAL SECTION No. 10

This portion of the work will be done by: (check one)   ☐ Owner   ☐ Contractor   ☐ Sub-contractor $ _____

☐ Cost Estimate Attached   ☐ Yes   ☐ No
☐ Photo Furnished   ☐ Yes   ☐ No
☐ Diagram Furnished   ☐ Yes   ☐ No
☐ See description of materials Form #26-1852
                                See Item Nos.: _____
☐ Other documentation:
☐ Comments:

HUD CASE NUMBER:	PAGE:

11. FENCING

11. FENCING	Unit	$ Cost	Qty	Total
Install new fencing	LF			
Re-set existing fencing	LS			

Describe the work to be done, and itemize materials to be used.

Draw No.: 1 2 3 4 5
(Circle One)

SUB-TOTAL SECTION No. 11

This portion of the work will be done by: (check one) ☐ Owner ☐ Contractor ☐ Sub-contractor $ _____

☐ Cost Estimate Attached ☐ Yes ☐ No
☐ Photo Furnished ☐ Yes ☐ No
☐ Diagram Furnished ☐ Yes ☐ No
☐ See description of materials Form #26-1852
See item Nos.: _____

☐ Other documentation:
☐ Comments:

12. GRADING

12. GRADING	Unit	$ Cost	Qty	Total
Remove debris from yards, finish earth; then grade and seed.	LS			

Describe the work to be done, and itemize materials to be used.

Draw No.: 1 2 3 4 5
(Circle One)

SUB-TOTAL SECTION No. 12

This portion of the work will be done by: (check one) ☐ Owner ☐ Contractor ☐ Sub-contractor $ _____

☐ Cost Estimate Attached ☐ Yes ☐ No
☐ Photo Furnished ☐ Yes ☐ No
☐ Diagram Furnished ☐ Yes ☐ No
☐ See description of materials Form #26-1852
See item Nos.: _____

☐ Other documentation:
☐ Comments:

13. WINDOWS

13. WINDOWS	Unit	$Cost	Qty	Total
Install new replacement windows	EA			
Replace rotted or defective sash	EA			
Replace all rotted sills at exterior	EA			
Replace basement windows	EA			
Replace cracked/broken glass	EA			
Replace missing glazing putty	EA			
Repair/Replace missing screens	EA			

Describe the work to be done, and itemize materials to be used.

Draw No.: 1 2 3 4 5
(Circle One)

SUB-TOTAL SECTION No. 13

This portion of the work will be done by: (check one) ☐ Owner ☐ Contractor ☐ Sub-contractor $ _____

☐ Cost Estimate Attached ☐ Yes ☐ No
☐ Photo Furnished ☐ Yes ☐ No
☐ Diagram Furnished ☐ Yes ☐ No
☐ See description of materials Form #26-1852
See item Nos.: _____

☐ Other documentation:
☐ Comments:

HUD CASE NUMBER:	PAGE:

◆ 14. WEATHER-STRIPPING

14. WEATHER-STRIPPING	Unit	$ Cost	Qty	Total
Install new weatherstripping at all exterior doors	EA			
Weatherstrip all windows	EA			
Install metal interlocking thresholds at exterior doors	EA			

Describe the work to be done, and itemize materials to be used.

Draw No.: 1   2   3   4   5
(Circle One)

SUB-TOTAL SECTION No. 14

This portion of the work will be done by: (check one) ☐ Owner ☐ Contractor ☐ Sub-contractor $ _____

☐ Cost Estimate Attached   ☐ Yes   ☐ No
☐ Photo Furnished   ☐ Yes   ☐ No
☐ Diagram Furnished   ☐ Yes   ☐ No
☐ See description of materials Form #26-1852
      See Item Nos.: _____
☐ Other documentation:
☐ Comments:

15. DOORS - EXTERIOR

15. DOORS - EXTERIOR	Unit	$ Cost	Qty	Total
Install new 1-3/4" exterior doors	EA			
Install three (3) new door butts	EA			
Install exterior door trim	LF			
Install new lockset	EA			

Describe the work to be done, and itemize materials to be used.

Draw No.: 1   2   3   4   5
(Circle One)

SUB-TOTAL SECTION No. 15

This portion of the work will be done by: (check one) ☐ Owner ☐ Contractor ☐ Sub-contractor $ _____

☐ Cost Estimate Attached   ☐ Yes   ☐ No
☐ Photo Furnished   ☐ Yes   ☐ No
☐ Diagram Furnished   ☐ Yes   ☐ No
☐ See description of materials Form #26-1852
      See item Nos.: _____
☐ Other documentation:
☐ Comments:

16. DOORS-INTERIOR

16. DOORS-INTERIOR	Unit	$ Cost	Qty	Total
Replace defective doors	EA			
Install new doors with new locksets	EA			
Install lockset where missing or malfunctioning	EA			
Readjust all doors for proper closing	EA			
Install bedroom closet doors	EA			
Install bi-fold doors	EA			
Install trim around doors	EA			

Describe the work to be done, and itemize materials to be used.

Draw No.: 1   2   3   4   5
(Circle One)

SUB-TOTAL SECTION No. 16

This portion of the work will be done by: (check one) ☐ Owner ☐ Contractor ☐ Sub-contractor $ _____

☐ Cost Estimate Attached   ☐ Yes   ☐ No
☐ Photo Furnished   ☐ Yes   ☐ No
☐ Diagram Furnished   ☐ Yes   ☐ No
☐ See description of materials Form #26-1852
      See Item Nos.: _____
☐ Other documentation:
☐ Comments:

HUD CASE NUMBER:	PAGE:

17. PARTITION

	Unit	$ Cost	Qty	Total
Framing of new walls and partitions (Do not include drywall costs.)	SF			

Describe the work to be done, and itemize materials to be used.

Draw No.: 1 2 3 4 5
(Circle One)

SUB-TOTAL SECTION No. 17

$ _____

This portion of the work will be done by: (check one) ☐ Owner ☐ Contractor ☐ Sub-contractor

☐ Cost Estimate Attached ☐ Yes ☐ No
☐ Photo Furnished ☐ Yes ☐ No
☐ Diagram Furnished ☐ Yes ☐ No
☐ See description of materials Form #26-1852
See item Nos.: _____

☐ Other documentation:
☐ Comments:

18. PLASTER/DRYWALL

	Unit	$ Cost	Qty	Total
Patch all defective plaster/ drywall; finish smooth with existing wall or ceiling finish	LS			
Install new drywall	SF			

Describe the work to be done, and itemize materials to be used.

Draw No.: 1 2 3 4 5
(Circle One)

SUB-TOTAL SECTION No. 18

$ _____

This portion of the work will be done by: (check one) ☐ Owner ☐ Contractor ☐ Sub-contractor

☐ Cost Estimate Attached ☐ Yes ☐ No
☐ Photo Furnished ☐ Yes ☐ No
☐ Diagram Furnished ☐ Yes ☐ No
☐ See description of materials Form #26-1852
See item Nos.: _____

☐ Other documentation:
☐ Comments:

19. DECORATING

	Unit	$ Cost	Qty	Total
Paint all interior walls & trim *All old defective paint to be removed in accordance with lead paint removal procedures.*	LS			
Remove all existing wallpaper	SF			
Wallpaper walls	SF			

Describe the work to be done, and itemize materials to be used.

Draw No.: 1 2 3 4 5
(Circle One)

SUB-TOTAL SECTION No. 19

$ _____

This portion of the work will be done by: (check one) ☐ Owner ☐ Contractor ☐ Sub-contractor

☐ Cost Estimate Attached ☐ Yes ☐ No
☐ Photo Furnished ☐ Yes ☐ No
☐ Diagram Furnished ☐ Yes ☐ No
☐ See description of materials Form #26-1852
See item Nos.: _____

☐ Other documentation:
☐ Comments:

HUD CASE NUMBER:		PAGE:

20. WOOD-TRIM	Unit	$ Cost	Qty	Total
Replace all cracked, broken, mismatched trim, jambs, etc.	LF			
Remove all unused hinges, curtain rod hangers, nails, screws, etc.	EA			
Replace all wood trim at interior door units, base, shoe & other trim	LF			
Replace defective wall paneling	SF			

Describe the work to be done, and itemize materials to be used.

Draw No.: 1   2   3   4   5
              (Circle One)

SUB-TOTAL SECTION No. 20

This portion of the work will be done by: (check one)   ☐ Owner   ☐ Contractor   ☐ Sub-contractor $ _____

☐ Cost Estimate Attached   ☐ Yes   ☐ No
☐ Photo Furnished   ☐ Yes   ☐ No
☐ Diagram Furnished   ☐ Yes   ☐ No
☐ See description of materials Form #26-1852
              See Item Nos.: _____

☐ Other documentation:
☐ Comments:

21. STAIRS	Unit	$ Cost	Qty	Total
Replace bad bsmt., treads, & risers	LF			
Replace main stairs, treads & risers	LF			
Replace broken &/or missing baluster	LF			
Provide hand rails, etc.	LF			
Install new stairs at basement	LS			
Install new stairs	LS			

Describe the work to be done, and itemize materials to be used.

Draw No.: 1   2   3   4   5
              (Circle One)

SUB-TOTAL SECTION No. 21

This portion of the work will be done by: (check one)   ☐ Owner   ☐ Contractor   ☐ Sub-contractor $ _____

☐ Cost Estimate Attached   ☐ Yes   ☐ No
☐ Photo Furnished   ☐ Yes   ☐ No
☐ Diagram Furnished   ☐ Yes   ☐ No
☐ See description of materials Form #26-1852
              See item Nos.: _____

☐ Other documentation:
☐ Comments:

22. CLOSETS	Unit	$ Cost	Qty	Total
Install new shelves	LF			
Install new clothes rods.	LF			

Describe the work to be done, and itemize materials to be used.

Draw No.: 1   2   3   4   5
              (Circle One)   SUB-TOTAL SECTION No. 22

This portion of the work will be done by: (check one)   ☐ Owner   ☐ Contractor   ☐ Sub-contractor $ _____

☐ Cost Estimate Attached   ☐ Yes   ☐ No
☐ Photo Furnished   ☐ Yes   ☐ No
☐ Diagram Furnished   ☐ Yes   ☐ No
☐ See description of materials Form #26-1852
              See item Nos.: _____

☐ Other documentation:
☐ Comments:

HUD·CASE NUMBER:	PAGE:

23. WOOD FLOORS

23. WOOD FLOORS	Unit	$ Cost	Qty	Total
Replace all defective flooring, holes in floors, etc. with wood flooring to match existing floors	SF			
Sand, fill and refinish wood floors	SF			
Install new hardwood floors	SF			

Describe the work to be done, and itemize materials to be used.

Draw No.:   1   2   3   4   5
(Circle One)

SUB-TOTAL SECTION No. 23

This portion of the work will be done by: (check one)   ☐ Owner   ☐ Contractor   ☐ Sub-contractor $ _____

☐ Cost Estimate Attached	☐ Yes	☐ No
☐ Photo Furnished	☐ Yes	☐ No
☐ Diagram Furnished	☐ Yes	☐ No

☐ See description of materials Form #26-1852
See Item Nos.: _____

☐ Other documentation:

☐ Comments:

24. FINISH FLOORS

24. FINISH FLOORS	Unit	$ Cost	Qty	Total
Install vinyl asbestos tile or sheet goods with 1/4" underlayment				
Kitchen:	SY			
Bath:	SY			
Install carpet & pad	SY			

Describe the work to be done, and itemize materials to be used.

Draw No.:   1   2   3   4   5
(Circle One)

SUB-TOTAL SECTION No. 24

This portion of the work will be done by: (check one)   ☐ Owner   ☐ Contractor   ☐ Sub-contractor $ _____

☐ Cost Estimate Attached	☐ Yes	☐ No
☐ Photo Furnished	☐ Yes	☐ No
☐ Diagram Furnished	☐ Yes	☐ No

☐ See description of materials Form #26-1852
See Item Nos.: _____

☐ Other documentation:

☐ Comments:

25. CERAMIC TILE

25. CERAMIC TILE	Unit	$ Cost	Qty	Total
Install ceramic tile wainscot in bathtub area for shower height	SF			
Install ceramic tile floor	SF			
Install Marlite wainscot in bathtub area for shower height	SF			
Replace defective tile in bath	SF			
Replace defective tile in vestibule	SF			
Replace defective tile in kitchen	SF			

Describe the work to be done, and itemize materials to be used.

Draw No.:   1   2   3   4   5
(Circle One)

SUB-TOTAL SECTION No. 25

This portion of the work will be done by: (check one)   ☐ Owner   ☐ Contractor   ☐ Sub-contractor $ _____

☐ Cost Estimate Attached	☐ Yes	☐ No
☐ Photo Furnished	☐ Yes	☐ No
☐ Diagram Furnished	☐ Yes	☐ No

☐ See description of materials Form #26-1852
See Item Nos.: _____

☐ Other documentation:

☐ Comments:

HUD CASE NUMBER:	PAGE:

26. BATH ACCESSORIES	Unit	$ Cost	Qty	Total
Replace medicine cabinet in bath	EA			
Install paper holder	EA			
Install towel bar	EA			
Install soal dish	EA			
Install grab bar in tub/shower	EA			

Describe the work to be done, and itemize materials to be used.

Draw No.:   1   2   3   4   5
(Circle One)

SUB-TOTAL SECTION No. 26

This portion of the work will be done by: (check one)   ☐ Owner   ☐ Contractor   ☐ Sub-contractor $ _____

☐ Cost Estimate Attached   ☐ Yes   ☐ No
☐ Photo Furnished   ☐ Yes   ☐ No
☐ Diagram Furnished   ☐ Yes   ☐ No
☐ See description of materials Form #26-1852
                See Item Nos.: _____
☐ Other documentation:
☐ Comments:

27. PLUMBING	Unit	$ Cost	Qty	Total
Install new hot & cold water piping	LF			
Install 30 gal. (min.) glass lined gas hot water heater (52 gal. if electric)	EA			
Install new kitchen sink	EA			
Install three (3) peice bathroom with shower over tub	LS			
Install laundry tray with faucet	EA			
Replace washers at faucets	EA			
Replace defective sewer lines	LF			
Replace defective kitchen faucets	EA			
Replace defective bath faucets	EA			

Describe the work to be done, and itemize materials to be used.

Draw No.:   1   2   3   4   5
(Circle One)

SUB-TOTAL SECTION No. 27

This portion of the work will be done by: (check one)   ☐ Owner   ☐ Contractor   ☐ Sub-contractor $ _____

☐ Cost Estimate Attached   ☐ Yes   ☐ No
☐ Photo Furnished   ☐ Yes   ☐ No
☐ Diagram Furnished   ☐ Yes   ☐ No
☐ See description of materials Form #26-1852
                See Item Nos.: _____
☐ Other documentation:
☐ Comments:

28. INSULATION	Unit	$ Cost	Qty	Total
Install in crawl space: R-	SF			
Install batts attic: R-	SF			
Install R-13 batts in exterior walls	SF			

Describe the work to be done, and itemize materials to be used.

Draw No.:   1   2   3   4   5
(Circle One)

SUB-TOTAL SECTION No. 28

This portion of the work will be done by: (check one)   ☐ Owner   ☐ Contractor   ☐ Sub-contractor $ _____

☐ Cost Estimate Attached   ☐ Yes   ☐ No
☐ Photo Furnished   ☐ Yes   ☐ No
☐ Diagram Furnished   ☐ Yes·   ☐ No
☐ See description of materials Form #26-1852
                See Item Nos.: _____
☐ Other documentation:
☐ Comments:

HUD CASE NUMBER:	PAGE:

29. HEATING	Unit	$ Cost	Qty	Total
Install new forced warm air heater	EA			
Install new hot water boiler	EA			
Install automatic flow control valve	EA			
Install temp. control valve at boiler	EA			
Install heat supply outlet in each room.	LS			
Install heat (FWA) grills	EA			

Describe the work to be done, and itemize materials to be used.

Draw No.: 1   2   3   4   5
(Circle One)

SUB-TOTAL SECTION No. 29

This portion of the work will be done by: (check one)   ☐ Owner   ☐ Contractor   ☐ Sub-contractor $ _____

☐ Cost Estimate Attached   ☐ Yes   ☐ No
☐ Photo Furnished   ☐ Yes   ☐ No
☐ Diagram Furnished   ☐ Yes   ☐ No
☐ See description of materials Form #26-1852
See item Nos.: _____
☐ Other documentation:
☐ Comments:

30. ELECTRICAL	Unit	$ Cost	Qty	Total
Install 100 amp. service	LS			
Replace all frayed exterior wire from service to main & into exterior panel box	LS			
Install new ceiling-light wall switches	EA			
Install new lighting fixtures	EA			
Install new exterior lighting	EA			
Replace wall receptacles	EA			
Install three (3) way switch	EA			
Smoke detector(s)	EA			
Exterior wall exhaust fan(s)	EA			
Install GFI outlets	EA			

Describe the work to be done, and itemize materials to be used.

Draw No.: 1   2   3   4   5
(Circle One)

SUB-TOTAL SECTION No. 30

This portion of the work will be done by: (check one)   ☐ Owner   ☐ Contractor   ☐ Sub-contractor $ _____

☐ Cost Estimate Attached   ☐ Yes   ☐ No
☐ Photo Furnished   ☐ Yes   ☐ No
☐ Diagram Furnished   ☐ Yes   ☐ No
☐ See description of materials Form #26-1852
See item Nos.: _____
☐ Other documentation:
☐ Comments:

31. CABINETRY	Unit	$ Cost	Qty	Total
Base cabinets	LF			
Kitchen countertop	LS			
Wall cabinets	LF			
Vanities	EA			
Vanity countertop(s)	LS			

Describe the work to be done, and itemize materials to be used.

Draw No.: 1   2   3   4   5
(Circle One)

SUB-TOTAL SECTION No. 31

This portion of the work will be done by: (check one)   ☐ Owner   ☐ Contractor   ☐ Sub-contractor $ _____

☐ Cost Estimate Attached   ☐ Yes   ☐ No
☐ Photo Furnished   ☐ Yes   ☐ No
☐ Diagram Furnished   ☐ Yes   ☐ No
☐ See description of materials Form #26-1852
See item Nos.: _____
☐ Other documentation:
☐ Comments:

HUD CASE NUMBER:	PAGE:

32. APPLIANCES	Unit	$ Cost	Qty	Total
Range	EA			
Refrigerator	EA			
Dishwasher	EA			
Disposal	EA			

Describe the work to be done, and itemize materials to be used.

Draw No.: 1   2   3   4   5
(Circle One)

SUB-TOTAL SECTION No. 32

This portion of the work will be done by: (check one)   ☐ Owner   ☐ Contractor   ☐ Sub-contractor $ _____

☐ Cost Estimate Attached   ☐ Yes   ☐ No
☐ Photo Furnished   ☐ Yes   ☐ No
☐ Diagram Furnished   ☐ Yes   ☐ No
☐ See description of materials Form #26-1852
See item Nos.: _____

☐ Other documentation:
☐ Comments:

33. BASEMENTS	Unit	$ Cost	Qty	Total
Install a min. 3" thick concrete floor	SF			
Cement parge basement walls	SF			
Provide dry basement	LS			
Install new sump pump	EA			
Replace damaged joists (termite damage)	EA			
Termite treatment	LS			

Describe the work to be done, and itemize materials to be used.

Draw No.: 1   2   3   4   5
(Circle One)

SUB-TOTAL SECTION No. 33

This portion of the work will be done by: (check one)   ☐ Owner   ☐ Contractor   ☐ Sub-contractor $ _____

☐ Cost Estimate Attached   ☐ Yes   ☐ No
☐ Photo Furnished   ☐ Yes   ☐ No
☐ Diagram Furnished   ☐ Yes   ☐ No
☐ See description of materials Form #26-1852
See item Nos.: _____

☐ Other documentation:
☐ Comments:

34. CLEANUP	Unit	$ Cost	Qty	Total
Remove debris from property exterior	LS			
Remove debris from property interior	LS			
Broom clean floors, clean ALL windows	LS			
Clean all plumbing fixtures and appliances	LS			

Describe the work to be done, and itemize materials to be used.

Draw No.: 1   2   3   4   5
(Circle One)

SUB-TOTAL SECTION No. 34

This portion of the work will be done by: (check one)   ☐ Owner   ☐ Contractor   ☐ Sub-contractor $ _____

☐ Cost Estimate Attached   ☐ Yes   ☐ No
☐ Photo Furnished   ☐ Yes   ☐ No
☐ Diagram Furnished   ☐ Yes   ☐ No
☐ See description of materials Form #26-1852
See item Nos.: _____

☐ Other documentation:
☐ Comments:

HUD CASE NUMBER: PAGE:

35. MISCELLANEOUS: (Describe any main dwelling materials, equipment or construction items not shown elsewhere; or use to provide additional information where the space provided was inadequate. Always reference by item number to correspond to numbering used on this form.)

RECAP OF SUB-TOTALS	TOTAL
1. Masonry	$
2. Siding	
3. Gutters & Downspouts	
4. Roof	
5. Shutters	
6. Exteriors	
7. Walks	
8. Driveways	
9. Paint (exterior)	
10. Caulking	
11. Fencing	
12. Grading	
13. Windows	
14. Weatherstripping	
15. Doors (exterior)	
16. Doors (interior)	
17. Partition Walls	
18. Plaster/Drywall	
19. Decorating	
20. Wood Trim	
21. Stairs	
22. Closets	
23. Wood Floors	
24. Finish Floors	
25. Ceramic Tile	
26. Bath Accessories	
27. Plumbing	
28. Insulation	
29. Heating	
30. Electrical	
31. Cabinetry	
32. Appliances	
33. Basements	
34. Cleanup	
35. Miscellaneous	
TOTAL COST OF REPAIRS	$
36. Allowance Fees (list)	
❖ _____ % Contingency Reserve	
❖ 5 Inspections @ $ _____ ea.	
Total Cost of Allowable Fees	$
TOTAL OF ITEMS 1 - 36	$

SUB-TOTAL SECTION No. 35 **$** _____

Applicant(s) and Contractor (if any) to sign and date upon final acceptance
_____
Signature and Date

X _____
Signature and Date

X _____
Signature and Date

X _____

CHANGE ORDER

Change Order # 1   Date:
Escrow # 81-75-20-E45

The following is a clarification and/or change to the original Contract
dated March 7, 1982   between:

OWNER: Ruth K. and Sam P. Smith
CONTRACTOR: XYZ Construction
PROPERTY ADDRESS: 4330 North La Mont

This Change Order is made in order to modify, change, or clarify the
work under the above-captioned Contract and this Order is made a part
of the Contract. This Change Order supercedes any previous drawings,
work orders, specifications, and agreements.

The changes, modifications, and clarifications are as follows:

ITEMS	EXTRAS TO CONTRACT	CREDITS TO CONTRACT

1. Remove existing wood fencing on south, east and north property
   lines from site. Install new 4'-0" high chain link fence as
   outlined:

   a. South side: 35 lf from east property line west to end of
      building. Install 3'-0" wide gate at west end, service walk.

   b. North side: 15 lf from south side of garage to south prop-
      erty line.

   c. East side: 12 lf from south side of garage to south property
      line. Install 3'-0" wide gate at south side, at service walk.

All dimensions are approximate. Contractor to verify in field before
beginning any work. Installation is to be in accordance with the NHS
Performance Manual

Total Extras or Credits to Contract for this Change Order	$500.00	$ 0

	Net Value of Contract	Total Value of Contract
Amount of Original Contract	$15,500.00	$16,000.00
Previous Extras to Contract (+)	0	
Previous Credits to Contract (-)	0	
Previous Adjusted Total Contract	15,500.00	
Net Previously Paid	9,800.00	
Balance Due Prior to This Change Order	5,700.00	
Extras to Contract from This Change Order (+)	500.00	
Credits to Contract from This Change Order (-)	0	
Adjusted Total Contract	16,000.00	
Balance Due on Adjusted Contract	6,200.00	

CONTRACTOR IS AUTHORIZED TO PROCEED WITH WORK SPECIFIED IN THIS CHANGE ORDER.

Approved By
Owner(s) _____ Date: _____

Approved By
Contractor _____ Date: _____

Draw Request
Section 203(k)

**U.S. Department of Housing
and Urban Development**
Office of Housing
Federal Housing Commissioner

OMB Approval No. 2502-0386 (exp. 6-30-92)

Public reporting burden for this collection of information is estimated to average 1.09 hours per response, including the time for reviewing instructions, searching existing data sources, gathering and maintaining the data needed, and completing and reviewing the collection of information. Send comments regarding this burden estimate or any other aspect of this collection of information, including suggestions for reducing this burden, to the Reports Management Officer, Office of Information Policies and Systems, U.S. Department of Housing and Urban Development, Washington, D.C. 20410-3600 and to the Office of Management and Budget, Paperwork Reduction Project (2502-0386), Washington, D.C. 20503.

Mortgagor's Name and Property Address	Mortgagee's Name and Address	FHA Case Number		
		This Draw Number		Date

	Construction Item	Total Escrow	Previous Draw Totals	%	Request for This Draw	Total of Previous and This Request	%	HUD/DE Accepted Amounts Total	%	
1.	Masonry									1.
2.	Siding									2.
3.	Gutters/Downspouts									3.
4.	Roof									4.
5.	Shutters									5.
6.	Exteriors									6.
7.	Walks									7.
8.	Driveways									8.
9.	Painting (Ext.)									9.
10.	Caulking									10.
11.	Fencing									11.
12.	Grading									12.
13.	Windows									13.
14.	Weatherstrip									14.
15.	Doors (Ext.)									15.
16.	Doors (Int.)									16.
17.	Partition Wall									17.
18.	Plaster/Drywall									18.
19.	Decorating									19.
20.	Wood Trim									20.
21.	Stairs									21.
22.	Closets									22.
23.	Wood Floors									23.
24.	Finished Floors									24.
25.	Ceramic Tile									25.
26.	Bath Accesories									26.
27.	Plumbing									27.
28.	Electrical									28.
29.	Heating									29.
30.	Insulation									30.
31.	Cabinetry									31.
32.	Appliances									32.
33.	Basements									33.
34.	Cleanup									34.
35.	Miscellaneous									35.
36.	**Totals**									36.

This draw request is submitted for payment. All completed work has been done in a workmanlike manner. It is understood that a 10% holdback will not be released until all work is complete and it is determined that no mechanic's and materialmen's liens have been placed on the property.

Mortgagor's Signature	Date	General Contractor's Signature (if any)	Date

The above draw amounts are acceptable except as modified above in **HUD/DE Accepted** column. *Compliance Inspection Report*, form HUD-92051, is attached.

Fee Inspector's Signature	I.D. Number	Date

Approved for Release

	This Draw	Totals to Date
Total from Above	$	$
Less 10% Holdback	$	$
Net Amount Due Mortgagor	$	$
Additional Amounts Released from Allowable Fees	$	$

The Mortgagee is hereby authorized to release the following funds from the escrow account:

Payable to the Mortgagor $_____ ;

Payable to the Fee Inspector $_____ ;

Payable to _____ $_____

Signature   Date:

☐ HUD Authorized Agent   ☐ DE Underwriter   I.D. Number

form **HUD-9746-A** (7/89)
ref. handbook 4240.4

RED FLAGS INSPECTION CHECKLIST

_____ Property

_____ Agent

_____ Date

Red Flags Property Inspection Guide page numbers provided for reference.

CIRCLE APPROPRIATE SYMBOL OR MARK ☒

	Red Flag	Possible Red Flag	Nothing Observed or Not Applicable

1. INSPECTING FOR RED FLAGS OUTSIDE THE HOME

	Red Flag	Possible Red Flag	Nothing Observed
Cracks in sidewalks, driveways, or decks? (2/4)	⚑	⚐	☐
Cracks in foundation? (2/5)	⚑	⚐	☐
Cracks in fireplace? (2/26)	⚑	⚐	☐
Visually distorted structure? (2/7)	⚑	⚐	☐
Visual evidence of drainage problems? (2/8)	⚑	⚐	☐
Building ventilation screens damaged? (2/10)	⚑	⚐	☐
Visual evidence of hillside instability, landsliding? (2/11)	⚑	⚐	☐
Visual evidence of erosion? (2/12)	⚑	⚐	☐
Visual evidence of roof deterioration? (2/15)	⚑	⚐	☐
Hazardous vegetation observed? (2/16)	⚑	⚐	☐
Hazardous deck or stair railings? (2/18)	⚑	⚐	☐
Hazardous stairs? (2/19)	⚑	⚐	☐
Hazardous walkways or steps? (2/20)	⚑	⚐	☐
Visual evidence of failing retaining walls? (2/39)	⚑	⚐	☐
Swimming pool out-of-level? (2/40)	⚑	⚐	☐
Cracks in swimming pool? (2/40)	⚑	⚐	☐
Hazardous play structure or treehouse? (2/41)	⚑	⚐	☐
_____	⚑	⚐	☐

2. INSPECTING FOR RED FLAGS INSIDE THE HOME

	Red Flag	Possible Red Flag	Nothing Observed
Cracks in basement walls? (2/21)	⚑	⚐	☐
Water stains, or white powdery deposits on basement walls? (2/21)	⚑	⚐	☐
Sump pump(s)? (2/21)	⚑	⚐	☐
Water stains on ceiling or around windows? (2/14)	⚑	⚐	☐
Wall or ceiling cracks? (2/22)	⚑	⚐	☐
Hidden wall cracks? (2/23)	⚑	⚐	☐
Any noticeable sloping floors? (2/24)	⚑	⚐	☐
Cracks in tile floors? (2/24)	⚑	⚐	☐
Sticking doors or windows? (2/25)	⚑	⚐	☐
Uneven spaces between doors and frames? (2/26)	⚑	⚐	☐
Cracks in fireplace? (2/26)	⚑	⚐	☐
Hazardous fireplace hearth? (2/27)	⚑	⚐	☐
Visual evidence of sagging beams? (2/28)	⚑	⚐	☐
Burned or damaged electrical outlets? (2/29)	⚑	⚐	☐
Any extension cords under carpet or stapled to wall? (2/29)	⚑	⚐	☐
Any exposed wiring? (2/30)	⚑	⚐	☐
Electrical panel accessible and intact? (2/30)	⚑	⚐	☐
Gas shut-off valve accessible? (2/32)	⚑	⚐	☐
Hazardous water heater? (ie. no pressure valve, etc.) (2/33)	⚑	⚐	☐
Visual evidence of illegal additions? (2/34)	⚑	⚐	☐
Hazardous steps? (2/35)	⚑	⚐	☐
_____	⚑	⚐	☐

3. DURING YOUR INSPECTION DID YOU OBSERVE?

CIRCLE YES OR NO

Safety glass emblem on sliding doors (2/36)	Yes	No
Ground fault interrupters (2/31)	Yes	No
Safety wire on garage door springs (2/37)	Yes	No
Smoke alarm(s) (2/37)	Yes	No
_____	Yes	No

This form is designed to be used in conjunction with the Red Flags Property Inspection Guide. In California the completed checklist may be made an attachment to the Real Estate Transfer Disclosure Statement (Statutory Form) part 3 or 4 as applicable. (PPC 109.3 & 109.4 CAL)

FORM   109 RF   (10-87)   COPYRIGHT © 1987 BY PROFESSIONAL PUBLISHING CORP. 122 PAUL DR. SAN RAFAEL. CA 94903 (415) 472-1964   ■ PROFESSIONAL PUBLISHING

BUYER'S PROPERTY INSPECTION REPORT

TO: ...., the seller

of the real property commonly known as ....

Noted below are my/our findings of the physical condition of the above mentioned real property, as of

.........., 19.... Items not marked as "UNSATISFACTORY" are considered to be in satisfactory condition.

	UNSATISFACTORY	ESTIMATED COST OF REPAIR
GROUNDS		
Landscaping		
Pool		
Other		
HEATING AND AIR CONDITIONING SYSTEMS		
Furnace		
Air Conditioning		
Water Heater		
BUILT-IN APPLIANCES AND EQUIPMENT		
Ovens		
Burners		
Microwave		
Dishwasher		
Disposal		
Smoke Detectors		
Intercom		
Electric Garage Door Opener		
Other		
ELECTRICAL SYSTEMS		
Interior Lighting		
Exterior Lighting		
Other		
PLUMBING		
Bathrooms		
Kitchen		
Laundry		
Sprinklers		
Sewers or Septic Tank		
GLASS		
Windows		
Glass Doors		
Shower Glass		
Tub Enclosures		
Mirrors		
Other		
PERSONAL PROPERTY		
Carpets		
Draperies		

REMARKS:

Date: ....   Purchaser: ....

....   Purchaser: ....
      (Qualified Technician)

INSPECTION ADDENDUM

In reference to the ☐ PURCHASE AGREEMENT, ☐ EXCHANGE AGREEMENT, ☐ LEASE OPTION — covering the real property commonly known as: _____,
dated _____, between _____
_____, and _____ _____
_____

Within two (2) days following acceptance hereof Purchaser shall order an inspection report(s) from a representative of Purchaser's choice, and at Purchaser's expense, which shall include the items marked ☒ below. Copies of the report(s) shall be delivered to the agents of Purchaser and Seller who are authorized to receive the same on behalf of their principals. Approval of the report(s), at the discretion of the Purchaser which shall not be unreasonably withheld, to be given in writing **within three (3) days of receipt** of same. In the event the Purchaser does not approve of the report(s) Purchaser shall be entitled to a full refund of all deposits excluding the cost of said inspection report(s) and both parties shall be relieved of all obligations hereunder.

- ☐ Roof, gutters, downspouts
- ☐ Exterior siding
- ☐ Doors and windows
- ☐ Interior walls, ceilings and floors
- ☐ Foundation and basement or crawlspace
- ☐ Plumbing system
- ☐ Electrical system
- ☐ Heating system
- ☐ Cooling system
- ☐ Fireplace(s)
- ☐ Smoke detectors
- ☐ Built-in appliances
- ☐ Solar energy system
- ☐ Pool
- ☐ Spa or hot tub
- ☐ Sauna
- ☐ Landscape sprinkler system
- ☐ Drainage system including sump pump
- ☐ Septic tank
- ☐ Well
- ☐ _____
- ☐ _____
- ☐ _____

Seller agrees to provide reasonable access to the property to Purchaser and inspectors representing Purchaser. Purchaser acknowledges that he has not received or relied upon statements or representations by the undersigned Agent(s) regarding the condition of any of the above referenced items which are not herein expressed.

Additional terms and conditions: _____
_____
_____
_____
_____
_____
_____
_____
_____
_____
_____
_____

The herein agreement, upon its execution by both parties, is herewith made an integral part of the aforementioned Agreement of Sale.

DATED: _____ TIME: _____   DATED: _____ TIME: _____
_____ PURCHASER   _____ SELLER
_____ PURCHASER   _____ SELLER
_____ AGENT   _____ AGENT

FORM 101-BI (1-86) COPYRIGHT · 1986, BY PROFESSIONAL PUBLISHING CORP. 122 PAUL DR. SAN RAFAEL, CA 94903

PROFESSIONAL PUBLISHING

6

Real Estate Forms and Reference

SAMPLE REAL ESTATE FORMS AND REFERENCE

The forms shown in this chapter are generic forms. Check the filing requirements of your real estate's locality for particular documents needed.

Notice to Prospective Real Estate Buyers*
List of States That Use Mortgages and Trust Deeds
Buyer's Broker Employment Agreement*
Comparative Residential Market Analysis*
Residential Purchase Agreement and Deposit Receipt*
Counter Offer*
Seller's Property Disclosure Statement*
Contingency Release Clause*
Residential Lease with Option to Purchase*
Option to Purchase and Exercise of Option*
Land Purchase Agreement*
Real Estate Transfer Disclosure Statement*
Real Estate Transfer Disclosure Supplement*
Estimated Seller's Proceeds*
Hazardous Materials Addendum*
A Detailed Home Evaluation Report

* Reprinted by permission of the copyright owner, Professional Publishing Corporation, © Copyright PROFESSIONAL PUBLISHING CORPORATION, 122 PAUL DRIVE, SAN RAFAEL, CA 94903 (415) 472-1964.

NOTICE TO PROSPECTIVE
REAL ESTATE BUYERS

As a prospective buyer you should know that:

- Generally, the listing and cooperating ("selling") brokers are the agents of the seller.

- Their fiduciary duties of loyalty and faithfulness are owed to their client (the seller).

- Although neither broker is your agent, they are able to provide you with a variety of valuable market information and assistance in your decision-making process.

For example, a real estate broker representing the seller can:

- Provide you with information about available properties and sources of financing.

- Show you available properties and describe their attributes and amenities.

- Assist you in submitting an offer to purchase.

Both the listing broker and the cooperating broker are obligated by law to treat you honestly and fairly. They must:

- Present all offers to the seller promptly.

- Respond honestly and accurately to questions concerning the property.

- Disclose material facts the broker knows or reasonably should know about the property.

- Offer the property without regard to race, color, religion, sex, familial status, handicap, or national origin.

You can, if you feel it necessary, obtain agency representation of a lawyer or a real estate broker, or both.

If you choose to have a real estate broker represent you as your agent, you should:

- Enter into a written contract that clearly establishes the obligations of both parties.

- Specify how your agent will be compensated.

If you have any questions regarding the roles and responsiblities of real estate brokers, please do not hesitate to ask.

I have received, read, and understand the information in this "Notice to Prospective Real Estate Buyers."	I certify that I have provided the Prospective Buyer with a copy of this "Notice to Prospective Buyers."
Buyer: _____	Broker: _____
Buyer: _____	By: _____
Address: _____	Date: _____
_____	
Telephone: _____	
Date: _____	

List of States That Use Mortgages and Trust Deeds

State	Security Instrument
Alabama	Mortgage
Alaska	Deed of Trust
Arizona	Deed of Trust
Arkansas	Mortgage
California	Deed of Trust
Colorado	Deed of Trust
Connecticut	Mortgage
Delaware	Mortgage
District of Columbia	Deed of Trust
Florida	Mortgage
Georgia	Security Deed
Hawaii	Deed of Trust
Idaho	Deed of Trust
Illinois	Mortgage
Indiana	Mortgage
Iowa	Mortgage
Kansas	Mortgage
Kentucky	Mortgage
Louisiana	Mortgage
Maine	Mortgage
Maryland	Deed of Trust
Massachusetts	Mortgage
Michigan	Mortgage
Minnesota	Mortgage
Mississippi	Deed of Trust
Missouri	Deed of Trust
Montana	Deed of Trust
Nebraska	Deed of Trust
Nevada	Deed of Trust
New Hampshire	Mortgage
New Jersey	Mortgage
New Mexico	Mortgage
New York	Mortgage
North Carolina	Deed of Trust
North Dakota	Mortgage
Ohio	Mortgage
Oklahoma	Mortgage
Oregon	Deed of Trust
Pennsylvania	Mortgage
Rhode Island	Mortgage
South Carolina	Mortgage
South Dakota	Mortgage
Tennessee	Deed of Trust

State	Security Instrument
Texas	Deed of Trust
Utah	Deed of Trust
Vermont	Mortgage
Virginia	Deed of Trust
Washington	Deed of Trust
West Virginia	Deed of Trust
Wisconsin	Mortgage
Wyoming	Mortgage
Virgin Islands	Mortgage
Puerto Rico	Mortgage

☐ *ZipForm™* **Computer Alignment**
NCR (No Carbon Required)

BUYER'S BROKER EMPLOYMENT AGREEMENT

The undersigned _____, hereinafter designated as CLIENT,
hereby employs _____, hereinafter designated as BROKER,
for the purpose of exclusively assisting Client to locate property of a nature outlined below or other property acceptable to Client, and to negotiate terms and
conditions acceptable to Client for purchase, exchange, lease, or option of or on such property. This agreement shall commence this date and terminate at
midnight of _____, 19_____.

GENERAL NATURE, LOCATION, AND REQUIREMENTS OF PROPERTY.

_____
_____
_____
_____
_____
_____

PRICE RANGE, AND OTHER TERMS AND CONDITIONS.

_____
_____
_____
_____
_____
_____
_____
_____
_____
_____
_____
_____

COMPENSATION TO BROKER. Client agrees to pay Broker, as compensation:

a) For locating property acceptable to Client and for negotiating the purchase or exchange, a fee of $_____, or _____% of the acquisition
price, or $_____ per hour.

b) For obtaining an option on a property acceptable to Client, a fee of $_____, and to pay Broker the balance of a fee equal to _____% of the
purchase price in the event the option is exercised or assigned prior to expiration of the option.

c) For locating a property acceptable to Client and negotiating a lease thereon, a fee of _____.

IF:

1. Client or any other person acting for Client or in Client's behalf, purchases, exchanges, obtains an option for, or leases any real property of the nature
described herein, during the term hereof, through the services of Broker or otherwise.

2. Client or any other person acting for Client or in Client's behalf, purchases, exchanges, obtains an option for, or leases any real property of the nature
described herein, within one year after termination of this agreement, which property Broker, Broker's agent, or cooperating brokers presented or
submitted to Client during the term hereof and the description of which Broker shall have submitted in writing to Client, either in person or by mail, **within
ten (10) days after termination of this agreement.**

**NOTICE: The amount or rate of real estate commissions is not fixed by law. They are set by each broker individually
and may be negotiable between the buyer and the broker.**

AGENCY RELATIONSHIP. Broker agrees to act as agent for Client only in any resulting transaction, provided that Broker may cooperate with other
brokers and their agents in an effort to locate property or properties in accordance with this agreement, and may divide fees in any manner acceptable to them.
If Broker receives compensation from anyone other than Client, Broker shall make full disclosure, and such compensation shall be credited against Client's
obligation hereunder.

In addition, Broker will provide appropriate Agency Disclosure as required by law.

BROKER'S OBLIGATIONS. In consideration of Client's agreement set forth above, Broker agrees to use diligence to achieve the purpose of this
agreement.

CLIENT'S OBLIGATIONS. Client agrees to provide Broker, upon request, relevant personal and financial information to assure Client's ability to
acquire property outlined above. Client further agrees to view or consider property of the general nature set forth in this Agreement, and to negotiate in good
faith to acquire such property if acceptable to Client. In the event completion of any resulting transaction is prevented by Client's default, Client shall pay Broker
the compensation provided for herein upon such default.

ATTORNEY FEE. If any action is brought to enforce the terms of this agreement, or arising out of the execution of this agreement, or to collect fees, the
prevailing party shall be entitled to receive from the other party a reasonable attorney fee to be determined by the court in which such action is brought.

ENTIRE AGREEMENT. Time is of the essence. The terms hereof constitute the entire agreement and supersede all prior agreements, negotiations and
discussions between the parties. This Agreement may be modified only by a writing signed by each of the parties.

Receipt of a copy of this agreement is hereby acknowledged.   DATED: _____ TIME: _____

Buyer's Broker: _____   _____ Client

By: _____   _____ Client

Address: _____   Address: _____

Phone: _____   Phone: _____

COMPARATIVE RESIDENTIAL MARKET ANALYSIS

FORM 123

Prepared for: Mr. & Mrs. John Doe .... Location of Subject Property: 123 Cedar Way, (Your City)

Type House: 2 Story Mediterranean .... Square Footage: 3,000 .... Total No. of Rooms: 8 .... Bedrooms: 5 .... Baths: 3 .... Age: 6

(Comparable properties recently sold must be similar to subject property in the above features)

Comparable Properties Sold		PROPERTY A	PROPERTY B	PROPERTY C	PROPERTY D	SUBJECT PROPERTY
Use as many comparables as available	Location	10 Appleberry	72 Oak Circle	37 Cottonwood	17 Mulberry	
	Date listed	January 10, 1986	November 12, 1985	February 23, 1986	January 22, 1986	
	Date sold	March 17, 1986	February 5, 1986	February 28, 1986	April 15, 1986	
	Terms of sale	Cash over Conv. Loan	New FHA	New FHA	Assumption-$5,000 2nd	
SALE PRICE ①		$155,000 ①	$167,000 ①	$158,000 ①	$161,000 ①	
LESS: Outstanding Features† ②		$6,000 ②	$13,000 ②	$6,000 ②	$8,000 ②	
Value of Basic Property (Line ① minus ②) ③		$149,000 ③	$154,000 ③	$152,000 ③	$153,000 ③	
PLUS: Fixing-up Cost* ④		$2,000 ④	$ - - - ④	$1,500 ④	$1,000 ④	
Value of Basic Property in Good Condition (Line ③ plus ④) ⑤		$151,000 ⑤	$154,000 ⑤	$153,500 ⑤	$154,000 ⑤	

SUM OF AMOUNTS ON LINE ⑤ DIVIDED BY THE NUMBER OF COMPARABLES USED = BASIC VALUE OF SUBJECT PROPERTY IN GOOD CONDITION . . . . . $153,125 ⑥

PLUS: Outstanding Features† of Subject Property (Itemize below) . . . . . $15,000 ⑦

SUB-TOTAL (Line ⑥ plus line ⑦) . . . . . $168,125 ⑧

LESS: Fixing-up Cost* of Subject Property (Itemize below) . . . . . $2,000 ⑨

ANTICIPATED SALE PRICE OF SUBJECT PROPERTY IN ITS PRESENT CONDITION (Line ⑧ minus line ⑨) . . . . . $166,125 ⑩

The ANTICIPATED SALE PRICE is merely an estimate and is based on the assumption that the property will be exposed to the open market for a reasonable period of time and is further based on the owner's full cooperation with broker during the term of the listing.

	PROPERTY A	PROPERTY B	PROPERTY C	PROPERTY D	SUBJECT PROPERTY
†Outstanding Features	All weather lanai, Lawn Sprinklers	Pool, Deck and excellent landscaping, Patio, Built-in Barbecue	Family room with wet bar	Pool	Pool, Patio, Family room
*Fixing-up Costs	Exterior paint		Interior paint	Front lawn needs to be replaced	Exterior paint

†Outstanding Features — Examples: Sprinkler system, pool, added rooms, superior landscaping, view lot, special equipment, etc.—ALLOW FOR OVER-IMPROVEMENTS!

*Fixing-up Costs — Examples: Necessary painting, renovating, landscaping, necessary repairs or replacements, etc., in order to bring property into good condition.

Date: April 15, 1986 .... Prepared by: James King .... Office: Oliver, Cox and Associates .... Telephone: 123-4567

COMPARABLE PROPERTIES FOR SALE NOW

ADDRESS	EXTRAS	CONDITION	PRICE	LISTING DATE

COMPARABLE LISTINGS EXPIRED DURING LAST 12 MONTHS

ADDRESS	EXTRAS	CONDITION	PRICE	LIST PERIOD

FHA — VA APPRAISALS OF COMPARABLE PROPERTIES

ADDRESS	EXTRAS	CONDITION	APPRAISAL

☐ *ZipForm*™ Computer Alignment
NCR (No Carbon Required)   **RESIDENTIAL PURCHASE AGREEMENT AND DEPOSIT RECEIPT**
                          For Resale Property

DEFINITIONS

BROKER includes cooperating brokers and all sales persons. *DAYS* means calendar days unless otherwise specified. *DATE OF ACCEPTANCE* means the date the Seller accepts the offer or the Buyer accepts the counter offer. *DELIVERED* means personally delivered or transmitted by facsimile machine, pursuant to **Item 40**, or mailed by certified mail; in the event of mailing, delivery shall be deemed to have been made **on the third day following the date of mailing**, evidenced by the postmark on the envelope containing the delivered material. *DATE OF CLOSING* means the date title is transferred. The *MASCULINE* includes the feminine and the *SINGULAR* includes the plural. *TIME LIMITS* for contingency removal are shown in **bold print**. *UNUSED DEPOSITS* means all deposits less expenses incurred by or on account of Buyer **to date of termination**. *PROPERTY* means the real property and any personal property included in the sale as provided herein.

RECEIVED from _____

_____, hereinafter designated as BUYER, the amount set forth below as **DEPOSIT (Item 1-A)** on account of the

PURCHASE PRICE of $_____ (_____**DOLLARS**),

for the real property situated in _____, County of _____, State of _____,

described as _____

_____

☐ **Buyer does**   ☐ **Buyer does not** intend to occupy the property as his/her residence.

1.   FINANCING TERMS AND LOAN PROVISIONS.

A. $_____   **DEPOSIT** evidenced by ☐ Check or ☐ Other: _____, payable to _____
held uncashed until acceptance and one day thereafter deposited with: _____

B. $_____   **ADDITIONAL CASH DEPOSIT In escrow** ☐ within_____days of acceptance, ☐ upon receipt of Loan
Commitment per **Item 2**, ☐ other: _____

C. $_____   **BALANCE OF CASH PAYMENT needed to close.**

D. $_____   **NEW FIRST LOAN:** ☐ CONVENTIONAL, ☐ FHA, ☐ VA:
☐ FIXED RATE: For _____ years, Interest not to exceed _____%, payable at approximately $_____ p/mo.
☐ Taxes and Insurance included in above monthly payments.
☐ ARM: For _____ years, Initial Interest Rate not to exceed _____%, with Initial Monthly Payments of $_____
and Maximum Life Time Rate not to exceed _____%, ☐ Taxes & Insurance included in above monthly payments.
☐ OTHER TERMS: _____
Loan origination fee not to exceed _____% plus $_____, paid by ☐ Buyer, ☐ Seller.
Seller agrees to pay Discount Points not to exceed _____%. Buyer agrees to pay Discount Points not to exceed _____%.
☐ FHA-MIP, ☐ VA Funding Fee, ☐ PMI, if any, to be ☐ financed, ☐ paid in cash, ☐ paid monthly.
Appraisal fee to be paid by ☐ Buyer, ☐ Seller.
In the event of FHA or VA financing, the **FHA or VA AMENDMENT, Item 10 or 11** on Page 2, is made a part of this agreement.

E. $_____   **EXISTING FINANCING:** ☐ FIRST LOAN, ☐ SECOND LOAN:
☐ **ASSUMPTION OF,** ☐ **SUBJECT TO** marked existing loan of record:
☐ FHA, ☐ VA, ☐ CONVENTIONAL, ☐ PRIVATE _____, ☐ FIXED RATE, ☐ ARM: _____
☐ OTHER: _____

payable at $_____ per month, with interest currently at _____%, ☐ Taxes and Insurance included in
above monthly payments, with Interest Rate to be adjusted not to exceed _____%. Other terms: _____
_____. Date balance due:_____.
Held by: _____. Assumption Fee, if any, not to exceed _____%.
All charges related to assumption shall be paid by Buyer.
☐ **ASSUMPTION OF LOAN WITH RELEASE OF LIABILITY:** Buyer shall assume Seller's Potential Indemnity
Liability to the U.S. Government for the repayment of the loan.
☐ **ASSUMPTION OF VA LOAN WITH SUBSTITUTION OF ENTITLEMENT.**
Paragraph 1-E is conditioned upon Buyer's approval of terms of said loan pursuant to **Item 4**, EXISTING LOANS.

F. $_____   **SELLER FINANCING:** ☐ FIRST LOAN, ☐ SECOND LOAN, ☐ THIRD LOAN,
secured by the property, payable at $_____ per month, or more, including _____% interest, with the
balance due _____ years from date of conveyance, ☐ due on sale.
A late charge of $_____ shall be due on monthly payments tendered **more than** _____ **days late.**
See **Item 6**, CREDIT APPROVAL.

G. $_____   **OTHER FINANCING:**_____
_____
_____
_____
_____
_____
_____

H. $_____   **TOTAL PURCHASE PRICE (not including closing costs).** Any net differences between the approximate balances
of encumbrances shown above, which are to be assumed or taken subject to, and the actual balances **at closing** shall be
adjusted in ☐ Cash, ☐ Other:_____

Buyer [_____] [_____] and Seller [_____] [_____] have read this page.

2. **LOAN APPROVAL.** Conditioned upon Buyers' ability to obtain a commitment for new financing for the herein property from a lender of Buyers' choice. and/or consent to assumption of existing financing provided for in this agreement, **within _____ days of acceptance.** Buyer shall notify Seller in writing whether or not such commitment was obtained **within said time.** Buyer shall use his best efforts to qualify for and obtain said financing and shall complete and submit a loan application **within five (5) days of acceptance.**

   In the event a loan commitment or consent is obtained but not honored without fault of Buyer and lender furnishes written verification that the loan will not be funded, then Buyer may terminate this agreement and have all deposits returned less expenses incurred **to the date of termination of this transaction.**

3. **BONDS AND ASSESSMENTS.** In the event there is a Bond or Assessment which has an outstanding principal balance and is a lien upon this property, such principal shall be [   ] paid by Seller, or [   ] assumed by Buyer. In the event of assumption, said obligation(s) [   ] shall, [   ] shall not be credited to Buyer **at closing.** This agreement is conditioned upon both parties verifying and approving in writing the amount of any bond or assessment **within ten (10) days of receipt** of the preliminary title report. The disapproving party may terminate this agreement, in which case all unused deposits shall be returned to Buyer.

4. **EXISTING LOANS.** Seller shall, **within three (3) days of acceptance,** provide Buyer with all Notes and Deeds of Trust to be assumed or taken subject to, and **within five (5) days of receipt thereof** Buyer shall in writing notify Seller of his approval or disapproval of the terms of said documents, which shall not be unreasonably withheld. **Within three (3) days of acceptance,** Seller shall submit written request for a current Statement of Condition on the above loan. Seller warrants that all loans in the transaction will be current **at close of escrow.**

5. **DUE ON SALE CLAUSE. If the note and deed of trust or mortgage for any existing loan contains an acceleration or DUE ON SALE clause, the lender may demand full payment of the entire loan balance as a result of this transaction. Both parties acknowledge that they are not relying on any representation by the other party or the broker with respect to the enforceability of such a provision in existing notes and deeds of trust or mortgages, or deeds of trust or mortgages to be executed in accordance with this agreement. Both parties have been advised by the broker to seek independent legal advice with respect to these matters.**

6. **CREDIT APPROVAL.** In the event of Seller Financing, Buyer shall furnish Seller **within three (3) days of acceptance,** a customary financial statement for the sole purpose of credit approval, which approval shall not be unreasonably withheld. Buyer authorizes Seller to engage the services of a reputable credit reporting agency for this purpose at Buyer's expense and Seller shall notify Buyer **within ten (10) days of receipt** of financial statement, of approval or disapproval of Buyer's credit.

7. **BALLOON PAYMENT. Both parties acknowledge they have not relied upon any statements or representations made to them by Broker regarding availability of funds, or rate of interest at which funds might be available, when Buyer becomes obligated to refinance or pay off the remaining balance of any loan pursuant to the terms of this agreement.**

8. **PRORATIONS.** Rents, taxes, interest, payments on Bonds and Assessments assumed by Buyer, Homeowner Association fees, and other expenses of the property to be prorated **as of the date of recordation** of the deed. Security deposits, advance rentals, or considerations involving future lease credits shall be credited to Buyer.

9. **REASSESSMENT OF PROPERTY TAX.** Buyer is advised that the property may be reassessed upon change of ownership which may result in a tax increase.

10. **FHA FINANCING. In the event of FHA financing, it is expressly agreed that, notwithstanding any other provisions of this contract, the Buyer shall not be obligated to complete the purchase of the property described herein or to incur any penalty by forfeiture of earnest money deposits or otherwise unless the Seller has delivered to the Buyer a written statement issued by the Federal Housing Commissioner, setting forth the appraised value of the property, (excluding closing costs) of not less than the amount specified as the purchase price, which statement the Seller hereby agrees to deliver to the Buyer promptly after such appraised value statement is made available to the Seller. The Buyer shall, however, have the privilege and option of proceeding with the consummation of the contract without regard to the amount of the appraised valuation made by the Federal Housing Commissioner.**

   THE APPRAISED VALUATION IS ARRIVED AT TO DETERMINE THE MAXIMUM MORTGAGE THE DEPARTMENT OF HOUSING AND URBAN DEVELOPMENT WILL INSURE. HUD DOES NOT WARRANT THE VALUE OR THE CONDITION OF THE PROPERTY. THE BUYER SHOULD SATISFY HIMSELF/HERSELF THAT THE PRICE AND CONDITION OF THE PROPERTY ARE ACCEPTABLE.

11. **VA FINANCING. In the event of VA financing, it is expressly agreed that, notwithstanding any other provisions of this contract, the Buyer shall not incur any penalty by forfeiture of earnest money or otherwise be obligated to complete the purchase of the property described herein, if the contract purchase price or cost exceeds the Reasonable Value of the property established by the Veterans Administration. The Buyer shall, however, have the privilege and option of proceeding with the consummation of this contract without regard to the amount of the Reasonable Value established by the Veterans Administration. Escrow Fee to be paid by Seller.**

12. **TIME IS OF THE ESSENCE.** Time is of the essence of this agreement. All modifications and extensions shall be in writing and signed by all parties.

13. **CONDITIONS SATISFIED/WAIVED IN WRITING.** Each condition or contingency, approval and disapproval herein shall be satisfied according to its terms or waived in writing by the benefiting party **within the time limits specified (or any extension** thereof agreed to by the parties in writing), or this agreement shall terminate and all unused deposits shall be returned. This paragraph contemplates that each party shall diligently pursue the completion of this transaction.

   In this agreement **bold print** is used where such time limits are specified.

14. **INSURANCE.** In the event of Seller Financing, Buyer shall obtain hazard insurance prepaid **for one year** in an amount satisfactory to the loan holders and covering one hundred percent replacement cost of improvements, and to name holders of the secured loans as additional loss payees. Buyer agrees further to annually increase said insurance if necessary, to equal the current replacement cost of the property during the term of the loan holders' mortgages. Buyer shall instruct the insurance carrier to deliver to Seller **before closing** a certificate providing for **30 days written notice** in the event of cancellation.

15. **DESTRUCTION OF IMPROVEMENTS.** If the improvements of the property are destroyed, materially damaged, or found to be materially defective **prior to closing,** Buyer may terminate the transaction by written notice delivered to Seller's broker or agent, and all unused deposits shall be returned. In the event Buyer does not elect to terminate the agreement, Buyer shall be entitled to receive in addition to the property any insurance proceeds payable on account of the damage or destruction.

16. **NOTICE OF VIOLATIONS.** By acceptance hereof Seller warrants that he has no written notice of violations relating to the property from City, County, or State agencies.

Buyer [_____] [_____] and Seller [_____] [_____] have read this page.

FORM   101-R.1(a)   (10-91)   COPYRIGHT © 1991. BY PROFESSIONAL PUBLISHING CORP. 122 PAUL DR. SAN RAFAEL, CA 94903 (415) 472-1964   **PROFESSIONAL PUBLISHING**

17. EXAMINATION OF TITLE. In addition to any encumbrances referred to herein, Seller shall convey title to the property subject only to: [1] Real Estate Taxes not yet due, and [2] Covenants, Conditions, Restrictions, Rights of Way, and Easements of record, if any, which do not materially affect the value or intended use of the property.

Within three (3) days from acceptance Buyer shall order a preliminary Title Report and CC&R's if applicable. **Ten (10) days from receipt** thereof are allowed the Buyer to examine the title to the property and to report in writing any valid objections thereto. All exceptions to the title contained in such report (other than monetary liens) shall be deemed approved unless written objection is delivered to Seller **within said ten (10) days.** If Buyer objects to any exceptions to the title, Seller shall use due diligence to remove such exceptions at his own expense **before closing.** But if such exceptions cannot be removed **before closing,** all rights and obligations hereunder may, at the election of the Buyer, terminate and the deposit shall be returned to Buyer less expenses incurred by Buyer **to date of termination,** unless he elects to purchase the property subject to such exceptions. If Seller concludes he is unwilling or unable to remove such objections, Seller shall so notify Buyer **within ten (10) days of receipt of said objections.** In that event Buyer may terminate this agreement and all unused deposits shall be returned.

18. SURVIVAL. The omission from escrow instructions of any provision herein shall not waive the right of any party. All representations or warranties shall survive the conveyance of the property.

19. DEFAULT. In the event Buyer shall default in the performance of this agreement, Seller may, subject to any rights of the broker herein, retain Buyer's deposit on account of damages sustained and may take such actions as he deems appropriate to collect such additional damages as may have been actually sustained, and Buyer shall have the right to take such action as he deems appropriate to recover such portion of the deposit as may be allowed by law. **In the event that Buyer shall so default, unless Buyer and Seller have agreed to Liquidated Damages, Buyer agrees to pay the Broker(s) entitled thereto such commission as would be payable by Seller in the absence of such default.**

20. ATTORNEY FEES. In any action or proceeding involving a dispute between Buyer, Seller and/or Broker, arising out of the execution of this agreement or the sale, or to collect commissions, the prevailing party shall be entitled to receive from the other party a reasonable attorney fee to be determined by the court or arbitrator(s).

21. CLOSING. [ ] On or before _____, [ ] within _____ days of acceptance, both parties shall deposit with an authorized Escrow Holder, to be selected by [ ] Buyer, [ ] Seller, all funds and instruments necessary to complete the sale in accordance with the terms hereof. [ ] Where customary, signed Escrow Instructions to be delivered to Escrow Holder **within _____ days of acceptance.**
Escrow Fee to be paid by_____. Transfer Tax(es), if any, to be paid by _____.

22. EVIDENCE OF TITLE, in the form of [ ] a policy of Title Insurance, [ ] Other:_____ paid by _____

23. PHYSICAL POSSESSION. Physical possession of the property, with keys to all property locks, alarms, and garage door openers, shall be delivered to Buyer (check the appropriate box): [ ] **Upon recordation of the deed, OR** [ ] **After recordation of the deed, but not later than midnight of _____.**
In the event physical possession is to be delivered **after recordation,** Seller agrees to pay Buyer the sum of [ ] Buyer's Principal, Interest, Taxes and Insurance or [ ] $_____ per day, as a day to day tenant, **from recordation to the date hereinabove set forth** (or any lesser sum in proportion **to the actual date possession is delivered),** to leave in escrow a sum equal to the above per diem amount **multiplied by the number of days from date of closing to date allowed above** for delivery of possession, and that all or so much of said sum as may be appropriate shall be delivered to the person(s) entitled thereto **on the date possession is delivered or on the date set forth above, whichever is sooner.**

Seller understands that continued occupancy **beyond the date specified above** constitutes a breach of this agreement in the absence of any written agreement between the parties to the contrary.

24. FIXTURES. All items permanently attached to the property, including light fixtures, attached floor coverings, draperies, blinds and shades including window hardware, window and door screens, storm sash, combination doors, awnings, TV antennas, burglar, fire and smoke alarms, pool and spa equipment, solar systems, attached fireplace screens, electric garage door openers with controls, outdoor plants and trees (other than in movable containers), are included in the purchase price free of liens, **EXCLUDING:**_____.

25. PERSONAL PROPERTY. The following personal property, on the premises when inspected by Buyer, is included in the purchase price and shall be transferred to Buyer free of liens by a Bill of Sale **at closing.** No warranty is implied as to the condition of said property: _____.

26. MAINTENANCE. Seller covenants that the heating, air-conditioning, electrical, solar, septic system, gutters and downspouts, sprinkler, and plumbing systems including the water heater, pool and spa systems, as well as built-in appliances and other mechanical apparatus shall be in **working order** on the **date possession is delivered.** Seller shall replace any cracked or broken glass including windows, mirrors, shower and tub enclosures. **Until possession is delivered** Seller shall maintain all structures, landscaping, grounds and pool. Seller agrees to deliver the property in a neat and clean condition with all debris and personal belongings removed. The following items are specifically excluded from the above: _____.

Buyer and Seller understand and acknowledge that Broker shall not in any circumstances be liable for any breach in this clause.

27. PRE-CLOSING WALK-THROUGH. Buyer may conduct a walk-through inspection of the property **within _____ days prior to closing** to verify Seller's compliance with **Item 26,** MAINTENANCE.

28. SELLER'S PROPERTY DISCLOSURE STATEMENT. Seller [ ] shall, [ ] shall not provide Buyer **as soon as practicable before transfer of title** a completed Seller's Property Disclosure Statement. Such statement may be provided on PPC Form #110.11, 110.12 and 110.13.

28-A. BUYER'S APPROVAL. If such Disclosure Statement is delivered to Buyer **after the execution of this offer to purchase,** the Buyer is allowed to terminate this agreement by written notice delivered to Seller or Seller's agent **within three (3) days after delivery in person, or five (5) days after delivery by deposit in the mail** and all unused deposits returned.

Buyer [ ] [ ] and Seller [ ] [ ] have read this page.

28-B. DISCLAIMER. Buyer understands that the Seller's Property Disclosure Statement is no substitute for property inspections by experts, including but not limited to engineers, geologists, architects, general contractors, specialty contractors, such as roofing contractors and structural pest control operators. Buyer is urged to retain such experts as he believes are appropriate. Buyer understands and acknowledges that the brokers and agents in the transaction cannot warrant the condition of the property or guarantee that all defects have been disclosed by Seller.

Neither the real property nor the fixtures and personal property referred to in **Items 24**, FIXTURES, and **25**, PERSONAL PROPERTY, are new, and have been subject to normal wear and tear. The obligations of Seller under **Item 26**, MAINTENANCE, are not intended to create a warranty with respect to the condition of the property to be maintained, or to create an obligation upon the part of the Seller to repair any item which may fail **after closing**. Buyer understands that, except as may be provided to the contrary in **Item 33**, ADDITIONAL TERMS AND CONDITIONS, Seller makes no express or implied warranty with respect to the condition of any of the real property or any personal property included in the sale.

Both parties acknowledge that **Broker(s) will not be investigating the status of permits, zoning, location of property lines, and/or code compliance. Square footage of structure is approximate** and neither Seller nor Broker guarantee accuracy. Buyer is to satisfy himself concerning these issues.

Buyer acknowledges that he has not relied upon any representations by either the Broker or the Seller with respect to the condition of the property which are not contained in this agreement or in the disclosure statements.

Seller agrees to hold harmless all brokers and agents in the transaction and to defend and indemnify them from any claim, demand, action or proceedings resulting from any omission or alleged omission by Seller in his Disclosure Statement.

29.   ACCESS TO PROPERTY.   Seller agrees to provide reasonable access to the property to Buyer and inspectors representing Buyer as provided in this agreement and to representatives of lending institutions for appraisal purposes.

30.   HAZARDOUS MATERIALS ADDENDUM   (PPC Form 110.61) [   ] is, [   ] is not attached hereto.

31.   COMPLIANCE WITH LOCAL LAWS.   Seller shall comply with any local laws applicable to the sale or transfer of the property.

32.   PROVISIONS ON THE REVERSE SIDE.   The provisions *initialed below* by Buyer, *printed in full on the reverse side (page 4)*, are included in this agreement.

[_____] A. Pest Control Inspection, paid by: [ ] Buyer, [ ] Seller	[_____] G. Flood Hazard Zone Disclosure
Other structures:_____	[_____] H. Home Protect. Contract [ ] Plan
Section (2) work to be paid by: [ ] Buyer, [ ] Seller	[ ] paid by _____ [ ] waived by _____
[_____] B. Existing Pest Control Report Dated:_____,	[_____] I. Contingent upon the sale of _____
By _____.	_____. Waiver within _____ days of acceptance.
[_____] C. Subject to Buyer's Approval of Pest Control Report	[_____] J. Owners Association Disclosure
[_____] D. Waiver of Pest Control Inspection	[_____] K. Rental Property
[_____] E. Inspections of Physical Condition of Property, to be	[_____] L. Rent Control Ordinance
approved or disapproved within _____ days of acceptance	[_____] M. Smoke Detector(s)
[_____] F. Maintenance Reserve in the amount of $ _____.	[_____] N. Tax Deferred Exchange (Investment Property)

_____ **32-A. PEST CONTROL INSPECTION.** Within ten (10) days of acceptance Seller shall furnish Buyer, at the expense of the party specified in **Item 32-A**, a current written inspection report by a registered structural pest control operator, covering the main building, and other structures on the property, listed in **Item 32-A**. (Said inspection report shall **not** include the roof coverings, which are included under the heading INSPECTIONS OF PHYSICAL CONDITION OF PROPERTY.)

If further inspection of inaccessible areas is recommended in the report, Buyer may require that said areas be inspected. If no infestation or infection is found, the additional cost of inspecting such inaccessible areas and the work required to return the property to its original condition shall be paid by Buyer.

The inspector shall be requested to separately report:

Section (1) — Work recommended (a) to correct infestation and/or infection of wood destroying pests or organisms, (b) to repair damage caused by such infestation and infection, and (c) to repair plumbing and other leaks, including repair of leaking shower stalls and pans.

Section (2) — Work recommended to correct conditions which are deemed likely to lead to infestation or infection, but where no infestation or infection exists at the time.

If no infestation or infection of wood destroying pests or organisms is found, the report shall include a written Certification that on the date of inspection "no evidence of active infestation or infection was found."

Work recommended under Section (1) of said report to be paid by Seller. Work recommended under Section (2) of said report to be paid by the party specified in **Item 32-A**.

Work to be performed at Seller's expense may be performed by Seller or through others, provided that all permits and final inspections are obtained and that, upon completion of said work, a written Certification is issued by a registered structural pest control operator showing that the inspected property "is now free of evidence of active infestation or infection."

Funds for work specified in said report, to be done at Seller's expense, shall be held in escrow and disbursed by escrow holder upon receipt of Certification statement by a licensed structural pest control operator, certifying that the property is free of evidence of active infestation or infection.

As soon as the same are available, copies of the report, and any certification or other proof of completion of the work shall be delivered to the agents of Buyer and Seller who are authorized to receive the same on behalf of their principals.

_____ **32-B. EXISTING PEST CONTROL REPORT ACCEPTED BY BUYER.**   Buyer accepts existing pest control report on the property by the licensed structural pest control operator listed under **Item 32-B**. Seller's obligations shall be as set forth in **Item 32-A** above.

_____ **32-C. SUBJECT TO BUYER'S APPROVAL OF PEST CONTROL REPORT.**   Property to be purchased in its present condition with no charge to Seller for any pest control work. However, Buyer shall have the right to have the property inspected and to obtain a report from a licensed structural pest control operator. Buyer shall be deemed to have approved said report unless written notice to the contrary is delivered to Seller or his agent **within fifteen (15) days of acceptance**. In the event Buyer does not approve the report, he may have his deposit returned and both parties shall be relieved of all obligations hereunder.

Buyer acknowledges that he has not relied upon any representations by either the Broker or the Seller, with respect to the condition of the property.

_____ **32-D. WAIVER OF PEST CONTROL INSPECTION.**   Buyer has satisfied himself about the condition of the property and agrees to purchase the property in its present condition without the benefit of a structural pest control inspection.

Buyer acknowledges that he has not relied upon any representations by either the Broker or the Seller, with respect to the condition of the property.

_____ **32-E. INSPECTION OF PHYSICAL CONDITION OF PROPERTY.**   Buyer shall have the right to retain, at his expense, licensed experts including but not limited to engineers, geologists, contractors, and structural pest control operators, to inspect the property for any structural and nonstructural conditions, including but not limited to matters concerning roof, electrical, plumbing, heating, cooling, electrical appliances, well, septic tank, pool, survey, geological and environmental hazards, toxic substances including but not limited to asbestos, formaldehyde, radon gas, lead-based paint and any items listed in the MAINTENANCE CLAUSE (**Item 26**). Buyer, if requested by Seller in writing, shall furnish Seller, at no cost, copies of all inspection reports obtained. Buyer shall approve or disapprove in writing, all inspection reports obtained, **within the number of days specified under Item 32-E**. If Seller does not agree in writing to correct any unacceptable conditions **within three (3) days from receipt of such notice**, Buyer may elect to terminate this agreement and all unused deposits shall be returned.

Buyer [_____] [_____] and Seller [_____] [_____] have read this page.

FORM   101-R.2(a) (10-91)   COPYRIGHT © 1991, BY PROFESSIONAL PUBLISHING CORP., 122 PAUL DR., SAN RAFAEL, CA 94903 (415) 472-1964

PROFESSIONAL PUBLISHING

_____ **32-F. MAINTENANCE RESERVE.** Seller agrees to leave in escrow a maintenance reserve in the amount **specified under Item 32-F.** If in the reasonable opinion of a qualified technician any of the terms listed under **Item 26**, MAINTENANCE, are not in working order, Buyer shall furnish Seller a copy of said technician's inspection report and/or submit written notice to Seller of non-compliance of any of the conditions under MAINTENANCE **within seven (7) days from date occupancy is delivered.**

In the event Seller fails to make the repairs and/or corrections **within five (5) days of receipt of said report or notice,** Seller herewith authorizes the escrow holder to disburse to Buyer against bills for such repairs or corrections the sum of such bills, not to exceed the amount reserved. Said reserve shall be disbursed to Buyer or returned to Seller **not later than fifteen (15) days from date occupancy is delivered.**

_____ **32-G. FLOOD HAZARD ZONE.** Buyer has been advised that the property is located in an area which the Secretary of HUD has found to have special flood hazards and that, pursuant to the National Flood Insurance Program, it will be necessary to purchase flood insurance in order to obtain any loan secured by the property from any federally regulated financial institution or a loan insured or guaranteed by an agency of the U.S. Government. The purpose of the Program is to provide flood insurance at reasonable cost. For further information consult your lender or insurance carrier.

_____ **32-H. HOME PROTECTION CONTRACT,** paid for by the party specified under **Item 32-H,** shall become effective **upon closing for not less than one year,** unless both parties have waived such Home Protection Contract, as specified under **Item 32-H.** The brokers herein have informed both parties that such protection programs are available, but do not approve or endorse any particular program.

_____ **32-I. CONTINGENCY RELEASE CLAUSE.** Subject to the sale and conveyance of "Buyer's Property", described in **Item 32-I, within the time specified for closing** of Seller's property. Provided further that if this condition is not satisfied or waived by Buyer **within the time specified in Item 32-I,** Seller may, in his sole discretion, terminate this agreement and all unused deposits shall be returned. Seller may continue to offer the herein property for sale and to accept written offers subject to the rights of Buyer. Should Seller accept such an offer, then Buyer shall be delivered written notice of such acceptance. If Buyer will not waive this condition in writing **within three (3) days of receipt of such notice,** this agreement shall terminate and all unused deposits shall be returned. Upon removal of this contingency Buyer warrants that adequate funds needed to close will be available and that Buyer's ability to obtain financing is not conditioned upon sale and/or closing of any property.

_____ **32-J. OWNERS ASSOCIATION DISCLOSURE.** Buyer shall take title subject to the governing documents of the development, furnished at Seller's expense, including Declaration of Restrictions, By-Laws, Articles of Incorporation, Rules and Regulations currently in force, and Financial Statement of the Owners Association, as applicable to common interests including Condominiums, PUD's, Stock Cooperatives, or Time Shares, to be delivered to Buyer for his approval **within fifteen (15) days of acceptance.** Buyer shall be deemed to have approved said documents unless written notice to the contrary is delivered to Seller or his agent **within five (5) days of receipt** by Buyer, in which case all unused deposits shall be returned.

In addition, Seller shall deliver to Buyer **before closing** a written statement from the owners association documenting the amount of any delinquent assessments including penalties, attorney's fees, and other charges provided for in the management documents. Such charges shall be credited to Buyer **at closing.**

_____ **32-K. RENTAL PROPERTY.** Buyer to take property subject to existing leases and rights of parties in possession on month-to-month tenancies. **Within seven (7) days of acceptance** Seller shall deliver to Buyer for his approval copies of existing leases and rental agreements as well as copies of any outstanding notices sent to tenants, and a written statement of all oral agreements with tenants, incurred defaults by Seller or tenants, claims made by or to tenants, a statement of all tenants' deposits held by Seller, and a complete statement of rental income and expenses, all of which Seller warrants to be true and complete.

Conditioned upon Buyer's inspection and approval of all rental units **within five (5) days of acceptance.** Said documents shall be deemed to have been approved unless written notice to the contrary is delivered to Seller **within seven (7) days of receipt** of said documents. In case of disapproval Buyer may terminate this agreement and all unused deposits shall be returned.

During the pendency of this transaction Seller agrees that no changes in the existing leases or rental agreements shall be made, nor new leases or rental agreements entered into, nor shall any substantial alterations or repairs be made or undertaken without the written consent of the Buyer.

Security deposits, advance rentals, or considerations involving future lease credits shall be credited to Buyer in escrow.

Seller shall furnish Buyer with copies of any service and/or equipment rental contracts with respect to the property **which run beyond closing.**

_____ **32-L. RENT CONTROL ORDINANCE.** Buyer is aware that a local ordinance is in effect which regulates the rights and obligations of property owners. It may also affect the manner in which future rents can be adjusted.

_____ **32-M. SMOKE DETECTOR(S).** Smoke detectors shall be installed at the expense of the Seller.

_____ **32-N. TAX DEFERRED EXCHANGE (INVESTMENT PROPERTY).** In the event that Seller wishes to enter into a tax deferred exchange for the real property described herein, or if Buyer wishes to enter into a tax deferred exchange with respect to property owned by him in connection with this transaction, each of the parties agrees to cooperate with the other party in connection with such exchange, including the execution of such documents as may be reasonably necessary to effectuate the same. Provided that: (a) The other party shall not be obligated to **delay the closing,** (b) All additional costs in connection with the exchange should be borne by the party requesting the exchange, and (c) The other party shall not be obligated to execute any note, contract, deed, or other document providing for any personal liability which would survive the exchange, nor shall the other party be obligated to take title to any property other than the property described in this agreement. The other party shall be indemnified and held harmless against any liability which arises or is claimed to have arisen on account of the acquisition of the exchange property.

33. ADDITIONAL TERMS AND CONDITIONS.

_____

_____

_____

_____

_____

_____

_____

_____

_____

_____

_____

_____

_____

34. ADDENDA: The following addenda are attached and made a part of this agreement: _____

35. FAIR HOUSING. Buyer and Seller understand that the Federal Housing Law prohibits discrimination in the sale, rental, appraisal, financing or advertising of housing on the basis of race, color, religion, sex, familial status, handicap, and national origin.

Buyer [_____] [_____] and Seller [_____] [_____] have read this page.

FORM 101-R.1(a) (10-91) COPYRIGHT © 1991 BY PROFESSIONAL PUBLISHING CORP. 122 PAUL DR. SAN RAFAEL, CA 94903 (415) 472-1964 **PROFESSIONAL PUBLISHING**

36.   F.I.R.P.T.A. (Foreign Investment and Real Property Tax Act) The Foreign Investment and Real Property Tax Act requires a Buyer of real property to withhold ten percent (10%) of the sale price and to deposit that amount with the Internal Revenue Service **upon closing**, if the Seller is a foreign person, foreign corporation or partnership, or non-resident alien, unless the property qualifies for an exemption under the act.

Unless it is established that the transaction is exempt because the purchase price is $300,000 or less and the Buyer intends to use the property as his primary residence, Seller agrees to:

    a. Provide Broker with a Non-Foreign Seller Affidavit (PPC Form 101-V) stating under penalty of perjury that Seller is not a foreign person; OR:

    b. Provide Broker with a Certificate from the Internal Revenue Service establishing that no federal income tax withholding is required; OR:

    c. Subparagraphs (a) or (b) to be provided to Buyer **within _____ days of acceptance** or Seller consents to withholding ten percent (10%) from the sale proceeds, to be deposited with the Internal Revenue Service.

37.   AGENCY RELATIONSHIP CONFIRMATION. The following agency relationship is hereby confirmed for this transaction:

LISTING AGENT: _____ is the agent of (check one):

                       (Print Firm Name)

             ☐ **the Seller exclusively; or**   ☐ **both the Buyer and Seller.**

SELLING AGENT: _____ (if not the same as the Listing Agent) is the agent of (check one):

                       (Print Firm Name)

      ☐ **the Buyer exclusively; or**   ☐ **the Seller exclusively; or**   ☐ **both the Buyer and Seller.**

Note: This confirmation DOES NOT take the place of any AGENCY DISCLOSURE form which may be required by law (PPC Form 110.51 NAR).

38.   EXPIRATION OF OFFER. This offer shall expire unless acceptance is delivered to Buyer or to _____
on or before _____ ☐ A.M., ☐ P.M., _____, 19_____.

39.   COUNTERPARTS. This agreement may be executed in one or more counterparts, each of which is deemed to be an original hereof, and all of which shall together constitute one and the same instrument.

40.   FAX TRANSMISSION. The facsimile transmission of a signed copy hereof or any counter offer to the other party or his/her agent, followed by faxed acknowledgement of receipt, shall constitute delivery of said signed document. The parties agree to confirm such delivery by mailing or personally delivering a signed copy to the other party or his/her agent.

41.   ENTIRE AGREEMENT. This document contains the entire agreement of the parties and supersedes all prior agreements or representations with respect to the property which are not expressly set forth herein. This agreement may be modified only by a writing signed and dated by both parties. **Both parties acknowledge that they have not relied on any statements of the real estate agent or broker which are not herein expressed.**

A Real Estate Broker or Agent is qualified to advise on Real Estate. If you have any questions concerning the legal sufficiency, legal effect or tax consequences of this document or the transaction related thereto, consult with your Attorney or Accountant.

The undersigned Buyer acknowledges that he/she has thoroughly read and approved each of the provisions contained herein and agrees to purchase the herein described property for the price and on the terms and conditions specified. Buyer acknowledges receipt of a copy of this agreement.

DATED: _____

Selling Broker _____   DATED: _____ TIME: _____

By _____   Buyer _____

Broker's Initials _____ Date _____   Buyer _____

                                                      Buyer _____

ACCEPTANCE

Seller accepts the foregoing offer and agrees to sell the herein described property for the price and on the terms and conditions herein specified.

42.   COMMISSION. Seller agrees to pay in cash the following real estate commission for services rendered, which commission Seller hereby irrevocably assigns from escrow:

_____% of the accepted price, or $ _____, to the listing broker: _____

_____% of the accepted price, or $ _____, to the selling broker: _____ , and

irrespective of the agency relationship. Escrow instructions with respect to commissions may not be amended or revoked without the written consent of the broker(s) herein.

If Seller receives Liquidated Damages upon default by Buyer, Seller agrees to pay broker(s) the lesser of the amount provided for above or one half of the Liquidated Damages after deducting any costs of collection.

Commission shall also be payable upon any default by Seller, or the mutual recission by Buyer and Seller without the written consent of the broker(s) herein, which prevents completion of the sale. This agreement shall not limit the rights of Broker and Seller provided for in any existing listing agreement.

Seller acknowledges that he/she has read and understands the provisions of this agreement and agrees to sell the herein described property for the price and on the terms and conditions specified.

Seller acknowledges receipt of a copy of this agreement. Authorization is hereby given the Broker(s) in this transaction to deliver a signed copy hereof to Buyer and to disclose the terms of sale to members of a Multiple Listing Service or Board of REALTORS at closing.

Subject to: _____

DATED: _____

Listing Broker _____   DATED: _____ TIME: _____

By _____   Seller _____

Broker's Initials _____ Date _____   Seller _____

Buyer acknowledges receipt of a copy of the accepted agreement. DATE: _____ TIME: _____ Buyer _____

CONTINGENCY LOG
(Not a part of the Purchase Agreement)

☐ *ZipForm™* Computer Alignment

A	B	C	D	E	F	G
	PROPERTY:					
	Date of Acceptance:					
		PARTY	DAYS	Days from	CONTINGENCY DEADLINE	CONTINGENCY
		responsible for	FROM	Receipt	(Add number of days	REMOVAL
ITEM	CONTINGENCY	REMOVAL	ACCEPTANCE	of Report	to Date of Acceptance)	DATE
1-B	ADDITIONAL DEPOSIT	Buyer				
2	LOAN APPROVAL					
	Loan Commitment	Buyer				
	Submit Loan Application	Buyer	5			
4	EXISTING LOANS					
	Copies Loan Doc's to Buyer	Seller	3			
	Approval Loan Doc's by Buyer	Buyer		5		
	Order Statement Condition	Seller	3			
6	CREDIT APPROVAL					
	Financial Statement to Seller	Buyer	3			
	Approval Financial Statement	Seller		10		
17	EXAMINATION OF TITLE					
	Preliminary Title Report Order	Buyer	3			
	Report Objections to Title	Buyer		10		
21	CLOSING					
	Days to Close	Buyer/Seller				
	Escrow Instructions	Buyer/Seller				
28-A	BUYER'S APPROVAL					
	Approval of Form 110.11/12/13	Buyer		3 or 5		
32-A	PEST CONTROL INSPECTION					
32-B	EXISTING PEST CONTROL REPORT					
32-C	SUBJECT TO BUYERS APPROVAL	Buyer	15			
32-E	PHYSICAL PROPERTY CONDITION					
	Approval Inspection Report	Buyer				
32-F	MAINTENANCE RESERVE					
	Notice of Non-Compliance	Buyer	7 days from date of occupancy			
32-I	CONTINGENT SALE PROPERTY					
	Waiver within days	Buyer				
	Contingency Removal by Buyer	Buyer		3		
32-J	OWNERS ASSOCIATION					
	Condo Doc's to Buyer	Seller	15			
	Approval of Doc's by Buyer	Buyer		5		
32-K	RENTAL PROPERTY					
	Copies of Leases, etc.	Seller	7			
	Inspection of Rental Units	Buyer	5			
	Approval of Loan Documents	Buyer		7		
FORM 101-R.1/2/3 (10-91)						

INSTRUCTIONS

1) In Row 4, Column C fill-in the Date of Acceptance
2) In the windows of Column D fill-in the Number of Days for Contingency Removal
3) In the windows of Column F fill-in the Sum of Date of Acceptance and the Number of Days in the windows of Column D

☐ *ZipForm*™ Computer Alignment
NCR (No Carbon Required)

COUNTER OFFER

Date: _____ Time: _____

In response to the OFFER ☐ TO PURCHASE, ☐ TO EXCHANGE, ☐ TO LEASE — ☐ the real property,
☐ the business, ☐ the premises — commonly known as: _____
_____,
made by _____, herein referred to as Offeror,
dated _____, **the following counter offer is hereby submitted:**

_____
_____
_____
_____
_____
_____
_____
_____
_____
_____
_____
_____
_____
_____
_____
_____
_____
_____
_____
_____
_____
_____
_____
_____
_____
_____
_____
_____
_____
_____

OTHER TERMS: All other terms to remain the same.
RIGHT TO ACCEPT OTHER OFFERS: Owner reserves the right to accept any other offer prior to Offeror's written acceptance
of this counter offer. Acceptance shall not be effective until a copy of this Counter Offer, dated and signed by Offeror, is
personally received by _____, the agent of the Owner.
_____(LISTING AGENT'S NAME)_____

EXPIRATION: This counter offer shall expire unless a copy hereof with Offeror's written acceptance is delivered to Owner
or his agent on or before _____ o'clock ☐ AM ☐ PM, on _____, 19_____.

_____ Owner

_____ Owner

Dated: _____ Time: _____

The undersigned Offeror accepts the above counter offer.

_____ Offeror

_____ Offeror

Receipt of acceptance is hereby acknowledged.   Dated:_____ Time: _____

_____   _____

SELLER'S PROPERTY DISCLOSURE STATEMENT
(Including the main structure and any outbuildings)

This document provides disclosures with respect to the property known to the Seller as of the date of this statement. It is not a warranty of any kind and is not a substitute for property inspections by experts which the Buyer may wish to obtain. Buyer understands and acknowledges that the broker(s) in this transaction cannot warrant the condition of the property or guarantee that all defects have been disclosed by the Seller.

PROPERTY ADDRESS _____

SELLER'S NAME _____

1. TITLE AND ACCESS

a. Is the property currently leased? .... ☐ Yes ☐ No

b. Has anyone right of refusal to buy, option, or lease the property? .... ☐ Yes ☐ No

c. Do you know of any existing, pending or potential legal actions concerning the property or Owners Association? .... ☐ Yes ☐ No

d. Has a Notice of Default been recorded against the property? .... ☐ Yes ☐ No

e. Any bonds, assessments, or judgements which are liens upon the property? .... ☐ Yes ☐ No

f. Do you own real property adjacent to, across the street from, or in the same sub-division as subject property? .... ☐ Yes ☐ No

g. Any boundary disputes, or third party claims affecting the property (rights of other people to interfere with the use of the property in any way)? .... ☐ Yes ☐ No

2. ENVIRONMENTAL

Are you aware of the following with respect to the property?

a. Any noises from airplanes, trains, trucks, freeways, etc.? .... ☐ Yes ☐ No

b. Any odors caused by toxic waste, gas, industry, agriculture, animals, pets, etc.? .... ☐ Yes ☐ No

c. Formaldehyde gas emitting materials, especially urea-formaldehyde foam insulation? .... ☐ Yes ☐ No

d. Asbestos insulation or fireproofing? .... ☐ Yes ☐ No

e. Elevated radon levels on the property? .... ☐ Yes ☐ No

f. Elevated radon levels in the neighborhood? .... ☐ Yes ☐ No

g. Use of lead-base paint on any surfaces? .... ☐ Yes ☐ No

h. Contamination of well or other water supply? .... ☐ Yes ☐ No

i. Any past or present flooding or drainage problems? .... ☐ Yes ☐ No

j. Any past or present flooding or drainage problems on adjacent properties? .... ☐ Yes ☐ No

k. Any standing water after rainfalls? .... ☐ Yes ☐ No

l. Any sump pumps in basement or crawlspace? .... ☐ Yes ☐ No

m. Any active springs? .... ☐ Yes ☐ No

n. Is property located wholly or partially within Flood Hazard Zone, as determined by the National Flood Insurance Program? .... ☐ Yes ☐ No

o. Is the house built on landfill (compacted or otherwise)? .... ☐ Yes ☐ No

p. Is there landfill on any portion of the property? .... ☐ Yes ☐ No

q. Any soil settling, slippage, sliding, or similar problems? .... ☐ Yes ☐ No

r. Any sinkholes or voids on or near the property? .... ☐ Yes ☐ No

s. Any depressions, mounds, or soft spots? .... ☐ Yes ☐ No

t. Any pending real estate development in your area (such as common interest developments, planned development units, subdivisions, or property for commercial, industrial, sport, educational, or religious use)? .... ☐ Yes ☐ No

u. Any federal or state areas once used for military training purposes, within one mile of the property? .... ☐ Yes ☐ No

v. Traces of concrete, metal, or asphalt indicating prior commercial or industrial use? .... ☐ Yes ☐ No

w. Proximity of property to former, current or proposed mines or gravel pits? .... ☐ Yes ☐ No

x. Proximity of property to former or current waste disposal sites? .... ☐ Yes ☐ No

y. Ravines or earth embankment that may indicate former dumping? .... ☐ Yes ☐ No

z. Pipelines carrying oil, gas, or chemicals underneath or adjacent to the property? .... ☐ Yes ☐ No

aa. Existence of pipeline rights-of-way or easements over or adjacent to the property? .... ☐ Yes ☐ No

bb. Discoloring of soil or vegetation? .... ☐ Yes ☐ No

cc. Oil sheen in wet areas? .... ☐ Yes ☐ No

3. STRUCTURAL

a. Approximate age of the house: _____

b. Do you know of any condition in the original or existing design or workmanship of the structures upon the property that would be considered substandard? .... ☐ Yes ☐ No

c. Do you know of any structural additions or alterations, or the installation, alteration, repair, or replacement of significant components of the structures upon the property, completed during the term of your ownership or that of a prior owner without an appropriate permit or other authority for construction from a public agency having jurisdiction? .... ☐ Yes ☐ No

d. Do you know of any violations of government regulations, ordinances, or zoning laws regarding this property? .... ☐ Yes ☐ No

e. Do you know of any excessive settling, slippage, sliding, or other soil problems, past or present? .... ☐ Yes ☐ No

f. Any problems with retaining walls cracking or bulging? .... ☐ Yes ☐ No

g. Swimming pool out of level? .... ☐ Yes ☐ No

h. Do you know of any past or present problems with driveways, walkways, sidewalks, patios (such as large cracks, potholes, raised sections)? .... ☐ Yes ☐ No

i. Any significant cracks in any of the following: .... ☐ Yes ☐ No

☐ foundations, ☐ exterior walls, ☐ interior walls, ☐ ceilings, ☐ fireplaces, ☐ chimneys, ☐ decks, ☐ slab floors, ☐ garage floors?

j. Any slanted floors? .... ☐ Yes ☐ No

k. Any distorted door frames (uneven spaces between doors and frames)? .... ☐ Yes ☐ No

l. Any sticking windows? .... ☐ Yes ☐ No

Property Address _____

m. Any sagging exposed ceiling beams? .... ☐ Yes ☐ No
n. Any structural woodmembers (including mudsills) below soil level? .... ☐ Yes ☐ No
o. Crawl space, if any, below soil level? .... ☐ Yes ☐ No
p. Any structures (including play structures, tree house, etc.) that could be hazardous? .... ☐ Yes ☐ No

4. ROOF, GUTTERS, DOWNSPOUTS

a. Type of roof: ☐ Tar and Gravel, ☐ Asphalt Shingle, ☐ Wood Shingle, ☐ Tile, ☐ Other _____. Age of roof: _____
b. Has roof been resurfaced? _____ If so, what year? _____
c. Is there a guarantee on the roof? _____ For how long? _____ By whom? _____
d. Has roof ever leaked since you owned the property? _____
   If so, what was done to correct the leak? _____ ☐ Explanation attached.
e. Are gutters and downspouts free of holes and excessive rust? _____
f. Do downspouts empty into drainage system or onto splash blocks? _____
g. Is water directed away from structure? _____

5. PLUMBING SYSTEM

a. Source of water supply: ☐ Public, ☐ Private Well. If well water, when was water sample last checked for safety? _____
   Result of test: _____ ☐ Explanation attached.
b. Well water pump: _____ Date installed: _____ Condition: _____ Sufficient water during late summer? _____
c. Are water supply pipes copper or galvanized? _____
d. Are you aware of below normal water pressure in your water supply lines (normal is 50 to 70 lbs.)? _____
e. Are you aware of excessive rust stains in tubs, lavatories and sinks? _____
f. Are you aware of water standing around any of the lawn sprinkler heads? _____
g. Are there any plumbing leaks around and under sinks, toilets, showers, bathtubs, and lavatories? _____ If so, where? ☐ Explanation attached.
h. Pool: Age: _____ Pool Heater: ☐ Gas, ☐ Electric, ☐ Solar. Pool Sweep? _____ Date of last inspection: _____
   By whom? _____ Regular maintenance? _____
i. Hot Tub/Spa: _____ Date of last inspection: _____ By whom? _____
j. ☐ City Sewer, ☐ Septic Tank: ☐ Fiberglass, ☐ Concrete, ☐ Redwood. Capacity: _____ Is septic tank in working order? _____

6. ELECTRICAL SYSTEM

a. 220 Volt? .... ☐ Yes ☐ No
b. Is the electrical wiring Copper? .... ☐ Yes ☐ No
c. Are there any damaged or malfunctioning receptacles? .... ☐ Yes ☐ No
d. Are you aware of any damaged or malfunctioning switches? .... ☐ Yes ☐ No
e. Are there any extension cords stapled to baseboards or underneath carpets or rugs? .... ☐ Yes ☐ No
f. Does outside TV antenna have a ground connection? .... ☐ Yes ☐ No
g. Are you aware of any defects, malfunctioning, or illegal installation of electrical equipment in or outside the house? .... ☐ Yes ☐ No

7. HEATING, AIR CONDITIONING, OTHER EQUIPMENT

a. Is the house insulated? .... ☐ Yes ☐ No
b. Type of Heating System: _____
c. Is furnace room or furnace closet adequately vented? .... ☐ Yes ☐ No
d. Are fuel-consuming heating devices adequately vented to the outside, directly or through a chimney? .... ☐ Yes ☐ No
e. Heating Equipment in working order? .... ☐ Yes ☐ No
f. Solar heating in working order? .... ☐ Yes ☐ No
g. Air Conditioning in working order? .... ☐ Yes ☐ No
h. Does Fireplace have a damper? .... ☐ Yes ☐ No
i. Provision for outside venting of clothes dryer? .... ☐ Yes ☐ No
j. Water Heater in working order? .... ☐ Yes ☐ No
k. Is heater equipped with temperature pressure relief valve, which is a required safety device? ... ☐ Yes ☐ No
l. Electric garage door opener in working order .... ☐ Yes ☐ No
m. Burglar alarm in working order? .... ☐ Yes ☐ No
n. Smoke Detectors in working order .... ☐ Yes ☐ No
o. Lawn Sprinklers in working order? .... ☐ Yes ☐ No
p. Water Softener in working order? .... ☐ Yes ☐ No
q. Sump pump: in working order? .... ☐ Yes ☐ No
r. Are you aware of any of the above equipment that is in need of repair or replacement or is illegally installed? .... ☐ Yes ☐ No

8. BUILT-IN APPLIANCES

a. Are you aware of any built-in appliances that are in need of repair or replacement? .... ☐ Yes ☐ No

9. CONDOMINIUMS — COMMON INTEREST DEVELOPMENTS

a. Please check the availability of copies of the following documents: ☐ CC&Rs, ☐ Condominium Declaration, ☐ Association Bylaws, ☐ Articles of Incorporation, ☐ Subdivision Report, ☐ Current Financial Statement, ☐ Regulations currently in force.
b. Does the Condominium Declaration contain any resale restrictions? _____
c. Does the Homeowners Association have the first right of refusal? _____
d. Please check occupancy restrictions imposed by the association, including but not limited to: ☐ Children, ☐ Pets, ☐ Storage of Recreational Vehicles or Boats on driveways or in common areas, ☐ Advertising or For Sale signs, ☐ Architectural or decorative alterations subject to association approval, ☐ Others: _____
e. In case of a conversion, have you an engineer's report on the condition of the building and its equipment? _____
f. Monthly/annual association dues:$ _____ What is included in the association dues? _____
g. Has your association notified you of any future dues increases or special assessments? _____
   If so, give details: _____ ☐ Explanation attached.

Seller(s) Initials [_____] [_____]

FORM 110.12 (10-91) COPYRIGHT © 1991, BY PROFESSIONAL PUBLISHING CORP. 122 PAUL DR, SAN RAFAEL, CA 94903 (415) 472-1964

PROFESSIONAL PUBLISHING

NCR (No Carbon Required)

Property Address _____

   h. Are all dues, assessments, and taxes current? _____

   i. I shall provide a statement from the Condominium Homeowners Association documenting the amount of any delinquent assessments, including penalties, attorney's fees, and any other charges provided for in the management documents to be delivered to Buyer. _____

   j. Security: ☐ Inter-com, ☐ Closed circuit TV, ☐ Guards, ☐ Electric gate, ☐ Other: _____

   k. Parking: Does each unit have its own designated parking spaces? _____

   l. Sound proofing adequate? _____ Are there noisy trash chutes? _____

   m. Property Management Co. _____

10. OWNERSHIP

   a. Are you a builder or developer? .... ☐ Yes ☐ No

   b. Are you a licensed real estate agent? .... ☐ Yes ☐ No

   c. Have all persons on the title signed the listing agreement? .... ☐ Yes ☐ No

   d. Please list all persons on the title who are not U.S. citizens: _____

_____

11. PERSONAL PROPERTY INCLUDED IN THE PURCHASE PRICE

   a. The following items of personal property are included in the purchase price: _____

_____

   b. Are there any liens against any of these items? _____ If so, please explain: _____

12. HOME PROTECTION PROGRAM

   a. Do you want to provide a Home Protection Program at your expense? .... ☐ Yes ☐ No

13. REPORTS

   a. Have you received or do you have knowledge of any of the following inspection reports or repair estimates made during or prior to your ownership?

REPORT	YES	NO	BY WHOM?	WHEN?	REPORT AVAILABLE?
Soils/Drainage					
Geologic					
Structural					
Roof					
Pest Control					
Well					
Septic					
Pool/Spa					
Heating					
Air Conditioning					
House Inspection					
Energy Audit					
Radon Test					
City/County Inspection					
Notice of Violation					

14. OTHER DISCLOSURES

   a. In addition to the disclosure statements made herein, the following facts are known or suspected by me/us which may materially affect the value or desirability of the subject property, now or in the future: _____ ☐ Explanation attached.

The foregoing answers and explanations are true and complete to the best of my/our knowledge and I/we have retained a copy hereof. I/we herewith authorize _____ **, the agent in this transaction, to disclose the information set forth above to other real estate brokers, real estate agents, and prospective buyers of the property.**

Seller agrees to hold harmless all brokers and agents in the transaction and to defend and indemnify them from any claim, demand, action or proceedings resulting from any omission or alleged omission by Seller in this Disclosure Statement.

Dated: _____ Seller: _____ Seller: _____

The undersigned Buyer understands that this document is a disclosure of Seller's knowledge of the condition of the property as of the date signed by the Seller. It is not a warranty of any kind and is not a substitute for property inspections by experts which the Buyer may wish to obtain. Buyer understands and acknowledges that the brokers in this transaction cannot warrant the condition of the property or guanantee that all defects have been disclosed by the Seller.

I/we acknowledge receipt of this SELLER'S PROPERTY DISCLOSURE STATEMENT, including additional explanations, if any, attached hereto.

Dated: _____ Buyer: _____ Buyer: _____

I am satisfied with the above SELLER'S PROPERTY DISCLOSURE STATEMENT.

Dated: _____ Buyer: _____ Buyer: _____

I am NOT satisfied with the above SELLER'S PROPERTY DISCLOSURE STATEMENT and herewith rescind my offer to purchase above property.

Dated: _____ Buyer: _____ Buyer: _____

I reserve the right to have the property inspected by the following professional(s) _____

_____,

and to submit a copy of the inspection report(s) to Seller's agent on or before _____.

Dated: _____ Buyer: _____ Buyer: _____

CONTINGENCY RELEASE CLAUSE

In reference to the Purchase Agreement and Deposit Receipt between...

...., the Purchaser and

...., the Seller,

dated.., covering the real property commonly known as ....,

the undersigned parties hereby agree that the purchase be contingent upon the sale and conveyance of Purchaser's real property commonly

known as..

within the time specified for closing of Seller's property. Seller shall have the right to continue to offer the herein property for sale and to accept offers subject to the rights of Purchaser. Should Seller accept such an offer, then Purchaser shall be given written notice of such

acceptance. In the event Purchaser will not waive the within condition in writing within .... calendar days of receipt of such notice, then this agreement shall be terminated and all deposits be returned to Purchaser. Said notice may be personally delivered or mailed by cer-

tified mail and addressed to ....
In the event of mailing, such notice shall be deemed to have been given on the date following the date of mailing evidenced by the postmark on the envelope containing such notice.

DATED:.. TIME:..................... DATED:.. TIME:...................

....Purchaser ....Seller

....Purchaser ....Seller

PROFESSIONAL
PUBLISHING
CORPORATION

- -

NOTICE TO PURCHASER
(Pursuant to Contingency-Release Clause)

TO PURCHASER: ....
              Name

....
              Address

Pursuant to the Purchase Agreement and Deposit Receipt dated ...., 19....... between you and the undersigned, you are hereby notified that the undersigned has, subject to your rights under the Contingency Release Clause, accepted a written offer for the purchase of the property. Unless you waive the condition with respect to the sale of your property commonly known as

....

within the number of calendar days specified in the Contingency-Release Clause, the Purchase Agreement shall be terminated.

DATED:..TIME:.............................

....Seller

RECEIPT
(If Delivered)

Receipt of this notice is acknowledged: DATED:..TIME:...........................

....Purchaser

WAIVER OF CONTINGENCY

The undersigned purchaser hereby waives the contingency referred to hereinabove. Purchaser acknowledges that pursuant to the Purchase Agreement and Deposit Receipt closing of the transaction is to take place on or before...

DATED:..TIME:.............................

....Purchaser

RECEIPT
(If Delivered)

Receipt of this notice is acknowledged: DATED:..TIME:...........................

....Seller

PROFESSIONAL
PUBLISHING
CORPORATION

☐ **ZipForm™** Computer Alignment
NCR No Carbon Required

RESIDENTIAL LEASE WITH OPTION TO PURCHASE

RECEIVED FROM _____

_____, hereinafter referred to as Optionee,

the sum of $ _____ (_____ DOLLARS),

evidenced by _____, as a deposit which, upon acceptance of this Lease, the Optionor

shall apply as follows:

DEPOSITS	TOTAL	RECEIVED	BALANCE DUE PRIOR TO OCCUPANCY
Non-Refundable Option Consideration	$ _____	$ _____	$ _____
Rent for the period from _____ to _____	$ _____	$ _____	$ _____
Security deposit	$ _____	$ _____	$ _____
Other	$ _____	$ _____	$ _____
TOTAL	$ _____	$ _____	$ _____

Upon acceptance hereof Optionee's deposit shall be placed in trust with _____

and Optionee shall **immediately, upon commencement of the term hereof, as specified in paragraph #1,** instruct escrow holder to release said funds to Optionor.

Optionee hereby offers to lease from the Optionor the premises situated in or near the City of _____

County of _____, State of _____, described as _____

_____

and consisting of _____

upon the following TERMS and CONDITIONS:

DEFINITIONS

BROKER includes cooperating brokers and all sales persons. **DAYS** means calendar days unless otherwise specified. **DATE OF ACCEPTANCE** means the date the Optionor accepts the offer or the Optionee accepts the counter offer. **DELIVERED** means personally delivered or transmitted by facsimile machine or mailed by certified mail; in the event of mailing, delivery shall be deemed to have been made on the day following the date of mailing, evidenced by the postmark on the envelope containing the delivered material. The **MASCULINE** includes the feminine and the **SINGULAR** includes the plural. **UNUSED DEPOSITS** means all deposits less expenses incurred by or on account of Optionee to date of termination, including any escrow and title cancellation fees. **PROPERTY** or **PREMISES** means the real property and any personal property included in the option as provided herein.

PRE-CONDITIONS

1. **CONDITIONS SATISFIED IN WRITING.** All conditions under paragraphs #2 through #12 shall have been satisfied in writing **before** _____
_____, 19_____, **the commencement date of the lease, or any extension thereof agreed to in writing.** In the event this agreement is terminated by Optionor or Optionee in accordance with the Pre-conditions, Optionee's unused deposit shall be refunded.

2. **EXAMINATION OF TITLE.** **Within three (3) days from acceptance of this agreement** Optionee shall order a preliminary Title Report and CC&R's, if applicable. Optionee may examine the title to the property and report in writing any valid objections thereto. All exceptions to the title contained in such report (other than monetary liens) shall be deemed approved unless written objection is delivered to Optionor **before the commencement date specified in paragraph #1.** If Optionee objects to any exceptions to the title, Optionor shall use due diligence to remove such exceptions at his own expense **before the commencement date specified in paragraph #1.** But if such exceptions cannot be removed **on or before said date,** this agreement may terminate, at the election of Optionee, unless Optionee elects to waive his objections with respect to such exceptions in writing **before the commencement date specified in paragraph #1.** If Optionor concludes he is unwilling or unable to remove such objections, Optionor shall so notify Optionee in writing **within ten (10) days of receipt of said objections.** In that event Optionee may terminate this agreement. Any exceptions not objected to by Optionee shall be deemed acceptable to Optionee in any subsequent examination of title.

3. **PEST CONTROL INSPECTION.** **Within two (2) days following acceptance** hereof Optionee shall order a structural pest control report from a licensed structural pest control operator at the expense of ☐ Optionee, ☐ Optionor. The inspector shall be requested to separately report: (1) Any portion of the structures where infestation or infection is evident, and (2) Where conditions are present which are deemed likely to lead to infestation or infection. Copies of report shall be delivered to agents of Optionee and Optionor who are authorized to receive same on behalf of their principals.
    Within three (3) days following receipt of the report, Optionor may [a] elect to pay the cost of all work recommended by such report; or [b] elect to pay none or only a portion of the cost of such work. Written notice of such election shall be delivered to Optionee or his agent.
    In the event Optionor shall not have agreed to pay for all such work, Optionee may elect to pay the balance of the cost of such work, or terminate this agreement. Written notice of such election shall be delivered to Optionor or his agent **within seven (7) days following receipt of Optionor's notice.** If no written election is made **within said seven (7) days,** Optionee shall have no right to terminate this agreement, and Optionor shall be responsible for that portion of the work which he elected to pay.
    In the event Optionor shall have elected to pay the cost of all such work, Optionor shall have the right to have the work performed by a licensed structural pest control operator of his choice. Optionor reserves the right to perform all or part of the work in accordance with above structural pest control operator's report; provided that, **upon completion of Optionor's work,** the property be re-inspected by a licensed structural pest control operator at Optionor's expense and the report recommends no further work. This agreement is conditioned upon Optionee's written satisfaction with Optionor's election to pay for work in accordance with the provisions of this paragraph **before the commencement date specified in paragraph #1.**

4. **INSPECTIONS OF PHYSICAL CONDITION OF PROPERTY.** Optionee shall have the right to retain, at his expense, licensed experts including but not limited to engineers, geologists, architects, contractors, and specialty contractors, to inspect the property for any structural and nonstructural conditions, including but not limited to matters concerning roofing, electrical, plumbing, heating, cooling, electrical appliances, well, septic system, pool, survey, geological and environmental hazards, toxic substances including but not limited to asbestos, formaldehyde, radon gas and any items listed in paragraph #24, MAINTENANCE, REPAIRS, ALTERATIONS. Optionee, if requested by Optionor in writing, shall furnish Optionor, at no cost, copies of all inspection reports obtained. Optionee shall approve or disapprove in writing, all inspection reports obtained, **before the commencement date specified in paragraph #1.** If Optionor does not agree, in writing, to correct any unacceptable conditions **within three (3) days from receipt of such notice,** Optionee may elect to terminate this agreement.

5. **OWNERS ASSOCIATION DISCLOSURE.** If the property is a common interest development, Optionee shall take title subject to the governing documents of the development, furnished at Optionor's expense, including Declaration of Restrictions or CC&R's, By-Laws, Articles of Incorporation, Rules and Regulations **currently in force,** and Financial Statement of the Owners Association, as applicable to common interests including Condominiums, PUD's, Stock Cooperatives, or Time Shares, to be delivered to Optionee for his approval **within fifteen (15) days of acceptance.** This agreement is conditioned upon Optionee's approval of said documents **before the commencement date specified in paragraph #1.**
    In addition, Optionor shall deliver to Optionee **before closing** a written statement from the owners association documenting the amount of any delinquent assessments including penalties, attorney's fees, and other charges provided for in the management documents. Such charges shall be credited to Optionee **at closing.**

6. **SMOKE DETECTORS.** Smoke detectors shall be installed at the expense of ☐ Optionee, ☐ Optionor and, if required, shall be inspected by the appropriate City or County agency and a compliance report obtained **prior to the commencement date specified in paragraph #1.**

7. **COMPLIANCE WITH LOCAL LAWS.** Optionor shall comply with any local laws applicable to the sale or transfer of the property, including but not limited to: Providing inspection(s) and/or report(s) for compliance with local building and permit regulations, including septic system inspection report(s); Compliance with minimum energy conservation standards; and Compliance with water conservation measures. All such inspections and reports shall be paid by _____
_____. If Optionor does not agree **before the commencement date specified in paragraph #1** to pay the cost of any repair or improvement required to comply with such laws, Optionee may terminate this agreement.

8. **CREDIT APPROVAL.** In the event of financing by Optionor, in accordance with paragraph #40, FINANCING BY OPTIONOR, Optionee shall furnish Optionor **within three (3) days of acceptance** a customary financial statement for the sole purpose of credit approval, which shall not be unreasonably withheld. Optionee authorizes Optionor to engage the services of a reputable credit reporting agency for this purpose at Optionee's expense and Optionor shall notify Optionee **before the commencement date specified in paragraph #1,** of approval or disapproval of Optionee's credit. In the event of disapproval, Optionor may terminate this agreement.

☐ **ZipForm**™ Computer Alignment
Property Address _____

9. **EXISTING LOANS.** In the event Optionee has the right to assume existing loans upon exercise of the option in accordance with paragraph #43, ASSUMPTION OF EXISTING LOANS, Optionor shall, **within five (5) days of acceptance**, provide Optionee with copies of Notes and Deeds of Trust of all existing Loans. **Before the commencement date specified in paragraph #1**, Optionee shall notify Optionor in writing of his approval or disapproval of the terms of said documents. In the event of disapproval, Optionee may terminate this agreement.

Optionor shall not prepay any existing loans, which Optionee has the right to assume or take subject to, in excess of obligatory payments.

10. **SELLER'S DISCLOSURE STATEMENT.** Optionor ☐ shall, ☐ shall not provide Optionee, **as soon as practicable before transfer of title**, a completed Property Disclosure Statement. Such statement may be provided on PPC Form #110.11, 110.12 and 110.13 (old Form #109.1, 109.2 and 109.3), SELLER'S PROPERTY DISCLOSURE STATEMENT.

OPTIONEE'S APPROVAL. If the Seller's Disclosure Statement is delivered **after the execution of an offer to purchase**, the Optionee may terminate the transaction by written notice delivered to Optionor or Optionor's agent **within three (3) days from receipt of said statement**.

DISCLAIMER. Optionee understands that the Seller's Disclosure Statement **is not a substitute for property inspections by experts**, including but not limited to engineers, geologists, architects, general contractors, specialty contractors, such as roofing contractors and structural pest control operators. Optionee is urged to retain such experts as he believes are appropriate. Optionee understands and acknowledges that the brokers and agents in the transaction cannot warrant the condition of the property or guarantee that all defects have been disclosed by Optionor.

Both parties acknowledge that **Broker(s) will not be investigating the status of permits, zoning, location of property lines, and/or code compliance. Square footage of structure is approximate** and neither Optionor nor Broker guarantee accuracy. Optionee is to satisfy himself concerning these issues.

Optionee acknowledges that **he has not received or relied upon any representations** by either the Broker or the Optionor with respect to the condition of the property which are not contained in this agreement or in the disclosure statements.

Optionor agrees to **hold harmless all brokers and agents** in the transaction and to defend and indemnify them from any claim, demand, action or proceedings resulting from any omissions or alleged omission by Optionor or his Seller's Disclosure Statement.

11. **FLOOD HAZARD ZONE DISCLOSURE.** [_____] [_____] By initialing here, Optionee acknowledges he has been advised that the property is located in an area which the Secretary of HUD has found to have special flood hazards and that, pursuant to the National Flood Insurance Program, it will be necessary to purchase flood insurance in order to obtain any loan secured by the property from any federally regulated financial institution or a loan insured or guaranteed by an agency of the U.S. Government. The purpose of the Program is to provide flood insurance at reasonable cost. For further information consult your lender or insurance carrier. Optionee shall be deemed to be satisfied with the result of such inquiries unless written notice to the contrary is delivered to Optionor or his agent **within seven (7) days of acceptance**, in which case Optionee may have his deposit returned and both parties shall be relieved of all obligations hereunder.

LEASE

12. **TERM AND PHYSICAL POSSESSION.** The term of the lease and physical possession **shall commence on the date specified in paragraph #1 and shall continue for a period of** _____ **months thereafter**.

If Optionor is unable to deliver possession of the premises **on the commencement date**, Optionor shall not be liable for any damage caused thereby, nor shall this agreement be void or voidable, but Optionee shall not be liable for any rent **until possession is delivered**. Optionee may terminate this agreement if possession is not delivered **within** _____ **days of the commencement date**.

13. **RENT.** Rent shall be $_____, per month, **payable in advance, upon the** _____ **day of each calendar month** to Optionor or his authorized agent, at the following address: _____

or at such other places as may be designated by Optionor **from time to time**. In the event rent is not paid **within five (5) days after due date**, Optionee agrees to pay a late charge of $_____ plus interest at _____% per month on the delinquent amount. Optionee further agrees to pay $_____ for each dishonored bank check. *

14. **UTILITIES.** Optionee shall be responsible for the payment of all utilities and services, except: _____
_____ , which shall be paid by Optionor.

15. **USE.** The premises shall be used as a residence with no more than _____ persons, and for no other purpose, without the written prior consent of the Optionor, except: _____

16. **ANIMALS.** No animals shall be brought on the premises without the prior consent of the Optionor.

17. **ORDINANCES AND STATUTES.** Optionee shall comply with all statutes, ordinances and requirements of all municipal, state and federal authorities now in force, or which may hereafter be in force, pertaining to the use of the premises.

18. **SUBLETTING.** Optionee shall not sublet any portion of the premises without prior written consent of the Optionor which may not be unreasonably withheld.

19. **INSURANCE DURING LEASE TERM.** Optionor shall maintain hazard insurance covering one hundred percent replacement cost of the improvements throughout the lease term, and shall name holders of any secured loans, as well as Optionee as additional loss payees. Optionor's Insurance does not cover Optionee's Personal Property.

20. **DESTRUCTION OF IMPROVEMENTS.** If the improvements of the property are destroyed, materially damaged, or found to be materially defective **prior to close of escrow**, Optionee may terminate the agreement by written notice delivered to Optionor's broker or agent specifically including the non-refundable option consideration. In the event Optionee does not elect to terminate the agreement Optionee, upon exercise of the option, shall be entitled to receive in addition to the property any insurance proceeds payable on account of the damage or destruction.

21. **INDEMNIFICATION.** Optionor shall not be liable for any damage or injury to Optionee, or any other person, or to any property, occuring on the premises or any part thereof, or in common areas thereof, except for damages or injury caused by the willful act or negligence of Optionor, his agents or employees. Optionee agrees to hold Optionor harmless from any claims for damages, no matter how caused, except for injury or damages caused by the willful act or negligence of Optionor, his agents or employees.

22. **CONDITION OF PROPERTY.** Optionor covenants that the heating, air-conditioning, electrical, solar, septic system, gutters and downspouts, sprinkler, and plumbing systems including the water heater, pool and spa systems, as well as built-in appliances and other mechanical apparatus shall be in **working order** on the **date possession is delivered**. Optionor shall replace any cracked or broken glass including windows, mirrors, shower and tub enclosures. **Until possession is delivered** Optionor shall maintain all structures, landscaping, grounds. Optionor agrees to deliver the property in a neat and clean condition with all debris and personal belongings removed. **The following items are specifically excluded from the above:** _____

Optionor and Optionee shall conduct a joint inspection of the property to determine compliance with this provision. (See Form 105-E, MOVE-IN CHECKLIST.)

23. **MAINTENANCE, REPAIR, ALTERATIONS.** If applicable, Optionor shall provide Optionee with a written inventory of furniture and furnishings on the premises (Form 105-A, FURNISHED RENTAL PROPERTY INVENTORY). Optionee shall be deemed to have possession of all said furniture and furnishings in good condition and repair, unless he objects thereto in writing **within five (5) days of receipt of such inventory**. Optionee shall, at his own expense and **at all times**, maintain the premises in a clean and sanitary manner, including all furniture and furnishings, shall maintain all equipment and appliances in working order and shall surrender the same **at termination of the lease** in as good condition as received, normal wear and tear excepted, unless such personal property shall be purchased with the real property if and when Optionee exercises the option to purchase. Optionee shall be responsible for damages caused by his negligence and that of his family, invitees and guests. Optionee shall not paint, paper or otherwise decorate or make alterations to the premises without the prior written consent of Optionor. Optionee shall irrigate and maintain any surrounding grounds, including lawns and shrubbery, and keep the same clear of rubbish and weeds, if such grounds are a part of the premises and are exclusively for use of Optionee.

---

* The late charge is not a grace period and Optionor is entitled to make written demand for any rent if not paid **when due**. Any unpaid balances remaining **after termination of occupancy** are subject to 1½% interest per month or the maximum allowed by law.

☐ *ZipForm*™ Computer Alignment
Property Address _____

24. DEFAULT. If Optionee fails to pay rent **when due**, or perform any term hereof, **after not less than three (3) days written notice of such default** given in the manner required by law, the Optionor at his option, may terminate all rights of Optionee hereunder, unless Optionee, **within said time**, shall cure such default. If Optionee abandons or vacates the property, while in default of the payment of rent, Optionor may consider any property left on the premises to be abandoned and may dispose of the same in any manner allowed by law. In the event the Optionor reasonably believes that such abandoned property has no value, it may be discarded. All property on the premises shall be subject to a lien for the benefit of Optionor securing the payment of all sums due hereunder, to the maximum extent allowed by law.

In the event of a default by Optionee, Optionor may elect to (a) continue the lease in effect and enforce all his rights and remedies hereunder, including the right to recover the rent **as it becomes due**, or (b) **at any time**, terminate all of Optionee's rights hereunder and recover from Optionee all damages he may incur by reason of the breach of the lease, including the cost of recovering the premises, and including the worth **at the time of such termination, or at the time of an award** if suit be instituted to enforce this provision, of the amount by which the unpaid rent for the balance of the term exceeds the amount of such rental loss which the Optionee proves could be reasonably avoided.

If required by a title company, Optionee shall execute a Quit Claim Deed to evidence the termination hereof.

25. NOTICE OF DEFAULT. Optionee is advised to record a Special Request for Notice of Default **before the commencement date specified in paragraph #1.**

26. OBLIGATIONS OF OPTIONOR. During the term of this lease, unless otherwise provided for herein, Optionor agrees to pay **prior to any delinquency**, all real property taxes and assessments upon the property, and all payments required under any note or other obligation secured by liens upon the real property. Optionee may record a request for notice of default with respect to any such liens. In the event Optionor fails to make any payment required, Optionee shall have the right to make such payment on behalf of Optionor and shall be entitled to repayment of the amount paid, together with interest at the rate of ten percent (10%) per annum, or may offset any such payment made against the obligations of Optionee hereunder.

27. SECURITY. The security deposit set forth above, if any, shall secure the performance of Optionee's obligations hereunder. Optionor may, but shall not be obligated to, apply all portions of said deposit on account of Optionee's obligations hereunder. Any balance remaining **upon termination** shall be returned to Optionee.

28. DEPOSIT REFUNDS. The balance of all deposits shall be refunded **within two weeks from date possession is delivered** to Optionor or his Authorized Agent, together with a statement showing any charges made against such deposits.

29. WAIVERS. No failure of Optionor to enforce any term hereof shall be deemed a waiver, nor shall any acceptance of a partial payment of rent be deemed a waiver of Optionor's right to the full amount thereof.

30. NOTICES. Any notice which either party may or is required to give, may be given by mailing the same, postage prepaid, to Optionee at the premises or to Optionor at the address shown below or at such other places as may be designated by the parties **from time to time.**

31. HEIRS, ASSIGNS, SUCCESSORS. This lease is binding upon and inures to the benefit of the heirs, assigns and successors in interest to the parties.

32. HOLDING OVER. Any holding over **after the expiration hereof**, with the consent of Optionor, shall become a month-to-month tenancy at a monthly rent of $_____ **payable in advance**, and otherwise subject to the terms hereof, as applicable until either party shall terminate the same by giving the other party **thirty (30) days written notice delivered by certified mail**. No such holding over or extension of this lease **shall extend the time** for the exercise of the option unless agreed upon in writing by Optionor.

33. ADDITIONAL TERMS OF LEASE.
_____
_____
_____
_____
_____
_____
_____
_____
_____
_____
_____
_____
_____
_____
_____
_____
_____
_____
_____
_____
_____
_____
_____
_____
_____
_____

OPTION

34. NON-REFUNDABLE OPTION CONSIDERATION. The option consideration received from Optionee is not refundable unless Optionor defaults in his obligations to convey the property upon exercise of the option.

35. OPTION. So long as Optionee is not in substantial default in the performance of any term of this lease, Optionee shall have the option to purchase the real property described herein for a PURCHASE PRICE of $_____(_____ DOLLARS). The purchase price shall be payable in cash unless otherwise provided for herein.

36. EXPIRATION OF OPTION. This option may be exercised at any time after _____, 19_____, **and shall expire at midnight** _____, 19_____, **unless exercised prior thereto. Upon expiration** Optionor shall be released from all obligations hereunder and all of Optionees' rights hereunder, legal or equitable, **shall cease. Upon expiration**: (a) All consideration paid for the option and all rent paid hereunder shall be retained by Optionor in consideration of the granting of the option; (b) Any security deposit shall be disbursed as provided herein; (c) If required by a title company, Optionee shall execute a Quit Claim Deed to evidence the termination hereof.

37. EXERCISE OF OPTION. The option shall be exercised by mailing or delivering written notice to the Optionor **prior to the expiration of this option** and by an additional payment, on account of the purchase price, in the amount of:
$_____(_____ DOLLARS)
for account of Optionor to the authorized escrow holder referred to above, **prior to the expiration of this option**.

Notice: If mailed, shall be by certified mail, postage prepaid, to the Optionor at the address set forth below, and shall be deemed to have been given **upon the day following the day shown** on the postmark of the envelope in which such notice is mailed.

38. OPTION CREDITS. In the event the option is exercised, the consideration paid for the option and _____% from the rent paid hereunder **prior to the exercise of the option** shall be credited upon the purchase price.

☐ *ZipForm*™ Computer Alignment
Property Address _____

39. FINANCING BY OPTIONOR:

[_____] [_____] By initialing here, Optionor agrees to carry a purchase money loan, secured by a ☐ first deed of trust, ☐ second deed of trust upon the property, upon the following terms:

    a. Loan amount not to exceed $_____, or _____% of the Purchase Price

    b. Interest shall be _____% per annum.

    c. Monthy payments including interest shall not exceed _____% of the face amount of the note, or shall be based upon _____ **years amortization**.

    d. Entire remaining balance shall be due and payable in full _____ **years from date of note.**

    e. Entire remaining balance ☐ shall, ☐ shall not be due and payable in full **upon sale or transfer of the property**.

    f. In the event monthly payments are not tendered **within** _____ **days after due date**, a late charge of $_____ plus interest at _____% **per month** on the delinquent amount shall be due. Optionee agrees to pay $_____ for each dishonored bank check.

    g. Optionor's loan shall be subject to: ☐ No prior loan, ☐ the existing first loan having an approximate balance of $_____, or ☐ a new first loan not to exceed $_____, made by a recognized financial institution, amortizable **over not less than** _____ **years, due in not less than** _____ **years**, and bearing interest at a rate not exceeding the current fixed or varible rate **at the date of closing.**

40. ASSUMPTION OF EXISTING LOANS. The Optionee ☐ shall, ☐ shall not have the right to assume existing loans secured by the property. In the event of assumption Optionor ☐ shall, ☐ shall not be released of all liability under said loan. Optionee shall pay for any assumption fee. Optionee understands that assumption of existing financing is conditional upon the lender's consent **prior to exercise of the option.**

41. AVAILABILITY OF FINANCING. Optionee acknowledges he has not received or relied upon any statements or representations made by Broker or Optionor regarding availability of new financing, or rate of interest at which financing might be available, prior to expiration of the Option.

42. DUE ON SALE CLAUSE. If the note and deed of trust or mortgage for any existing loan contains an acceleration or DUE ON SALE clause, the lender may demand full payment of the entire loan balance as a result of this transaction. Both parties acknowledge that they are not relying on any representation by the other party or the broker with respect to the enforceability of such a provision in existing notes and deeds of trust or mortgages, or deeds of trust or mortgages to be executed in accordance with this agreement. Both parties have been advised by the broker to seek independent legal advice with respect to these matters.

43. PRORATIONS. Rents, taxes, interest, payments on Bonds and Assessments assumed by Optionee, Homeowners Association fees, and other expenses of the property to be prorated **as of the date of recordation** of the deed. Security deposits, advance rentals, or considerations involving future lease credits shall be credited to Optionee.

44. CLOSING. Within _____ **days of exercise of the option** both parties shall deposit with an authorized escrow holder, to be selected by ☐ **Optionee,** ☐ **Optionor, all funds and instruments necessary to complete in accordance with the terms hereof.**

Escrow fee to be paid by _____.

Transfer fees to be paid by _____.

45. EVIDENCE OF TITLE, in the form of a ☐ ALTA, ☐ CLTA policy of title insurance, paid by _____

Title to the property shall be conveyed free and clear of all liens and encumbrances other than the lien for current real property taxes not yet due and to easements and restrictions of record accepted by Optionee in accordance with paragraph #2, unless otherwise provided for herein.

46. BONDS AND ASSESSMENTS. In the event there is a Bond or Assessment which has an outstanding principal balance and is a lien upon this property, such principal shall be ☐ paid by Optionor, or ☐ assumed by Optionee. In the event of assumption, said obligation(s) ☐ shall, ☐ shall not be credited to Optionee **at close of escrow.** (This paragraph does not apply to payments collected on the property tax bill for annual assessments.)

47. FIXTURES. All items permanently attached to the property, including light fixtures, attached floor coverings, draperies, blinds and shades including window hardware, window and door screens, storm sash, combination doors, awnings, TV antennas, burglar, fire and smoke alarms, pool and spa equipment, solor systems, attached fireplace screens, electric garage door openers with controls, outdoor plants and trees (other than in movable containers), are included in the purchase price free of liens, **EXCLUDING:** _____

48. PERSONAL PROPERTY. The following personal property, on the premises when inspected by Optionee, is included in the purchase price and shall be transferred to Optionee free of liens by a Bill of Sale **at close of escrow.** No warranty is implied as to the condition of said property: _____

☐ An inventory of personal property is attached hereto as Exhibit #_____ and made a part hereof.

49. MEDIATION OF DISPUTES. If a dispute arises out of or relates to this agreement or the breach thereof, by initialing in the spaces below

    [_____] [_____] **Optionee agrees**   [_____] [_____] **Optionee does not agree**

    [_____] [_____] **Optionor agrees**   [_____] [_____] **Optionor does not agree**

to first try in good faith to settle the dispute by non-binding mediation under the Commercial Mediation Rules of the American Arbitration Association, before resorting to court action or binding arbitration.

50. ARBITRATION OF DISPUTES. By initialing in the spaces below

    [_____] [_____] **Optionee agrees**   [_____] [_____] **Optionee does not agree**

    [_____] [_____] **Optionor agrees**   [_____] [_____] **Optionor does not agree**

that any dispute or claim in law or equity arising out of this contract or any resulting transaction shall be decided by neutral binding arbitration in accordance with the commercial rules of the American Arbitration Association and not by court action except as provided by law for judicial review of arbitration proceedings. Judgment upon the award rendered by the arbitrator(s) may be entered in any court having jurisdiction thereof. The parties shall have the right to discovery.

The following matters are excluded from arbitration hereunder: (a) a judicial or non-judicial foreclosure or other action or proceeding to enforce a deed of trust, mortgage or real property sales contract; (b) an unlawful detainer action; (c) the filing or enforcement of a mechanics lien; (d) any matter which is within the jurisdiction of a probate court or small claims court; (e) an action for bodily injury or wrongful death.

The parties further agree that the party or parties prevailing in such arbitration shall be entitled to receive from the other party or parties a reasonable attorney's fee and all costs incurred in connection with the arbitration in an amount to be determined by the arbitrator(s), and in the event that any party shall fail to pay the amount due under the award of the arbitrator(s), and legal action is commenced for the enforcement of the award, the prevailing party or parties shall be entitled to receive a reasonable attorney's fee incurred in such action to be determined by the court in which such action is brought.

51. ATTORNEY FEES. In any action or proceeding involving a dispute between Optionee, Optionor and/or Broker, arising out of the execution of this agreement or the sale, or to collect commissions, the prevailing party shall be entitled to receive from the other party a reasonable attorney fee, expert fees, appraisal fees and all other costs incurred in connection with said action or proceedings, to be determined by the court or arbitrator(s).

52. FAIR HOUSING. Optionee and Optionor understand that the Federal Housing Law prohibits discrimination in the sale, rental, appraisal, financing or advertising of housing on the basis of race, color, religion, sex, familial status, handicap, and national origin.

53. SURVIVAL. The omission from escrow instructions of any provision herein shall not waive the right of any party. All representations or warranties shall survive the conveyance of the property.

54. ASSIGNMENT. Optionee shall not assign this agreement without prior written consent of Optionor.

55. MEMORANDUM OF OPTION. A Memorandum of Option ☐ shall, ☐ shall not be recorded upon commencement of this agreement, in accordance with paragraph #1. All resulting fees and taxes shall be paid by Optionee.

☐ **ZipForm**™ Computer Alignment

Property Address _____

56. **F.I.R.P.T.A. (Foreign Investment and Real Property Tax Act)** The Foreign Investment and Real Property Tax Act requires a Seller of real property to withhold ten percent (10%) of the sale price and to deposit that amount with the Internal Revenue Service **upon close of escrow**, if the Seller is a foreign person, foreign corporation or partnership, or non-resident alien, unless the property qualifies for an exemption under the act.

Unless it is established that the transaction is exempt because the purchase price is $300,000 or less **and** the Optionee intends to use the property as his primary residence, Optionor agrees to:

    a. Provide Broker with a Non-Foreign Seller Affidavit (PPC Form 101-V) stating under penalty of perjury that Optionor is not a foreign person; OR:

    b. Provide Broker with a Certificate from the Internal Revenue Service establishing that no federal income tax withholding is required; OR:

    c. Consent to withholding ten percent (10%) from the sale proceeds, to be deposited with the Internal Revenue Service.

57. **AGENCY RELATIONSHIP.** The following agency relationship is hereby disclosed for this transaction:

    LISTING AGENT: _____ is the agent of (check one):
        (Print Firm Name)

        ☐ the Optionor exclusively; or   ☐ both the Optionee and Optionor.

    SELLING AGENT: _____ (if not the same as the Listing Agent) is the agent of (check one):
        (Print Firm Name)

    ☐ the Optionee exclusively; or   ☐ the Optionor exclusively; or   ☐ both the Optionee and Optionor.

58. **ADDITIONAL TERMS OF OPTION.**

_____

_____

_____

_____

_____

_____

_____

_____

_____

_____

_____

_____

_____

_____

59. **EXPIRATION OF OFFER.** This offer shall expire unless acceptance is delivered to Optionee or to _____

on or before _____ ☐ A.M., ☐ P.M., _____, 19_____.

60. **ENTIRE AGREEMENT.** This document contains the entire agreement of the parties and supersedes all prior agreements or representations with respect to the property which are not expressly set forth herein. This agreement may be modified only by a writing signed and dated by both parties. **Both parties acknowledge that they have not relied on any statements of the real estate agent or broker which are not herein expressed.**

Optionee understands he may be unable to qualify for new financing or for assumption of existing financing and that for lack of such financing he may not be able to purchase the property and could lose his investment. Both parties acknowledge they have not received or relied upon any statements or representations made to them by the broker(s) or agents(s) in this transaction with respect to availability of funds or rate of interest at which funds might be available at the time the option must be exercised.

A Real Estate Broker or Agent is qualified to advise on Real Estate. If you have any questions concerning the legal sufficiency, legal effect or tax consequences of this document or the transaction related thereto, consult with your Attorney or Accountant.

The undersigned Optionee acknowledges that he/she has thoroughly read and approved each of the provisions contained herein and agrees to purchase the herein described property for the price and on the terms and conditions specified. Optionee acknowledges receipt of a copy of this agreement.

Receipt for Deposit acknowledged: DATED: _____ TIME: _____

Real Estate Broker _____   Optionee _____

By _____   Optionee _____

Broker's Initials _____ Date _____   Optionee _____

ACCEPTANCE

61. **BROKERAGE FEE.** Upon excution hereof the Optionor agrees to pay to _____

_____, the Agent in this transaction, _____% of the option consideration

for securing said option plus the sum of $_____ (_____ DOLLARS)

for leasing services rendered and authorizes Agent to deduct said sum from the deposit received from Optionee. In the event the option is exercised, the Optionor agrees to pay Agent the additional sum of $_____ (_____ DOLLARS).

This agreement shall not limit the rights of Agent provided for in any listing or other agreement which may be in effect between Optionor and Agent. In the event legal action is instituted to collect this fee, or any portion thereof, the Optionor agrees to pay the Agent a reasonable attorney's fee and all costs in connection with such action.

62. **PROVISIONS TO BE INITIALED.** The following items must be initialed by Optionor to signify agreement, in order to accept the offer. In the event of disagreement Optionor should make a counter offer.

    Item 49. MEDIATION OF DISPUTES

    Item 50. ARBITRATION OF DISPUTES

Optionor acknowledges that he/she has read and understands the provisions of this agreement and agrees to sell the herein described property for the price and on the terms and conditions specified.

Optionor acknowledges receipt of a copy of this agreement. Authorization is hereby given the Broker(s) in this transaction to deliver a signed copy hereof to Optionee and to disclose the terms of sale to members of a Multiple Listing Service or Board or Association of REALTORS at close of escrow.

Subject to: _____

DATED: _____   DATED: _____ TIME: _____

Real Estate Broker _____   Optionor _____

By _____   Optionor _____

Broker's Initials _____ Date _____   Optionor _____

Optionee acknowledges receipt of a copy of the accepted agreement. DATE: _____ TIME: _____ Optionee _____

FORM 106-A.5 (3-91) COPYRIGHT © 1991, BY PROFESSIONAL PUBLISHING CORP. 122 PAUL DR. SAN RAFAEL, CA 94903, (415) 472-1964   **PROFESSIONAL PUBLISHING**

OPTION TO PURCHASE

In consideration of the payment by _____ _____
_____ , hereinafter referred to as Optionee, in the amount of
$ _____ (_____ DOLLARS),
receipt of which is hereby acknowledged, _____
_____ , hereinafter referred to as Optionor, grants to Optionee an option to purchase the real property situated in the
City of _____ , County of _____ , State of _____ ,
described as _____
_____

for a PURCHASE PRICE OF $ _____ (_____ DOLLARS),
upon the following TERMS and CONDITIONS:

ENCUMBRANCES: In addition to any encumbrances referred to above, Optionee shall take title to the property subject to: 1) Real Estate Taxes not yet due and 2) Covenants, conditions, restrictions, reservations, rights, rights of way and easements of record, if any, which do not materially affect the value or intended use of the property.
The amount of any bond or assessment which is a lien shall be ☐ paid, ☐ assumed by _____ .
EXAMINATION OF TITLE: Fifteen (15) days from date of exercise hereof are allowed the Optionee to examine the title to the property and to report in writing any valid objections thereto. Any exceptions to the title, which would be disclosed by examination of the records, shall be deemed to have been accepted unless reported in writing **within said fifteen (15) days.** If Optionee objects to any exceptions to the title, Optionor shall use all due diligence to remove such exceptions at his own expense **within 60 days thereafter.** But if such exceptions cannot be removed **within the 60 days allowed,** all rights and obligations hereunder may, at the election of the Optionee, terminate and end, and the option payment shall be returned to Optionee, unless he elects to purchase the property subject to such exceptions.
EVIDENCE OF TITLE shall be in the form of ☐ a policy of title insurance, ☐ other: _____ , to be paid for by _____ .
CLOSE OF ESCROW: Within _____ days from exercise of the option, or upon removal of any exceptions to the title by the Optionor, as provided above, **whichever is later,** both parties shall deposit with an authorized escrow holder, to be selected by the Optionee, all funds and instruments necessary to complete the sale in accordance with the terms and conditions hereof.
POSSESSION: Possession shall be delivered to Optionee: ☐ **Upon recordation of deed.** ☐ **After recordation, but not later than** _____ .
Unless Optionor has vacated the premises **prior to recordation of the deed,** Optionor agrees to pay Optionee $ _____ per day **from recordation to date possession is delivered** and to leave this sum in escrow, to be disbursed to the persons entitled thereto **on the date possession is delivered.**
PRORATIONS: Rents, taxes, premiums on insurance acceptable to Optionee, interest and other expenses of the property to be prorated **as of recordation of deed.** Security deposits, advance rentals or considerations involving future lease credits shall be credited to Optionee.
MAINTENANCE: Until possession is delivered Optionor agrees to maintain heating, sewer, plumbing and electrical systems and any built-in appliances and equipment in normal working order, to keep the roof watertight and to maintain the grounds.
NOTICES: By acceptance hereof, Optionor warrants that he has no notice of violations relating to the property from City, County, or State agencies.
TIME: Time is of the essence of this agreement.
EXPIRATION OF OPTION: If not exercised, this option shall expire _____ days from date and Optionor shall be released from all obligations hereunder and all of Optionee's rights hereunder, legal or equitable, shall cease and the consideration hereinabove receipted for by Optionor shall be retained by Optionor.
EXERCISE OF OPTION: The option shall be exercised by mailing or delivering written notice to the Optionor **prior to the expiration of this option** and by an additional payment, on account of the purchase price, in the amount of $ _____ (_____
_____ DOLLARS) for account of Optionor to the authorized escrow holder referred to above, **prior to the expiration of this option.**
Notice, if mailed, shall be by certified mail, postage prepaid, to the Optionor at the address set forth below, and shall be deemed to have been given **upon the day following the day shown** on the postmark of the envelope in which such notice is mailed.
In the event the option is exercised, the consideration hereinabove receipted for by Optionor ☐ shall, ☐ shall not be credited upon the purchase price.
NOTICE: The amount or rate of real estate commissions is not fixed by law. They are set by each Broker individually and may be negotiable between the Seller and Broker.
BROKERAGE FEE: Upon execution of this option the Optionor agrees to pay to _____ ,
the Agent in his transaction, the sum of $ _____ (_____ DOLLARS)
and in the event the option is exercised, Optionor agrees to pay Agent the additional sum of $ _____ (_____
_____ DOLLARS) for services rendered. This agreement shall not limit the rights of Agent provided for in any listing or other agreement which may be in effect between Owner and Agent. In the event legal action is instituted to collect this fee, or any portion thereof, the Optionor agrees to pay the Agent a reasonable attorney's fee and all costs in connection with such action.

DATED: _____

_____ Optionor   _____ Optionee

_____ Optionor   _____ Optionee

_____ Address   _____ Address

_____ Phone   _____ Phone

_____ Agent   _____ Agent's Address

By _____   _____ Agent's Phone

EXERCISE OF OPTION

To: _____ , Optionor

I hereby exercise the option set forth on the reverse hereof.

I have opened an escrow and deposited the sum of $ _____ _____ with:

Name _____

Address _____

Dated: _____ , 19_____.

_____
Optionee

RECEIPT

Optionor acknowledges receipt of the exercise of the option

this _____ day of _____ , 19_____.

_____
Optionor

FORM   108(a)   (6-80)   COPYRIGHT ⓒ 1980. BY PROFESSIONAL PUBLISHING CORP. 122 PAUL DR SAN RAFAEL CA 94903 (415) 472-1964

**PROFESSIONAL
PUBLISHING**

LAND PURCHASE AGREEMENT

RECEIVED FROM _____

_____, hereinafter designated as **BUYER**, the amount set forth below as **DEPOSIT** on account of the

PURCHASE PRICE of $_____ **(DOLLARS)**,

for the real property in the City of _____, County of _____, State of _____,

consisting of approximately _____ ☐ acres, ☐ sq. ft., described as _____

_____, upon the following **TERMS and CONDITIONS**:

1. **FINANCIAL TERMS.**

    1-A. $_____   **DEPOSIT** evidenced by ☐ Cash, ☐ Cashiers Check, ☐ Note, ☐ Personal Check, ☐ Other: _____

          to be deposited **within one (1) business day of acceptance,** and escrow opened with: _____.

    1-B. $_____   **ADDITIONAL CASH DEPOSIT** to be placed in escrow ☐ **within** _____ **days of acceptance,** ☐ upon removal of all

          contingencies.

    1-C. $_____   **BALANCE OF CASH PAYMENT AT CLOSE OF ESCROW.**

    1-D. $_____   **BONDS OR ASSESSMENTS** of record if assumed by Buyer.

    1-E. $_____   **ADDITIONAL FINANCING:**

          _____

          _____

          _____

          _____

          _____

    1-F. $_____   **TOTAL PURCHASE PRICE** (not including closing costs). Any net differences between the approximate balances of encumbrances

          shown above, which are to be assumed or taken subject to, and the actual balances of said encumbrances at close of escrow shall be

          adjusted in ☐ Cash, ☐ Other: _____.

2. **OTHER TERMS AND CONDITIONS:**

_____

_____

_____

_____

_____

_____

_____

3. **ADDENDA.** The following addenda are attached hereto.

  ☐ Form 421-A, ADDENDUM TO LAND PURCHASE AGREEMENT (Subordination, partial Reconveyances)

  ☐ Form 109.8, HAZARDOUS MATERIALS ADDENDUM

  ☐ OTHER: _____

4. **CLOSING.** ☐ On or before _____, ☐ within _____ **days of acceptance,** both parties shall deposit with an

authorized Escrow Holder to be selected by ☐ Buyer, ☐ Seller, all funds and instruments necessary to complete the sale in accordance with the terms hereof.

Until then, Buyer, Seller, and Broker agree not to disclose the terms of sale. The representations and warranties shall not be terminated by conveyance of the property.

Escrow fee to be paid by _____. Documentary transfer tax, if any, to be paid by _____.

5. **EVIDENCE OF TITLE** in the form of ☐ a policy of Title Insurance, ☐ Other _____, paid by _____.

6. **BROKER REPRESENTING BOTH PARTIES.** By placing their initials here: Buyer [_____] and Seller [_____] acknowledge that

_____, the broker in this transaction, represents both parties and Buyer and Seller consent thereto.

7. **PROVISIONS ON THE REVERSE SIDE.** The provisions checked below are included in this agreement on the reverse side.

  ☐ A. SOIL TESTS, within _____ days of acceptance, paid by _____

  ☐ B. SURVEY, paid by _____, based upon $_____ per ☐ acre, ☐ sq. ft.

  ☐ C. TAX DEFERRED EXCHANGE (Investment Property)

EXPIRATION. This offer shall expire unless a copy hereof with Seller's written acceptance is delivered to the Buyer or to his agent on or before

_____ ☐ AM, ☐ PM, on _____, 19_____.

The undersigned Buyer has read this agreement, _including Items 7 through 14 on the reverse side_ and acknowledges receipt of a copy hereof. Buyer acknowledges further that s/he has not received or relied upon any statements or representation by the undersigned Agent which are not herein expressed.

_____ Buyer's Broker   DATED: _____ TIME: _____

By _____ Agent   _____ Buyer

Broker's Initials: _____ Dated: _____   _____ Buyer

ACCEPTANCE

Seller accepts the foregoing offer and agrees to sell the herein described property for the price and on the terms and conditions herein specified.

Subject to: _____

COMMISSION. Seller hereby irrevocably assigns and agrees to pay to _____

_____

the Broker in this transaction, in Cash from proceeds **at close of escrow,** for services rendered: _____

In the event that Buyer defaults and fails to complete the sale, the Broker shall be entitled to receive one-half of Buyer's deposit, but not more than the commission earned, without prejudice to Broker's rights to recover the balance of the commission from Buyer. The mutual recission of this agreement by Buyer and Seller shall not relieve said parties of their obligations to Broker hereunder. This agreement shall not limit the rights of Broker provided for in any listing or other agreement which may be in effect between Seller and Broker, except that the amount of the commission shall be as specified herein.

The undersigned Seller hereby acknowledges receipt of a copy hereof and authorizes Broker to deliver a signed copy to Buyer.

_____ Seller's Broker   DATED: _____ TIME: _____

By _____   _____ Seller

Broker's Initials: _____ Dated: _____   _____ Seller

The undersigned Buyer hereby acknowledges receipt of a copy of the accepted agreement.

DATE: _____ TIME: _____   _____ Buyer

FORM 421 (10-90)   COPYRIGHT © 1990, BY PROFESSIONAL PUBLISHING CORP. 122 PAUL DR. SAN RAFAEL, CA 94903 (415) 472-1964   **PROFESSIONAL PUBLISHING**

7. A. SOIL TESTS. Upon acceptance of this agreement Buyer shall have the right to go upon the property to conduct soil tests, including percolation tests, to ascertain whether the property is suitable for the improvements which Buyer proposes to make. All expenses of such test shall be borne by **the person indicated under Item 7-A on the reverse side,** and Buyer shall be responsible for the repair and restoration of any damage to the property which may be caused by such tests. If in the reasonable opinion of the soil engineer, employed by Buyer, the property is not suitable for the proposed development, this agreement at the option of the Buyer, may be terminated and all deposits shall be refunded. Buyer shall be deemed to have waived this condition unless written notice to the contrary is delivered to Seller or his agent **within the number of days of acceptance specified under Item 7-A on the reverse side.**

B. SURVEY. Upon acceptance of this offer, the property shall be surveyed by a licensed surveyor at the expense of the party specified under **Item 7-B on the reverse side.** The surveyor shall set and flag all property pins, to be approved in writing by Buyer prior to close of escrow. The purchase price is based upon the price specified under **Item 7-B** and shall be adjusted in accordance with the area set forth in such a survey, if applicable.

C. TAX DEFERRED EXCHANGE (Investment Property). In the event that Seller wishes to enter into a tax deferred exchange for the real property described herein, or if Buyer wishes to enter into a tax deferred exchange with respect to property owned by him in connection with this transaction, each of the parties agrees to cooperate with the other party in connection with such exchange, including the execution of such documents as may be reasonably necessary to effectuate the same. Provided that: (a) The other party shall not be obligated to **delay the closing,** (b) All additional costs in connection with the exchange should be borne by the party requesting the exchange, and (c) The other party shall not be obligated to execute any note, contract, deed, or other document providing for any personal liability which would survive the exchange, nor shall the other party be obligated to take title to any property other than the property described in this agreement. The other party shall be indemnified and held harmless against any liability which arises or is claimed to have arisen on account of the acquisition of the exchange property.

8. EXAMINATION OF TITLE. In addition to any encumbrances referred to herein, Seller shall convey title to the property subject only to: [1] Real Estate Taxes not yet due, and [2] Covenants, Conditions, Restrictions, Rights of Way, and Easements of record, if any, which do not materially affect the value or indended use of the property. **Within three (3) days from date of acceptance** Buyer shall order a preliminary Title Report and CC&R's if applicable. **Ten (10) days from receipt** thereof are allowed the Buyer to examine the title to the property and to report in writing any valid objections thereto. All exceptions to title contained in such report (other than monetary liens) shall be deemed approved unless written objection is delivered to Seller **within said ten (10) days.** If Buyer objects to any exceptions to the title, Seller shall use due diligence to remove such exceptions at his own expense **before closing.** But if such exceptions cannot be removed **before closing,** all rights and obligations hereunder may, at election of the Buyer, terminate and the deposit shall be returned to Buyer less expenses incurred by Buyer **to date of termination** unless he elects to purchase the property subject to such exceptions. If Seller concludes he is unwilling or unable to remove such objections, Seller shall so notify Buyer **within ten (10) days of receipt of said objections.** In that event Buyer may terminate this agreement and have all deposits returned less expenses incurred **to date of termination.**

9. PRORATIONS. Rents, taxes, interest, and other expenses of the property to be prorated as of the date of recordation of the deed. Security deposits, advance rentals, or considerations involving future lease credits shall be credited to Buyer.

10. ENCUMBRANCES. In addition to any encumbrances referred to herein, Buyer shall take title to the property subject to: (1) Real Estate Taxes not yet due, and (2) Covenants, Conditions, Restrictions, Rights of Way, and Easements of Record, if any, which do not materially affect the value or intended use of the property.

11. DEFAULT. In the event that Buyer defaults in the performance of this agreement Seller may, subject to any rights of the Broker herein, retain Buyer's deposit on account of damages sustained and may take such actions as he deems appropriate to collect such additional damages as may have been actually sustained, and Buyer shall have the right to take such action as he deems appropriate to recover such portion of the deposit as may be allowed by law. In the event that Buyer so defaults Buyer agrees to pay the Broker(s) entitled thereto such commissions as would be payable by Seller in the absence of such default. In the event legal action is instituted by the Broker(s), or any party to this agreement, to enforce the terms of this agreement, or arising out of the execution of this agreement or the sale, or to collect commissions, the prevailing party shall be entitled to receive from the other party a reasonable attorney fee to be determined by the court in which such action is brought.

12. F.I.R.P.T.A. (Foreign Investment and Real Property Tax Act). The Foreign Investment and Real Property Tax Act requires a Buyer of real property to withhold ten percent (10%) of the sale price and to deposit that amount with the Internal Revenue Service **upon closing,** if the Seller is a foreign person, foreign corporation or partnership, or non-resident alien, unless the property qualifies for an exemption under the act.

Unless it is established that the transaction is exempt because the purchase price is $300,000 or less and the Buyer intends to use the property as his residence, Owner agrees to:

   a. Provide Broker with a Non-Foreign Seller Affidavit (PPC Form 101-V), stating under penalty of perjury that Seller is not a foreign person; OR:

   b. Provide Broker with a Certificate from the Internal Revenue Service establishing that no federal income tax withholding is required; OR:

   c. Consent to withholding 10% from the sale proceeds, to be deposited with the IRS, plus any amount that may be required by state law.

13. LAND USE RESTRICTIONS. Buyer shall satisfy himself through sources of information, other than the principals or real estate brokers or salespersons in this transaction, whether any public or private action in the form of a vote, initiative, referendum, local ordinance, law, or other measure presently in force or contemplated by a governing or other body may halt entirely or otherwise restrict Buyer's use of the subject property for improvement or other use, and Buyer acknowledges that he has not relied on any advice or representations by the principals or real estate representatives in this transaction for such independent information to any extent.

14. TIME. Time is of the essence of this agreement. All modifications and extensions shall be in writing and signed by all parties.

REAL ESTATE TRANSFER DISCLOSURE STATEMENT
(STATUTORY FORM)

THIS DISCLOSURE STATEMENT CONCERNS THE REAL PROPERTY SITUATED IN THE CITY OF _____
_____, COUNTY OF _____, STATE OF CALIFORNIA, DESCRIBED AS
_____.

THIS STATEMENT IS A DISCLOSURE OF THE CONDITION OF THE ABOVE DESCRIBED PROPERTY IN COMPLIANCE WITH SECTION 1102 OF THE CIVIL CODE AS OF _____, 19 ____. IT IS NOT A WARRANTY OF ANY KIND BY THE SELLER(S) OR ANY AGENT(S) REPRESENTING ANY PRINCIPAL(S) IN THIS TRANSACTION, AND IS NOT A SUBSTITUTE FOR ANY INSPECTIONS OR WARRANTIES THE PRINCIPAL(S) MAY WISH TO OBTAIN.

1. COORDINATION WITH OTHER DISCLOSURE FORMS

This Real Estate Transfer Disclosure Statement is made pursuant to Section 1102 of the Civil Code. Other statutes require disclosures, depending upon the details of the particular real estate transaction (for example: special study zone and purchase-money liens on residential property).

Substituted Disclosures: The following disclosures have or will be made in connection with this real estate transfer, and are intended to satisfy the disclosure obligations on this form, where the subject matter is the same: _____

_____

_____

(list all substituted disclosure forms to be used in connection with this transaction)

2. SELLERS INFORMATION

The Seller discloses the following information with the knowledge that even though this is not a warranty, prospective Buyers may rely on this information in deciding whether and on what terms to purchase the subject property. Seller hereby authorizes any agent(s) representing any principal(s) in this transaction to provide a copy of this statement to any person or entity in connection with any actual or anticipated sale of the property.

THE FOLLOWING ARE REPRESENTATIONS MADE BY THE SELLER(S) AND ARE NOT THE REPRESENTATIONS OF THE AGENT(S), IF ANY. THIS INFORMATION IS A DISCLOSURE AND IS NOT INTENDED TO BE PART OF ANY CONTRACT BETWEEN THE BUYER AND SELLER.

Seller ☐ is ☐ is not occupying the property.

A. The subject property has the items checked below (read across):

☐ Range	☐ Oven	☐ Microwave	Garage: ☐ Attached, ☐ Not Attached
☐ Dishwasher	☐ Trash Compactor	☐ Garbage Disposal	☐ Carport
☐ Washer/Dryer Hookups	☐ Window Screens	☐ Rain Gutters	Pool/Spa Heater: ☐ Gas ☐ Solar
☐ Burglar Alarms	☐ Smoke Detector(s)	☐ Fire Alarm	☐ Electric
☐ T.V. Antenna	☐ Satellite Dish	☐ Intercom	Water Heater: ☐ Gas ☐ Solar
☐ Central Heating	☐ Central Air Conditioning	☐ Evaporator Cooler(s)	☐ Electric
☐ Wall/Window Air Conditioning	☐ Sprinklers	☐ Public Sewer System	Water Supply: ☐ City ☐ Well
☐ Septic Tank	☐ Sump Pump	☐ Water Softener	☐ Private Utility
☐ Patio/Decking	☐ Built-in Barbeque	☐ Gazebo	☐ Other _____
☐ Sauna	☐ Pool	☐ Spa ☐ Hot Tub	Gas Supply: ☐ Utility ☐ Bottled
☐ Security Gate(s)	☐ Autom. Garage Door Opener(s)*	☐ Number Remote Controls	

Exhaust Fan(s) in _____ 220 Volt Wiring in _____ Fireplace(s) in _____
Gas Starter _____ Roof(s): Type: _____ Age: _____(approx.)
Other: _____

Are there, to the best of your (Seller's) knowledge, any of the above that are not in operating condition? ☐ Yes ☐ No. If yes, then describe. (Attach additional sheets if necessary): _____
_____
_____

B. Are you (Seller) aware of any significant defects/malfunctions in any of the following? ☐ Yes ☐ No. If yes, check appropriate box(es) below.
☐ Interior Walls ☐ Ceilings ☐ Floors ☐ Exterior Walls ☐ Insulation ☐ Roof(s) ☐ Windows ☐ Doors ☐ Foundation ☐ Slab(s)
☐ Driveways ☐ Sidewalks ☐ Walls/Fences ☐ Electrical Systems ☐ Plumbing/Sewers/Septics ☐ Other Structural Components (Describe: _____).

If any of the above is checked, explain. (Attach additional sheets if necessary): _____
_____
_____

C. Are you (Seller) aware of any of the following:

1. Substances, materials, or products which may be an environmental hazard such as, but not limited to, asbestos, formaldehyde, radon gas, lead-based paint, fuel or chemical storage tanks, and contaminated soil or water on the subject property .... ☐ Yes ☐ No
2. Features of the property shared in common with adjoining landowners, such as walls, fences, and driveways, whose use or responsibility for maintenance may have an effect on the subject property .... ☐ Yes ☐ No
3. Any encroachments, easements or similar matters that may affect your interest in the subject property .... ☐ Yes ☐ No
4. Room additions, structural modifications, or other alterations or repairs made without necessary permits .... ☐ Yes ☐ No
5. Room additions, structural modifications, or other alterations or repairs not in compliance with building codes .... ☐ Yes ☐ No
6. Landfill (compacted or otherwise) on the property or any portion thereof .... ☐ Yes ☐ No
7. Any settling from any cause, or slippage, sliding, or other soil problems .... ☐ Yes ☐ No
8. Flooding, drainage or grading problems .... ☐ Yes ☐ No
9. Major damage to the property or any of the structures from fire, earthquake, floods, or landslides .... ☐ Yes ☐ No
10. Any zoning violations, nonconforming uses, violations of "setback" requirements .... ☐ Yes ☐ No
11. Neighborhood noise problems or other nuisances .... ☐ Yes ☐ No
12. CC&R's or other deed restrictions or obligations .... ☐ Yes ☐ No
13. Homeowners' Association which has any authority over the subject property .... ☐ Yes ☐ No
14. Any "common area" (facilities such as pools, tennis courts, walkways, or other areas co-owned in undivided interest with others ... ☐ Yes ☐ No
15. Any notices of abatement or citations against the property .... ☐ Yes ☐ No
16. Any lawsuits against the seller threatening to or affecting this real property .... ☐ Yes ☐ No
17. The property is located within a wildland area which may contain substantial forest fire risks and hazards and is subject to the requirements of Sec. 4291 of the Public Resources Code .... ☐ Yes ☐ No

If the answer to any of these is yes, explain. (Attach additional sheets if necessary): _____
_____

Seller certifies that the information herein is true and correct to the best of the Seller's knowledge as of the date signed by the Seller.

Seller _____ Date _____

Seller _____ Date _____

*This garage door opener may not be in compliance with the safety standards relating to automatic reversing devices as set forth in Chapter 12.5 (commencing with Section 19890) of Part 3 of Division 13 of the Health and Safety Code.

FORM 110.21 CAL (old 109.3 CAL) (7-91) PROFESSIONAL PUBLISHING CORPORATION, 122 PAUL DR. SAN RAFAEL, CA 94903 (415) 472-1964 PROFESSIONAL PUBLISHING

DISCLOSURE OBLIGATIONS
(CALIFORNIA CIVIL CODE §1102, ET SEQ.)

SELLER'S OBLIGATIONS (Transferor)

Effective January 1, 1987. A Seller (Transferor) of residential real property (1 to 4 units) including stock cooperatives and pertaining to transfers made by Sale, Exchange, Installment Land Sale Contract (as defined in C.C. §2985), Lease with an Option to Purchase, any other Option to Purchase, or ground lease coupled with improvements must supply a Buyer (Transferee) with a completed REAL ESTATE TRANSFER DISCLOSURE STATEMENT in the form prescribed in California Civil Code §1102.6 (P.P.C. Form 109.3CAL).

AGENT'S OBLIGATIONS

The Agent of the Seller, and the Agent who has obtained the offer (when two agents are involved) are required to make "A REASONABLY COMPETENT AND DILIGENT VISUAL INSPECTION OF THE ACCESSIBLE AREAS OF THE PROPERTY, . . .," and upon completion state in writing their observations (P.P.C. Form 109.4CAL).

BUYER'S RIGHTS (Transferee)

"If any disclosure, or any material amendment of any disclosure, required to be made by this article, is delivered after the execution of an offer to purchase, the transferee shall have **three (3) days** after delivery in person or **five (5) days** after delivery by deposit in the mail, to terminate his or her offer by delivery of a written notice of termination to the Transferor or the Transferor's Agent."

TIMING OF DISCLOSURE

(a) "In the case of a sale, as soon as practicable before transfer of title."

(b) "In the case of transfer by a real property sales contract (Installment Land Sale Contract) . . . or by a Lease together with an Option to Purchase, or a ground lease coupled with improvements, as soon as practicable before execution of the contract . . . "Execution" means the making or acceptance of an offer."

EXEMPTED TRANSFERS

(a) Transfers requiring "a public report pursuant to §11018.1 of the Business & Professions Code" and transfers pursuant to §11010.4 of Business & Professions Code where no public report is required;

(b) "Transfers pursuant to court order" (such as probate sales, sales by a bankruptcy trustee, etc.);

(c) Transfers by foreclosure (including a deed in lieu of foreclosure and a transfer by a beneficiary who has acquired the property by foreclosure or deed in lieu of foreclosure);

(d) "Transfers by a fiduciary in the course of the administration of a decedent's estate, guardianship, conservatorship, or trust."

(e) "Transfers from one co-owner to one or more other co-owners."

(f) "Transfers made to a spouse" or to a direct blood relative;

(g) "Transfers between spouses" in connection with a dissolution of marriage or similar proceeding;

(h) Transfers by the State Controller pursuant to the Unclaimed Property Law;

(i) Transfers as a result of failure to pay property taxes;

(j) "Transfers or exchanges to or from any governmental entity."

PUBLISHER'S NOTICE

The above is a summary of the Disclosure Obligations contained in C.C. §1102, ET SEQ. Other disclosures may be required by other statutes, depending on the specifics of the transfer.

NCR (No Carbon Required) PROPERTY ADDRESS: _____

3. AGENTS INSPECTION DISCLOSURE – (Listing Agent)
(To be completed only if the Seller is represented by an agent in this transaction.)

THE UNDERSIGNED, BASED ON THE ABOVE INQUIRY OF THE SELLER(S) AS TO THE CONDITION OF THE PROPERTY AND BASED ON A REASONABLY COMPETENT AND DILIGENT VISUAL INSPECTION OF THE ACCESSIBLE AREAS OF THE PROPERTY IN CONJUNCTION WITH THAT INQUIRY, STATES THE FOLLOWING:

_____
_____
_____
_____
_____
_____
_____
_____
_____
_____
_____
_____
_____
_____
_____
_____

Agent (Broker
Representing Seller) _____ By _____ Date _____
         (Please Print)   (Associate Licensee or Broker-Signature)

4. AGENTS INSPECTION DISCLOSURE – (Selling Agent)
(To be completed only if the agent who has obtained the offer is other than the agent above.)

THE UNDERSIGNED, BASED ON A REASONABLY COMPETENT AND DILIGENT VISUAL INSPECTION OF THE ACCESSIBLE AREAS OF THE PROPERTY, STATES THE FOLLOWING:

_____
_____
_____
_____
_____
_____
_____
_____
_____
_____
_____
_____
_____
_____
_____
_____
_____

Agent (Broker
obtaining the Offer) _____ By _____ Date _____
         (Please Print)   (Associate Licensee or Broker-Signature)

5. BUYER(S) AND SELLER(S) MAY WISH TO OBTAIN PROFESSIONAL ADVICE AND/OR INSPECTIONS OF THE PROPERTY AND TO PROVIDE FOR APPROPRIATE PROVISIONS IN A CONTRACT BETWEEN BUYER(S) AND SELLER(S) WITH RESPECT TO ANY ADVICE/INSPECTIONS/DEFECTS.

I / WE ACKNOWLEDGE RECEIPT OF A COPY OF *BOTH PAGES* OF THIS STATEMENT.

Seller _____ Date _____
Seller _____ Date _____
Buyer _____ Date _____
Buyer _____ Date _____
Agent (Broker Representing Seller) _____ By _____ Date _____
                                      (Associate Licensee or Broker-Signature)
Agent (Broker obtaining the Offer) _____ By _____ Date _____
                                      (Associate Licensee or Broker-Signature)

A REAL ESTATE BROKER IS QUALIFIED TO ADVISE ON REAL ESTATE. IF YOU DESIRE LEGAL ADVICE, CONSULT YOUR ATTORNEY.

REAL ESTATE TRANSFER DISCLOSURE SUPPLEMENT

PROPERTY ADDRESS: _____

SELLER'S NAME: _____

This form supplements the requirements of Civil Code 1102 and is designed to give the Buyer additional information regarding the property. The following representations are made by the Seller(s) and are NOT the representations made by the Agent(s), if any.

1. IN REFERENCE TO THE REAL ESTATE TRANSFER DISCLOSURE STATEMENT (STATUTORY FORM)

SECTION 2-A: NOTICE: Make sure that only those items which are included in the sale are checked under Section 2-A.
Are any of the items listed in Section 2-A of the REAL ESTATE TRANSFER DISCLOSURE STATEMENT, or any additional items not so listed, leased? _____ If so, which ones: _____

SECTION 2-B: Are you aware of any repairs or replacements to any of the items listed in Section 2-B of the REAL ESTATE TRANSFER DISCLOSURE STATEMENT? If so, for each repair or replacement state (attach additional sheets, if necessary):
What was replaced or repaired? _____
When? _____ Why? _____
By whom? _____ Permit? _____

2. TITLE AND ACCESS

2.1 Property currently leased? _____ Until when? _____ Option to renew? _____
2.2 Does anyone have a first right of refusal to buy, option, or lease? _____ If so, who? _____
2.3 Has a Notice of Default been recorded against the property? _____ If so, please explain: _____
2.4 Any bonds, assessments, or judgements which are either liens upon the property or which limit its use? _____
2.5 Can the bonds, if any, be paid off without an interest penalty charge? _____
2.6 Any boundary disputes, or third party claims affecting the property (rights of other people to interfere with the use of the property in any way)? _____ If so, please explain: _____

3. ENVIRONMENTAL PROBLEMS

3.1 Any pending real estate development in your area (such as condominiums, planned development units, subdivisions, or property for commercial, educational, or religious use)? _____
3.2 Any excessive noises (such as from airplanes, trains, trucks, freeways, etc.)? _____
3.3 Any unusual odors (such as caused by toxic waste, agriculture, industry or animals)? _____

4. STRUCTURAL DISCLOSURES

4.1 Any problems with retaining walls (such as bulging or cracking)? _____
4.2 Any structural wood members including mudsills below soil level? _____
4.3 Is crawlspace, if any, below soil level? _____
4.4 Any sump pump in the crawlspace or basement? _____ If so, why? _____
4.5 Any abandoned septic tank? _____
4.6 Vapor or moisture barrier (plastic covering) in the sub-area? _____
4.7 Are you aware of any asbestos in the property? _____ If so, where? _____
4.8 Is structure insulated? _____ If so, where? _____

5. ROOF, GUTTERS, DOWNSPOUTS

5.1 Roof been resurfaced? _____ When? _____ Guaranteed until? _____ By whom? _____
5.2 Has roof ever leaked since you owned? _____ If so, what was done to correct it? _____
5.3 Gutters and downspouts free of holes and excessive rust? _____
5.4 Downspouts emptying into drainage system or onto splash blocks? _____ Water directed away from structure? _____

6. PLUMBING SYSTEM

6.1 ☐ Public water supply, ☐ Private well. If well water, date of last water safety check: _____ Test result: _____
6.2 Well water pump: _____ Date installed: _____ Condition: _____
6.3 Water standing around lawn sprinkler heads? _____
6.4 Plumbing leaks around and/or under: ☐ sinks, ☐ toilets, ☐ showers, ☐ bathtubs, ☐ _____

7. HEATING, AIR CONDITIONING, OTHER EQUIPMENT

7.1 Furnace room or enclosure adequately vented? _____
7.2 Fuel consuming heating devices (including clothes dryer) adequately vented to outside, directly or through chimney? _____
7.3 Water heater equipped with required temperature pressure relief valve? _____

8. COMMON INTEREST DEVELOPMENTS

8.1 Restrictions: ☐ resale, ☐ children, ☐ pets, ☐ storage of recreational vehicles or boats in driveways or common areas, ☐ advertising or For Sale signs, ☐ architectural alterations subject to association approval?
8.2 In case of a conversion, have you an engineer's report on the condition of the building and its equipment? _____
8.3 Association dues $ _____ per _____ Included: _____
8.4 Any pending dues increases or special assessments? _____
8.5 All dues, assessments, taxes current? _____
8.6 Soundproofing adequate? _____ Any noisy trash chutes? _____
8.7 Do you know of any pending or potential legal actions concerning the Homeowners Association? _____

9. OWNERSHIP

9.1 Are you a builder or developer? _____
9.2 Are you a licensed real estate broker/agent? _____
9.3 List all persons on the title who are not U.S. citizens: _____

10. REPORTS

Have you received or do you have knowledge of any of the following inspection reports or repair estimates made during or prior to your ownership?

REPORT	YES	NO	BY WHOM?	WHEN?	REPORT AVAILABLE?
Soils/Drainage					
Geologic					
Structural					
Roof					
Pest Control					
Well					
Septic					
Pool/Spa					
Heating					
Air Conditioning					
House Inspection					
Energy Audit					
Radon Test					
City/County Inspection					

In addition to the disclosure statements made herein, the following facts are known or suspected by me (us) which may materially affect the value or desirability of the subject property, now or in the future: _____ ☐ Explanation attached.

Seller certifies that the information herein is true and correct to the best of the Seller's knowledge as of the date signed by the Seller.

Seller _____ Seller _____ Date _____

Receipt acknowledged: Buyer _____ Buyer _____ Date _____

FORM 109.5 CAL (8-89) COPYRIGHT © 1988, BY PROFESSIONAL PUBLISHING CORP, 122 PAUL DR, SAN RAFAEL, CA 94903 (415) 472-1964

PROFESSIONAL PUBLISHING

ESTIMATED SELLER'S PROCEEDS

Based on Sellers price shown below and proration date of _____

Prepared by: _____ Date: _____

Office: _____ Phone: _____

Prepared for: _____

Property address: _____

(IF NOT APPLICABLE, FILL IN "NONE." DO NOT LEAVE BLANK SPACES!)

SELLING PRICE .... $_____

APPROXIMATE INDEBTEDNESS:
    First Loan .... $_____
    Second Loan .... $_____
    Other Liens .... $_____
        LESS: TOTAL APPROXIMATE INDEBTEDNESS .... $_____

GROSS EQUITY: .... $_____

ESTIMATED COSTS:
    Appraisal Fee .... $_____
    Inspection Fees (VA) .... $_____
    Escrow Fee (VA) .... $_____
    Document Prep. Fee (VA / FHA) .... $_____
    Warehouse & Misc. Loan Fees (VA / FHA) .... $_____
    Brokerage Commission .... $_____
    Escrow Fee .... $_____
    Title Insurance .... $_____
    Legal Fee .... $_____
    Prepayment Penalty .... $_____
    Documentary or Transfer Tax .... $_____
    City Inspection Report of Residential Building Record .... $_____
    Pest Control Inspection Fee .... $_____
    Pest Control Work .... $_____
    Repairs and Fixing-up Costs .... $_____
    Recording Fee .... $_____
    Discount Fee First Mortgage (FHA or VA points) .... $_____
    Trustee's Fee or Reconveyance Fee .... $_____
    Notary Fee .... $_____
    Prorated Taxes (if not paid to proration date) .... $_____
    Prorated Personal Property Tax (if not paid to proration date) .. $_____
    Interest (from due date last loan payment to proration date) .... $_____
    Loan Payments in Arrears .... $_____
    Prorated Rents .... $_____
    Security Deposits and Prepaid Rents on hand .... $_____
    Damage and Cleaning Deposits on hand .... $_____
    Home Protection Contract Fee .... $_____
    _____ $_____
    _____ $_____

        LESS: TOTAL ESTIMATED COSTS .... $_____

        SUB-TOTAL .... $_____

ESTIMATED CREDITS:
    Prorated Taxes (if paid beyond proration date) .... $_____
    Trust Fund or Impound Account Balance .... $_____ $_____

        PLUS: TOTAL ESTIMATED CREDITS .... $_____

ESTIMATED SELLER'S PROCEEDS: .... $_____

        LESS: LOAN CARRIED BY SELLER .... $_____

ESTIMATED CASH PROCEEDS: .... $_____

    PLUS: ESTIMATED PROCEEDS FROM SALE OF LOAN CARRIED BY SELLER $_____

ESTIMATED NET CASH PROCEEDS: .... $_____

The real estate licensee preparing the above estimate and/or his employing broker, does not warrant accuracy and assumes no responsibility for any errors or omissions.

FORM 126 (4-86) COPYRIGHT ᴌ 1986. BY PROFESSIONAL PUBLISHING CORP. 122 PAUL DR. SAN RAFAEL, CA 94903 **PROFESSIONAL PUBLISHING**

HAZARDOUS MATERIALS ADDENDUM

To the ☐ PURCHASE AGREEMENT, ☐ EXCHANGE AGREEMENT, ☐ LEASE AGREEMENT —
covering the real property commonly known as _____

_____ ,

between _____

and _____ ,

dated _____

Various materials utilized in the construction of any improvements to Property may contain materials that have been or may in the future be determined to be toxic, hazardous or undesirable and may need to be specially handled and/or removed from the Property. For example, some electrical transformers and other electrical components can contain PCBS, and asbestos has been used in a wide variety of building components such as fire-proofing, air duct insulation, acoustical tiles, spray-on acoustical materials, linoleum, floor tiles and plaster. Due to current or prior uses, the Property or improvements may contain materials such as metals, minerals, chemicals, hydrocarbons, biological or radioactive materials and other substances which are considered, or in the future may be determined to be, toxic wastes, hazardous materials or undesirable substances. Such substances may be in above-and below-ground containers on the Property or may be present on or in soils, water, building components or other portions of the Property in areas that may not be accessible or noticeable.

Current and future federal, state and local laws and regulations may require the clean-up of such toxic, hazardous or undersirable materials at the expense of those persons who in the past, present or future have had any interest in Property including, but not limited to current, past and future owners and users of the Property. The Parties are advised to consult with Independent legal counsel of their choice to determine the potential liability with respect to toxic, hazardous, or undesirable materials. The Parties should also consult with such legal counsel to determine what provisions regarding toxic, hazardous or undesirable materials they may wish to include in purchase and sale agreements, leases, options and other legal documentation related to transactions they contemplate entering into with respect to the Property.

The real estate salesperson and brokers in this transaction have no expertise with respect to toxic wastes, hazardous materials or undesirable substances. Proper inspections of the Property by qualified experts are an absolute necessity to determine whether or not there are any current or potential toxic wastes, hazardous materials or undesirable substances in or on the Property. The real estate salesperson and brokers in this transaction have not made, nor will make, any representations, either expressed or implied, regarding the existence or nonexistence of toxic wastes, hazardous materials, or undesirable substances in or on the Property. Problems involving toxic wastes, hazardous materials or undesirable substances can be extremely costly to correct. It is the responsibility of the Parties to retain qualified experts to deal with the detection and correction of such matters.

The Parties are directed to seek further information concerning any and all future correctional measures, if any, from Municipal, County, State and/or Federal Agencies.

DATED: _____

_____   _____
Seller/Lessor   Seller/Lessor

RECEIPT ACKNOWLEDGED:

DATED: _____

_____   _____
Buyer/Lessee   Buyer/Lessee

FORM 110.61 (old 109.8) (5-91)   PROFESSIONAL PUBLISHING CORPORATION, 122 PAUL DR. SAN RAFAEL, CA 94903 (415) 472-1964   **PROFESSIONAL PUBLISHING**

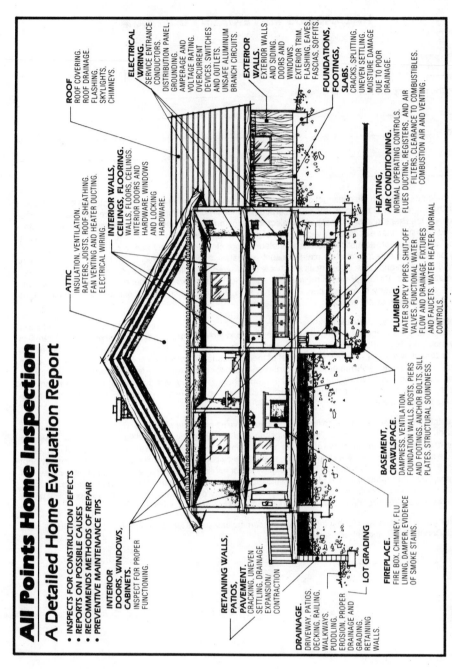

All Points Home Inspection

A Detailed Home Evaluation Report

- INSPECTS FOR CONSTRUCTION DEFECTS
- REPORTS ON POSSIBLE CAUSES
- RECOMMENDS METHODS OF REPAIR
- PREVENTIVE MAINTENANCE TIPS

ROOF
ROOF COVERING.
ROOF DRAINAGE.
FLASHING.
SKYLIGHTS.
CHIMNEYS.

ELECTRICAL WIRING.
SERVICE ENTRANCE CONDUCTORS.
DISTRIBUTION PANEL.
GROUNDING.
AMPERAGE AND VOLTAGE RATING.
OVERCURRENT DEVICES, SWITCHES AND OUTLETS.
UNSAFE ALUMINUM BRANCH CIRCUITS.

EXTERIOR WALLS.
EXTERIOR WALLS AND SIDING.
DOORS AND WINDOWS.
EXTERIOR TRIM.
FLASHING, EAVES, FASCIAS, SOFFITS.

FOUNDATIONS, FOOTINGS, SLABS.
CRACKS, SPLITTING, UNEVEN SETTLING.
MOISTURE DAMAGE DUE TO POOR DRAINAGE.

ATTIC
INSULATION, VENTILATION.
RAFTERS, JOISTS, ROOF SHEATHING.
FAN VENTING AND HEATER DUCTING.
ELECTRICAL WIRING.

INTERIOR WALLS, CEILINGS, FLOORING.
WALLS, FLOORS, CEILINGS.
INTERIOR DOORS AND HARDWARE, WINDOWS AND LOCKING HARDWARE.

HEATING, AIR CONDITIONING.
NORMAL OPERATING CONTROLS.
FLUES DUCTING, REGISTERS, AND AIR FILTERS. CLEARANCE TO COMBUSTIBLES.
COMBUSTION AIR AND VENTING.

PLUMBING.
WATER SUPPLY PIPES, SHUT-OFF VALVES. FUNCTIONAL WATER FLOW AND DRAINAGE. FIXTURES AND FAUCETS. WATER HEATER. NORMAL CONTROLS.

INTERIOR DOORS, WINDOWS, CABINETS.
INSPECT FOR PROPER FUNCTIONING.

RETAINING WALLS, PATIOS, PAVEMENT.
CRACKING, UNEVEN SETTLING, DRAINAGE, EXPANSION/ CONTRACTION.

DRAINAGE.
DRIVEWAY, PATIOS, DECKING, RAILING, WALKWAYS, PUDDLING, EROSION, PROPER DRAINAGE AND GRADING, RETAINING WALLS.

LOT GRADING

FIREPLACE.
FIRE BOX, CHIMNEY, FLU LINING, DAMPER, EVIDENCE OF SMOKE STAINS.

BASEMENT, CRAWLSPACE.
DAMPNESS, VENTILATION.
FOUNDATION WALLS, POSTS, PIERS AND FOOTINGS, ANCHOR BOLTS, SILL PLATES, STRUCTURAL SOUNDNESS.

Source: Reprinted with permission from Erik J. Kuoppamaki, All Points Home Inspection and the American Society of Home Inspection.

Appendix

Mortgage and Trust Deed Requirements

Alabama

> *Nature of Mortgage:*   Title
> *Customary Security Instrument:*   Mortgage
> *Predominant Method of Purchase:*   Power of Sale
> *Time Required to Complete Initial Action (Months):*   1
> *Redemption (Months):*   12
> *Possession:*   Purchaser

Alaska

> *Nature of Mortgage:*   Lien
> *Customary Security Instrument:*   Trust Deed
> *Predominant Method of Purchase:*   Power of Sale
> *Time Required to Complete Initial Action (Months):*   3
> *Redemption (Months):*   None
>
> Deed of Trust—however, if there is a judicial foreclosure, there is a 12-month redemption period and the transfer time to FHA is increased accordingly.
>
> *Possession:*

Arizona

> *Nature of Mortgage:*   Lien
> *Customary Security Instrument:*   Trust Deed
>
> Judicial foreclosure under mortgage is also available. Time to complete would be 4 months followed by a 6-month redemption. However, if

property was abandoned, the redemption can be reduced to 1 month if so stated in the Decree.

Predominant Method of Purchase: Power of Sale
Time Required to Complete Initial Action (Months):   4
Redemption (Months):   None

Judicial foreclosure under mortgage is also available. Time to complete would be 4 months followed by a 6-month redemption. However, if property was abandoned, the redemption can be reduced to 1 month if so stated in the Decree.

Possession:

Arkansas

Nature of Mortgage: Intermediate
Customary Security Instrument: Mortgage
Predominant Method of Purchase: Power of Sale
Time Required to Complete Initial Action (Months):   5
Redemption (Months):   None

Provided redemption rights have been expressly waived in the security instrument; if no waiver, redemption period is 12 months.

Possession:

California

Nature of Mortgage: Lien
Customary Security Instrument: Trust Deed
Predominant Method of Purchase: Power of Sale
Time Required to Complete Initial Action (Months):   5
Redemption (Months):   None

Deed of Trust—however, if there is a judicial foreclosure, there is a 12-month redemption period and the transfer time to FHA is increased accordingly.

Possession:

Colorado

Nature of Mortgage: Lien
Customary Security Instrument: Trust Deed
Predominant Method of Purchase: Power of Sale
Time Required to Complete Initial Action (Months):   2
Redemption (Months):   2-1/2

Redemption period is 5 months on security instruments executed before July 1, 1965; FHA transfer time is then 9 months.

Possession: Mortgagor

Connecticut

Nature of Mortgage: Intermediate
Customary Security Instrument: Mortgage
Predominant Method of Purchase: Strict Foreclosure
Time Required to Complete Initial Action (Months):   6
Redemption (Months):   None

> Redemption (law date) depends entirely on the equity in the property. If little or no equity exists, there is a 30-day law date prior to completion; otherwise, length is determined by the court.

Possession:

Delaware

Nature of Mortgage: Intermediate
Customary Security Instrument: Mortgage
Predominant Method of Purchase: Judicial
Time Required to Complete Initial Action (Months):   9
Redemption (Months):   None
Possession:

District of Columbia

Nature of Mortgage: Intermediate
Customary Security Instrument: Trust Deed
Predominant Method of Purchase: Power of Sale
Time Required to Complete Initial Action (Months):   2
Redemption (Months):   None
Possession:

Florida

Nature of Mortgage: Lien
Customary Security Instrument: Mortgage
Predominant Method of Purchase: Judicial
Time Required to Complete Initial Action (Months):   6
Redemption (Months):   None
Possession:

> VA may request eviction.

Georgia

Nature of Mortgage: Title
Customary Security Instrument: Security Deed
Predominant Method of Purchase: Power of Sale
Time Required to Complete Initial Action (Months):   1
Redemption (Months):   None
Possession:

Hawaii

Nature of Mortgage: Lien
Customary Security Instrument: Mortgage
Predominant Method of Purchase: Judicial

Foreclosure by Power of Sale or Entry and Possession also available under Deed of Trust.

Time Required to Complete Initial Action (Months):   6
Redemption (Months):   None

Foreclosure by Power of Sale or Entry and Possession also available under Deed of Trust.

Possession:

Idaho

Nature of Mortgage: Lien
Customary Security Instrument: Mortgage
Predominant Method of Purchase: Judicial

For properties over 20 acres, redemption is 12 months. Power of Sale Foreclosure also available under Trust Deed.

Time Required to Complete Initial Action (Months):   6
Redemption (Months):   6

For properties over 20 acres, redemption is 12 months. Power of Sale Foreclosure also available under Trust Deed.

Possession:

Illinois

Nature of Mortgage: Intermediate
Customary Security Instrument: Mortgage
Predominant Method of Purchase: Judicial
Time Required to Complete Initial Action (Months):   6
Redemption (Months):   6

Statute permits both Strict Foreclosure (where value of property does not exceed 90% of debt) and Foreclosure with Consent of the Mortgagor; in either case, the foreclosure sale is eliminated, the mortgagee waives deficiency judgment and the decree vests title directly in the mortgage subject to a 3-month redemption period. Transfer time to FHA and VA then both become 6 months.

Redemption is 6 months from sale if the judgment date is after January 1, 1982 (previously was 12 months from date of service).

Possession: Mortgagor

Receiver may be obtained to collect rents if authorized by security instrument.

Indiana

Nature of Mortgage: Lien
Customary Security Instrument: Mortgage
Predominant Method of Purchase: Judicial
Time Required to Complete Initial Action (Months):   7
Redemption (Months):   3

The redemption period precedes sale.

On security instruments executed before July 1, 1975, redemption period is 6 months before sale. Time to complete is then 10 months with a 12-month transfer time.

Possession: Mortgagor

Iowa

Nature of Mortgage: Lien
Customary Security Instrument: Mortgage
Predominant Method of Purchase: Judicial
Time Required to Complete Initial Action (Months):   6
Redemption (Months):   6

If security instrument specifically provides for 6-month redemption period and includes waiver of deficiency judgment as of 1977; otherwise, redemption period is 12 months and transfer time to FHA is then 20 months. If the property was abandoned, redemption can be reduced to 2 months.

Possession: Mortgagor

Kansas

Nature of Mortgage: Lien
Customary Security Instrument: Mortgage
Predominant Method of Purchase: Judicial
Time Required to Complete Initial Action (Months):   4
Redemption (Months):   12

Provided no suit is instituted for deficiency. Redemption period is reduced to 6 months in cases of abandoned property or on purchase money mortgages with less than 1/3 down. Transfer time to FHA then becomes 11 months.

Possession: Mortgagor

Kentucky

Nature of Mortgage: Lien
Customary Security Instrument: Mortgage
Predominant Method of Purchase: Judicial
Time Required to Complete Initial Action (Months):   9
Redemption (Months):   None

If foreclosure sale brings less than $2/3$ of appraised value (court appraiser), there is a 12-month redemption period and FHA transfer time then becomes 19 months.

Possession:

Louisiana

Nature of Mortgage: Lien
Customary Security Instrument: Mortgage
Predominant Method of Purchase: Judicial
Time Required to Complete Initial Action (Months):   4
Redemption (Months):   None
Possession:

Maine

Nature of Mortgage: Title
Customary Security Instrument: Mortgage
Predominant Method of Purchase: Entry and Possession
Time Required to Complete Initial Action (Months):   1
Redemption (Months):   12
Possession: Mortgage

Maryland

Nature of Mortgage: Title
Customary Security Instrument: Trust Deed
Predominant Method of Purchase: Power of Sale

Except in Baltimore, where decree of equity court orders sale.

Time Required to Complete Initial Action (Months):   2
Redemption (Months):   None
Possession:

Massachusetts

Nature of Mortgage: Intermediate
Customary Security Instrument: Mortgage
Predominant Method of Purchase: Power of Sale
Time Required to Complete Initial Action (Months):   9
Redemption (Months):   None
Possession:

Michigan

Nature of Mortgage: Lien
Customary Security Instrument: Mortgage
Predominant Method of Purchase: Power of Sale
Time Required to Complete Initial Action (Months):   4
Redemption (Months):   6

> Redemption period is 12 months on security instruments dated prior to January 1, 1965; transfer time to FHA is then 17 months. Redemption may be reduced if the property was abandoned.

Possession: Mortgagor

Minnesota

Nature of Mortgage: Lien
Customary Security Instrument: Mortgage
Predominant Method of Purchase: Power of Sale
Time Required to Complete Initial Action (Months):   3
Redemption (Months):   6

> If deed is executed after July 1, 1967, the redemption is 6 months, provided the deficiency judgment was waived.

Possession: Mortgagor

Mississippi

Nature of Mortgage: Title
Customary Security Instrument: Trust Deed
Predominant Method of Purchase: Power of Sale
Time Required to Complete Initial Action (Months):   1
Redemption (Months):   None
Possession:

Missouri

Nature of Mortgage: Lien
Customary Security Instrument: Trust Deed
Predominant Method of Purchase: Power of Sale
Time Required to Complete Initial Action (Months):   2
Redemption (Months):   None

> Within 10 days after sale, mortgagor may give notice of intention to redeem, including security deposit for taxes, interest, etc. Redemption period is then 12 months and transfer time to FHA becomes 15 months.

Possession:

Montana

Nature of Mortgage: Lien
Customary Security Instrument: Trust Deed
Predominant Method of Purchase: Power of Sale

For estates over 15 acres, a mortgage is used and foreclosed judicially; 1 year redemption.

Time Required to Complete Initial Action (Months):   1

Loan must be in default at least 120 days before day fixed for sale.

Redemption (Months):   None

For estates over 15 acres, a mortgage is used and foreclosed judicially; 1-year redemption.

Possession:

Nebraska

Nature of Mortgage: Lien
Customary Security Instrument: Mortgage
Predominant Method of Purchase: Judicial
Time Required to Complete Initial Action (Months):   7
Redemption (Months):   None

The redemption period precedes sale (court stays sale on mortgagor's request). Nebraska redeems only between day of sale and confirmation of sale. Foreclosure by Power of Sale is available under a Deed of Trust effective 1965. Time of completion would then be 3 months; no redemption following sale.

Possession:

Nevada

Nature of Mortgage: Lien
Customary Security Instrument: Trust Deed
Predominant Method of Purchase: Power of Sale
Time Required to Complete Initial Action (Months):   5
Redemption (Months):   None

Judicial foreclosure is available under a mortgage with a 12-month redemption following the sale.

Possession:

New Hampshire

Nature of Mortgage: Title
Customary Security Instrument: Mortgage
Predominant Method of Purchase: Power of Sale
Time Required to Complete Initial Action (Months):   2
Redemption (Months):   None
Possession:

New Jersey

Nature of Mortgage: Intermediate
Customary Security Instrument: Mortgage
Predominant Method of Purchase: Judicial
Time Required to Complete Initial Action (Months): 6
Redemption (Months): None

> Provided no suit is instituted for deficiency; otherwise, redemption is 6 months.

Possession:

New Mexico

Nature of Mortgage: Lien
Customary Security Instrument: Mortgage
Predominant Method of Purchase: Judicial
Time Required to Complete Initial Action (Months): 6
Redemption (Months): 1

> Provided mortgage specifically calls for shorter redemption period; otherwise, redemption period is 6 months.

Possession: Purchaser

New York

Nature of Mortgage: Lien
Customary Security Instrument: Mortgage
Predominant Method of Purchase: Judicial
Time Required to Complete Initial Action (Months): 8
Redemption (Months): None

Possession:

North Carolina

Nature of Mortgage: Intermediate
Customary Security Instrument: Trust Deed
Predominant Method of Purchase: Power of Sale
Time Required to Complete Initial Action (Months): 1
Redemption (Months): None

Possession:

North Dakota

Nature of Mortgage: Lien
Customary Security Instrument: Mortgage
Predominant Method of Purchase: Judicial
Time Required to Complete Initial Action (Months):   3
Redemption (Months):   6

If security instrument specifically provides for 6-month redemption period and includes a waiver of deficiency judgment as of 1977; otherwise, redemption period is 12 months and transfer time to FHA is then 20 months.

Possession: Mortgagor

Ohio

Nature of Mortgage: Lien
Customary Security Instrument: Mortgage
Predominant Method of Purchase: Judicial
Time Required to Complete Initial Action (Months):   8
Redemption (Months):   None

Possession:

Oklahoma

Nature of Mortgage: Lien
Predominant Method of Purchase: Judicial
Time Required to Complete Initial Action (Months):   6
Redemption (Months):   None

Provided sale is with court appraisement; otherwise, there is a 6-month redemption period preceding the sale.

Possession:

Oregon

Nature of Mortgage: Lien
Customary Security Instrument: Trust Deed
Predominant Method of Purchase: Power of Sale
Time Required to Complete Initial Action (Months):   9
Redemption (Months):   None

If security instrument was executed prior to May 25, 1959, judicial foreclosure is necessary with a 12-month redemption period following sale. Transfer time to FHA is then 17 months.

Possession:

Pennsylvania

Nature of Mortgage: Title
Customary Security Instrument: Mortgage
Predominant Method of Purchase: Judicial
Time Required to Complete Initial Action (Months):   6
Redemption (Months):   None
Possession:

Rhode Island

Nature of Mortgage: Title
Customary Security Instrument: Mortgage
Predominant Method of Purchase: Power of Sale
Time Required to Complete Initial Action (Months):   1
Redemption (Months):   None
Possession:

South Carolina

Nature of Mortgage: Lien
Customary Security Instrument: Mortgage
Predominant Method of Purchase: Judicial
Time Required to Complete Initial Action (Months):   5
Redemption (Months):   None

> Provided no suit is instituted for deficiency; otherwise, redemption is 6 months. The redemption is 1 month if a deficiency judgment was obtained.

Possession:

South Dakota

Nature of Mortgage: Lien
Customary Security Instrument: Mortgage
Predominant Method of Purchase: Judicial
Time Required to Complete Initial Action (Months):   6
Redemption (Months):   6

> If security instrument specifically provides for 6-month redemption period and includes a waiver of deficiency judgment as of 1977; otherwise, redemption period is 12 months and transfer time to FHA is then 20 months.

> Foreclosure by Power of Sale with Service is also available for properties under 40 acres.

> Redemption period can be extended to 24 months upon filing of affidavit by mortgagor including provision for accruing taxes, interest, etc. Transfer time to FHA then becomes 31 months.

Possession: Mortgagor

Tennessee

Nature of Mortgage: Title
Customary Security Instrument: Trust Deed
Predominant Method of Purchase: Power of Sale
Time Required to Complete Initial Action (Months):   1
Redemption (Months):   None

Provided redemption rights have been expressly waived in the security instrument. If no waiver, redemption period is 24 months.

Possession:

Texas

Nature of Mortgage: Lien
Customary Security Instrument: Trust Deed
Predominant Method of Purchase: Power of Sale
Time Required to Complete Initial Action (Months):   1
Redemption (Months):   None

Possession:

Utah

Nature of Mortgage: Lien
Customary Security Instrument: Trust Deed
Predominant Method of Purchase: Power of Sale
Time Required to Complete Initial Action (Months):   5
Redemption (Months):   3

The redemption period precedes sale (if foreclosure is by Power of Sale).

Judicial foreclosure is also available. If used, the 6-month redemption period precedes the sale and the VA transfer time then becomes 10 months. In Utah, the 6-month redemption would follow the sale.

Possession: Mortgagor

Vermont

Nature of Mortgage: Title
Customary Security Instrument: Mortgage
Predominant Method of Purchase: Strict Foreclosure
Time Required to Complete Initial Action (Months):   1
Redemption (Months):   6

For mortgages executed after April 1, 1968, the redemption period is 6 months from date of judgment unless a shorter period is granted per the complaint. Redemption is 12 months for mortgages executed before April 1, 1968.

Possession: Mortgagor

Virginia

Nature of Mortgage: Intermediate
Customary Security Instrument: Trust Deed
Predominant Method of Purchase: Power of Sale
Time Required to Complete Initial Action (Months):   2
Redemption (Months):   None

Possession:

Washington

Nature of Mortgage: Lien
Customary Security Instrument: Trust Deed
Predominant Method of Purchase: Power of Sale
Time Required to Complete Initial Action (Months):   1

Loan must be in default at least 120 days before day fixed for sale.

Redemption (Months):   None

Possession:

West Virginia

Nature of Mortgage: Lien
Customary Security Instrument: Trust Deed
Predominant Method of Purchase: Power of Sale
Time Required to Complete Initial Action (Months):   2
Redemption (Months):   None

Possession:

Wisconsin

Nature of Mortgage: Lien
Customary Security Instrument: Mortgage
Predominant Method of Purchase: Power of Sale

Judicial foreclosure is also available. If used, the 6-month redemption period precedes the sale and the VA transfer time then becomes 10 months.

Time Required to Complete Initial Action (Months):   3
Redemption (Months):   12

Judicial foreclosure is also available. If used, the 6-month redemption period precedes the sale and the VA transfer time then becomes 10 months.

Possession: Mortgagor

Wyoming

Nature of Mortgage: Lien
Customary Security Instrument: Mortgage
Predominant Method of Purchase: Power of Sale

Judicial foreclosure is also available. If used, the 6-month redemption period precedes the sale and the VA transfer time then becomes 10 months. In Wyoming, a 3-month redemption follows the sale plus 30 days for successive lien holders.

Time Required to Complete Initial Action (Months): 3
Redemption (Months): 3

Judicial foreclosure is also available. If used, the 6-month redemption period precedes the sale and the VA transfer time then becomes 10 months. In Wyoming, a 3-month redemption follows the sale plus 30 days for successive lien holders.

Possession: Financial Analysis

DEPARTMENT OF HOUSING AND URBAN DEVELOPMENT (HUD)

1. **REGION I (BOSTON)**
   Building, Room 375
   10 Causeway Street
   Boston, Massachusetts 02222-1092
   (617) 565-5234

2. **REGION II (NEW YORK)**
   26 Plaza
   New York, New York 10278-0068
   (212) 264-8053

3. **REGION III (PHILADELPHIA)**
   Liberty Square Building
   105 South Seventh Street
   Philadelphia, Pennsylvania 19106-3392
   (215) 597-2560

4. **REGION IV (ATLANTA)**
   Russell Building
   75 Spring Street SW
   Atlanta, Georgia 30303-3388
   (404) 331-5136

5. **REGION V (CHICAGO)**
   300 South Wacker Drive
   Chicago, Illinois 60606-6765
   (312) 353-5680

547 West Jackson Boulevard
Chicago, Illinois 60606-5760
(312) 353-7660

6. **REGION VI (FORT WORTH)**
1600 Throckmorton
Post Office Box 2905
Fort Worth, Texas 76113-2905
(817) 885-5401

7. **REGION VII (KANSAS CITY)**
Professional Building
1103 Grand Avenue
Kansas City, Missouri 64106-2496
(816) 374-2661

8. **REGION VIII (DENVER)**
Executive Tower Building
1405 Curtis Street
Denver, Colorado 80202-2349
(303) 844-4513

9. **REGION IX (SAN FRANCISCO)**
Burton Building & U.S. Courthouse
450 Golden Gate Avenue
Post Office Box 36003
San Francisco, California 94102-3448
(415) 556-4752

10. **REGION X (SEATTLE)**
Arcade Plaza Building
1321 Second Avenue
Seattle, Washington 98101-20542
(206) 442-5414

FEDERAL NATIONAL MORTGAGE ASSOCIATION (FANNIE MAE)

1. **WASHINGTON OFFICE**
3900 Wisconsin Avenue, NW
Washington, D.C. 20016-2899
(202) 537-7000

2. **SOUTHEASTERN REGIONAL OFFICE**
950 East Paces Ferry Road
Atlanta, Georgia 30326-1161
(404) 365-6000

3. **MIAMI OFFICE**
   11430 North Kendall Drive
   Suite 231
   Miami, Florida 33176-1006
   (312) 641-0740

4. **MIDWESTERN REGIONAL OFFICE**
   One South Wacker Drive
   Suite 3100
   Chicago, Illinois 60606-4667
   (312) 641-0740

5. **SOUTHWESTERN REGIONAL OFFICE**
   13455 Noel Road
   Suite 600
   Post Office Box 650043
   Dallas, Texas 75265-0043
   (214) 991-7771

6. **HOUSTON OFFICE**
   1616 South Voss
   Suite 900
   Houston, Texas 77057-2687
   (713) 972-9800

7. **OKLAHOMA CITY OFFICE**
   6525 North Meridian
   Suite 311
   Oklahoma City, Oklahoma 73116-1491
   (405) 722-9933

8. **WESTERN REGIONAL OFFICE**
   10920 Wilshire Boulevard
   Suite 1800
   Post Office Box 24019
   Los Angeles, California 90024-6519
   (213) 208-6234

9. **ANCHORAGE OFFICE**
   3201 "C" Street
   Suite 606
   Anchorage, Alaska 99503-3994
   (907) 561-0828

10. **NORTHEASTERN REGIONAL OFFICE**
    510 Walnut Street
    16th Floor
    Philadelphia, Pennsylvania 19106-3697
    (215) 574-1400

11. FANNIE MAE SOFTWARE SYSTEMS
3139 Campus Drive
Norcross, Georgia 30071-1402
(404) 446-2533
(800) 241-8291

FEDERAL NATIONAL HOUSING MORTGAGE CORPORATION (FREDDIE MAC)

1. ADMINISTRATIVE OFFICES
1759 Business Center Drive
6th Floor
Reston, Virginia 22090

2. NORTHEAST REGIONAL OFFICE
Crystal Park Three
2231 Crystal Drive
Suite 900
Crystal City, Virginia 22202
(703) 685-4500

3. NORTH CENTRAL REGIONAL OFFICE
333 West Wacker Drive
Suite 3100
Chicago, Illinois 60606
(312) 407-7400

4. SOUTHEAST REGIONAL OFFICE
2839 Paces Ferry Road
Suite 700
Atlanta, Georgia 30339-33718
(404) 438-3800

5. SOUTHWEST REGIONAL OFFICE
Four Forest Plaza
12222 Merit Drive
Suite 700
Dallas, Texas 75251
(214) 702-2000

6. WESTERN REGIONAL OFFICE
15303 Ventura Boulevard
Suite 500
Post Office Box 9114
Sherman Oaks, California 91403
(818) 905-0070

RESOLUTION TRUST CORPORATION—NATIONAL OFFICE AND FOUR REGIONAL OFFICES

1. David Cook
   Executive Director
   550 17th Street NW
   Washington, D.C.
   (800) 424-4334

2. William Dudley
   Regional Director
   245 Peachtree Avenue
   Suite 1100
   Atlanta, Georgia 30303
   (404) 522-1145

3. Carmen Sullivan
   Regional Director
   1910 Pacific Avenue
   Dallas, Texas 75201
   (214) 754-0098

4. Michael Martinelli
   Regional Director
   4900 Main Street
   Kansas City, Kansas 64112
   (816) 531-2212

5. Anthony Scalzi
   Regional Director
   1125 17th Street
   Suite 700
   Denver, Colorado 80202
   (303) 296-4703

Contact the asset managers of local thrifts, banks, credit unions, and insurance companies, and ask to be placed on their REO/ORE mailing list.

REGIONAL OFFICES OF THE VETERANS ADMINISTRATION (VA)

ALABAMA
VA Regional Office
474 South Court Street
Montgomery, AL 36104
Henry Moody (LGO)
Ralph Strickland (PMC)
(205) 832-7193

ALASKA
VA Regional Office
235 E. 8th Avenue
Anchorage, AK 99501
Terry Niendorf (LGO)
Curtis Brantley (PMC)
(907) 271-4562

ARIZONA
VA Regional Office
3225 North Central Avenue
Phoenix, AZ 85012
William Cipolla (LOG)
Bob Johnson (PMC)
(602) 241-1748

ARKANSAS
VA Regional Office
P.O. Box 1280, Ft. Roots N.
Little Rock, AR 72115
Wilma Graham (LGO)
Ed Johnson (PMC)
(501) 370-3758

CALIFORNIA
VA Regional Office Federal
Building
1100 Wilshire Boulevard
Los Angeles, CA 90024
Paul Schikal (LGO)
Angie Wild (PMC)
(213) 209-7838

VA Regional Office
211 Main Street
San Francisco, CA 94105
Charles Bidondo (LGO)
Peter O'Sullivan (PMC)
(415) 974-0204

COLORADO
VA Regional Office
Box 25126, 44 Union Boulevard
Denver, CO 80225
Julius Williams (LGO)
George Tucker (PMC)
(303) 980-2847

CONNECTICUT
VA Regional Office
450 Main Street
Hartford, CT 06103
Burke Bell (LGO)
Susan Labins (PMC)
(203) 244-2897

DISTRICT OF COLUMBIA
VA Regional Office
941 N. Capitol Street, NE
Washington, DC 20421
James Nalitz (LGO)
Walter Covington (PMC)
(202) 275-0611

FLORIDA
VA Regional Office
P.O. Box 1437
St. Petersburg, FL 33731
Ronald Veltman (LGO)
Ralph Harris (PMC)
(813) 893-3404

GEORGIA
VA Regional Office
730 Peachtree Street, NE
Atlanta, GA 30365
Wayne Beck (LGO)
Howard Yeager (PMC)
(404) 881-3474

HAWAII
VA Regional Office
P.O. Box 50188
Honolulu, HI 96850
Thomas Serocca (LGO/PMC)
(808) 546-2160

IDAHO
VA Regional Office
550 West Fort Street
Boise, ID 83724
Charles Brioschi (LGO)
Ray Sims (PMC)
(208) 334-1910

ILLINOIS
VA Regional Office
536 South Clark Street
P.O. Box 8136
Chicago, IL 60680
Alan Schneider (LGO)
David Stelzner (PMC)
(312) 353-4068

INDIANA
VA Regional Office
575 Pennsylvania Street
Indianapolis, IN 46204
Frank Kuehn (LGO)
Robert Amt (PMC)
(317) 269-7827

IOWA
VA Regional Office
210 Walnut Street
Des Moines, IA 50309
Jack Rivers (LGO)
Raymond Morris (PMC)
(515) 284-4657

KANSAS
VA Regional Office
901 George Washington
    Boulevard
Wichita, KS 67211
Danny Cross (LGO)
George Lyon (PMC)
(316) 269-6311

KENTUCKY
VA Regional Office
600 Federal Place
Louisville, KY 40202
Michele Culp (LGO)
Richard Sloan (PMC)
(502) 582-5866

LOUISIANA
VA Regional Office
701 Loyola Avenue
New Orleans, LA 70113
Paul Griener (LGO)
Darryl Crum (PMC)
(504) 589-6459

MAINE
VA Medical & Regional Office
Toqus, ME 04330
John Bales (LGO)
Ted Hodgdon (PMC)
(207) 623-5434

MARYLAND
VA Regional Office
31 Hopkins Plaza
Baltimore, MD 21201
Judy Eagan (LGO)
Don Dennehy (PMC)
(301) 962-4467

MASSACHUSETTS
VA Regional Office
John F. Kennedy Building
Boston, MA 02203
Arthur Snyder (LGO/PMC)
(617) 223-3052

MICHIGAN
VA Regional Office
477 Michigan Avenue
Detroit, MI 48226
Stan Brown (LGO)
Mike Johnson (PMC)
(313) 226-7561

MINNEAPOLIS
VA Regional Office
Ft. Snelling
St. Paul, MN 55111
Don Munro (LGO)
Ron Stowers (PMC)
(612) 725-4054

MISSISSIPPI
VA Regional Office
100 West Capitol Street
Jackson, MS 39269
Robert Finneran (LGO)
Ron Stowers (PMC)
(601) 960-4840

MISSOURI
VA Regional Office
1520 Market Street
St. Louis, MO 63103
James Mullins (LGO)
Gerald Jones (PMC)
(314) 425-5144

MONTANA
VA Regional Office & Medical
    Center
Fort Harrison, MT 59636
Albert Olsen (LGO)
Ruth Smith (PMC)
(406) 442-6410

NEBRASKA
VA Regional Office
100 Centennial Mall, N.
Lincoln, NE 68508
David Wiese (LGO)
Carol Swan (PMC)
(402) 471-5031

NEW HAMPSHIRE
VA Regional Office
275 Chestnut Street
Manchester, NH 03101
Robert Carstarphen (LGO)
Ray Arocha (PMC)
(603) 666-7656

NEW JERSEY
VA Regional Office
20 Washington Place
Newark, NJ 07102
Elmer DeRitter (LGO)
Russell Williams (PMC)
(201) 645-3607

NEW MEXICO
VA Regional Office
500 Gold Avenue, SW
Albuquerque, NM 87102
West Crone (LGO)
Jean McKinney (PMC)
(505) 766-2214

NEW YORK
VA Regional Office
111 West Huron Street
Buffalo, NY 14202
Keith Boerner (LGO)
Mike Meyer (PMC)
(716) 846-5296

VA Regional Office
252 7th Avenue
New York, NY 10001
Gerald Prizeman (LGO)
William Rooney (PMC)
(212) 620-6421

NORTH CAROLINA
VA Regional Office
251 North Main Street
Winston-Salem, NC 27155
John Koivisto (LGO)
Cedric Upchurch (PMC)
(919) 761-3494

OHIO
VA Regional Office
1240 East 9th Street
Cleveland, OH 44199
Thomas Vickroy (LGO)
Jim Haugh (PMC)
(216) 522-3583

OKLAHOMA
VA Regional Office
125 Main Street
Muskogee, OK 74401
Jean Mathis (LGO)
Harvey Sweet (PMC)
(918) 687-2161

OREGON
VA Regional Office
1220 S.W. Third Avenue
Portland, OR 97204
Phyllis Somers (LGO)
Richard Lewis (PMC)
(503) 221-2481

PENNSYLVANIA
VA Regional Office & Medical
    Center
5000 Wissahickon Avenue
Philadelphia, PA 19101
Richard Kesteven (LGO)
Stephen Loughnane (PMC)
(215) 951-5508

VA Regional Office
1000 Liberty Avenue
Pittsburgh, PA 15222
Carl Rueter (LGO)
Al Curotola (PMC)
(412) 644-6979

SOUTH CAROLINA
VA Regional Office
1801 Assembly Street
Columbia, SC 29210
Olin Westbrook (LGO)
David Ramsey (PMC)
(803) 765-5154

TENNESSEE
VA Regional Office
110 9th Avenue, S.
Nashville, TN 37203
Kenneth Harvey (LGO)
Billy Bushulen (PMC)
(615) 251-5241

TEXAS
VA Regional Office
2515 Murworth Drive
Houston, TX 77054
Mike McReaken (LGO)
Mike Moran (PMC)
(713) 660-4177

VA Regional Office
14000 N. Valley Mills Drive
Waco, TX 76799
Lee Kramer (LGO)
Bill Carr (PMC)
(817) 757-6869

UTAH
VA Regional Office
P.O. Box 11500
Salt Lake City, UT 84147
Gilbert Yocky (LGO)
Gerald Overstreet (PMC)
(801) 588-5983

VIRGINIA
VA Regional Office
210 Franklin Road, S.W.
Roanoke, VA 24011
Bill Hogan (LGO)
Robert Gibson (PMC)
(703) 982-6141

WASHINGTON
VA Regional Office
915 Second Avenue
Seattle, WA 98174
Leonette Kobiela (LGO)
Cheryle Lany (PMC)
(206) 442-7014

WEST VIRGINIA
VA Regional Office
640 4th Avenue
Huntington, WV 25701
Robert Shearin (LGO)
Margo Keyser (PMC)
(304) 529-5047

WISCONSIN
VA Regional Office
P.O. Box 6
Milwaukee, WI 53295
Thomas Malta (LGO)
Susan Lofton (PMC)
(414) 671-8171

Glossary

Abstract of title A summary of all of the recorded instruments and proceedings that affect the title to property, arranged in the order in which they were recorded.

Accrued interest Interest that has been earned but is not due and payable.

Acknowledgment A formal declaration, made before a duly authorized officer by a person who has executed an instrument, that such execution is the person's free act and deed.

Acquisition An act or process by which a person obtains property.

Ad valorem According to valuation.

Adjacent Lying near to but not necessarily in actual contact with.

Adjoining Continuous, attaching, in actual contact with.

Administrator A person appointed by a court to administer the estate of a person who died intestate, that is, without a will.

Adverse possession A means of acquiring title to property that has been occupied for a certain period.

Affidavit A written statement or declaration sworn to or affirmed before an authorized person.

Affirm To confirm, to ratify, to verify.

Agency The relationship that arises when an agent is employed to act on the principal's behalf in dealing with a third party.

Agent One who undertakes to act for another.

Agreement of sale A written agreement in which the purchaser agrees to buy and the seller agrees to sell. Terms and conditions are included in the agreement.

Alienation The transfer of property to another.

Alienation clause A provision that allows a lender to demand payment of the balance of a loan in full if the collateral is sold. Also known as a "due on sale" clause.

Amortization The repayment of a debt in installments.

Amortization mortgage A debt for which the periodic repayments are used to reduce the principal outstanding as well as to pay off the current interest charges.

Annuity A financial contract that provides for a series of periodic payments in the future.

Apportionment The adjustment of the income, expenses, or carrying costs of real estate that are usually computed to the date of closing of title so that the seller pays all expenses to that date. The buyer assumes all expenses from the date on which the deed is conveyed to the buyer.

Appraisal An estimate of a property's value made by an appraiser who is usually presumed to be an expert in this work.

Appraisal by comparison An estimate of value made by comparing the sale prices of other similar properties.

Appurtenance Something that is outside the property itself but belongs to the land and adds to its greater enjoyment, such as a right-of-way or a barn or dwelling.

Arbitration clause Sometimes appears in a long-term lease or other contract requiring the decision of a third-party referee in the event of a dispute.

Assessed valuation A valuation placed on property by a public officer or a board, as a basis for taxation.

Assessment A charge against real estate made by a unit of government to cover a proportionate cost of an improvement such as a street or sewer.

Assessor An official who has the responsibility of determining assessed valuation.

Assignment The method or manner by which a right or contract is transferred from one person (the assignor) to another (the assignee).

Assumption of mortgage Occurs when a person takes title to property and assumes liability for the payment of an existing note or bond secured by a mortgage against the property.

Attest To witness to, either by observation or by signature.

Balloon payment A final installment payment, larger than previous installments, that pays off a debt.

Bearer Lender in whose hands a promissory note remains until it is paid in full.

Beneficiary   The person who receives or is to receive the benefits of a certain act.

Bequeath   To leave by will.

Bequest   A gift made by will.

Betterment   A property improvement that increases the property's value.

Bill of sale   A document by which title to personal property is passed from seller to buyer.

Bona fide   In good faith; without fraud.

Capital gain or loss   The difference between the basis price (cost plus purchase expenses) of a capital asset and its sales price.

Capital improvement   Any permanent structure erected to extend the useful life and value of a property. (The replacement of a roof would be considered a capital improvement.)

Caveat emptor   Let the buyer beware. The buyer must examine the goods or property and buy at his or her own risk.

Chain of title   A history of the conveyances and encumbrances affecting a title from the time the original ownership was granted, or as far back as records are available.

Chattel   Personal property, such as household goods or fixtures.

Chattel mortgage   A mortgage on personal property.

Client   The one by whom a broker is employed and by whom the broker will be compensated (the principal).

Closing date   The date on which the buyer takes over the property.

Cloud on the title   An outstanding claim or encumbrance that, if valid, would affect or impair the owner's title.

Codicil   An addition to or amendment of a will.

Collateral   Additional security pledged for the payment of a debt.

Color of title   An apparent, invalid title.

Commission   A fee charged for brokerage services.

Commitment   A pledge; a promise; an affirmation agreement.

Complaint   (1) In civil law, the initial statement of the facts on which a complaint is based. (2) In criminal law, the preliminary charge made against the accused.

Condemnation   The acquisition of private property for public use, with fair compensation to the owner. See also *Eminent domain.*

Conditional sales   A contract for the sale of property stating that, although delivery is to be made to the buyer, the title is to remain vested in the seller until the conditions of the contract have been fulfilled.

Consideration   Anything given as an inducement to enter into a contract, such as money or personal services. Any contract, lease, obligation, or mortgage may subsequently be modified without consideration, provided that the change is made in writing and signed.

Constructive notice   Information that a person is assumed, by law, to have simply because it could be ascertained by proper diligence and enquiry, for example, information that is to be found in the public records.

Contract   A legally enforceable agreement.

Conversion   In terms of property, the exchange of personal or real property of one character or use for another.

Conveyance   The transfer of the title of land from one person to another.

Correlation   The final stage of the appraisal process in which the appraiser reviews the data and estimates the subject property's value.

Covenants   Agreements written into deeds and other instruments promising performance or nonperformance of certain acts, or stipulating certain uses or restrictions on the property.

Current value   The value at the time of an appraisal.

Damages   Compensation, required by law and paid in money, for loss or injury.

De facto   In fact or reality.

Debit   The amount charged as due or owing.

Debt service   Annual amount to be paid by a debtor for money borrowed.

Dedication   The action by which land is granted by its owner for some public use and is accepted for such use by an authorized official on behalf of the public.

Deed   An instrument in writing, duly executed and delivered, that conveys title to real property.

Deed restriction   A restriction imposed in a deed to limit the use of the land. A deed might include clauses preventing the sale of liquor or defining the size, type, value, or placement of improvements.

Default   Failure to fulfill a duty or promise, or to discharge an obligation; omission or failure to perform an act. In property foreclosure, usually the failure to pay loan installment repayments when they become due.

Defeasance clause   The clause in a mortgage that permits the mortgagor to redeem his or her property upon the payment of the obligations to the mortgagee.

Defendant   The party sued or called to answer in any lawsuit, civil or criminal.

Deficiency judgment   When the security for a loan is sold for less than the amount of the loan, the unpaid amount (the deficiency) is held by law (the judgment) to be the liability of the borrower unless the new owner has assumed the debt.

Delivery   The transfer of the possession of an object from one person to another.

Demand note   A note that is payable on demand of the holder.

Descent   When an owner of real estate dies intestate, the owner's property descends, by operation of law, to the owner's distributees.

Desist and refrain order   An order issued by a real estate commissioner to stop an action that violates the real estate law.

Devise   A gift of real estate made to the devisee in the will of the devisor.

Distributee   Person receiving or entitled to receive land as representative of the former owners. See also *Descent*.

Documentary evidence   Evidence in the form of written or printed papers.

Domicile   A place where a person lives or has a home; in a legal sense, the place where he or she has a true, fixed, permanent home and principal establishment, and to which place he or she has, whenever absent, the intention of returning.

Duress   A threat that prevents a person from acting of his or her own free will.

Earnest money   Down payment made by a purchaser of real estate as evidence of good faith.

Easement   A building, part of a building, or obstruction that intrudes upon the property of another.

Eminent domain   A right of the government to acquire property for public use; the owner must be fairly compensated.

Encumbrance   See *Incumbrance*.

Endorsement   Signing one's name on the back of a check, document, or note to verify acknowledgment.

Equity   In real estate, the difference between the value of the property and the amount owed on it. Also called the "owner's interest."

Equity cushion   The amount of equity required before a lender will make a loan.

Equity loan   Junior (subordinate) loan based on a percentage of the equity.

Equity of redemption   A right of the owner to avert foreclosure by paying the debt, interest, and costs.

Escheat   The reversion to the state of property, the owners of which have abandoned it or died without heirs.

Escrow   A written agreement between two or more parties providing that certain instruments or property be entrusted to a third party to be delivered to a designated person upon the fulfillment or performance of some act or condition.

Estate   The degree, quantity, nature, and extent of interest (ownership) that a person has in real property.

Estate for life   An estate or interest held during the term of a person's life.

Estate at will   The occupation of property by a tenant for an indefinite period, terminable by one or both parties at will.

Estoppel certificate   An instrument executed by the mortgagor setting forth the status of and the balance due on the mortgage as of the date of the execution of the certificate.

Eviction   A legal proceeding by a landlord to recover possession of real property.

Eviction, actual   Where one is, either by force or by process of law, physically put out of possession.

Eviction, constructive   Any disturbance of the tenant's possessions by the landlord whereby the premises are rendered unfit or unsuitable for the purpose for which they were leased.

Eviction, partial   Where the tenant is deprived of the use of the premises.

Exclusive agency   An agreement to employ one broker only. If the sale is made by any other broker, both are entitled to commissions.

Exclusive right to sell   An agreement to give a broker the exclusive right to sell for a specified period. If a sale during the term of the agreement is made by the owner or by any other broker, the broker holding the exclusive right is nevertheless entitled to compensation.

Executor   A male person or a corporate entity or any other type of organization named in a will to carry out its provisions.

Executrix   A woman appointed to perform the same duties as an executor.

Extension agreement   An agreement that extends the life of a mortgage.

Fee (fee simple, fee absolute)   The absolute ownership of real property. This type of estate gives the owner and his or her heirs unconditional power of disposition.

FHA mortgage loan   Mortgage loan insured by the Federal Housing Administration.

Fiduciary   A person who transacts business or handles money or property on behalf of another. The relationship implies great confidence and trust.

First lien   Debt recorded first against a property. See *First mortgage.*

First mortgage   Mortgage that has priority as a lien over all other mortgages. In cases of foreclosure, the first mortgage will be satisfied before other mortgages are paid off.

Fixtures   Personal property so attached to the land or its improvements as to become part of the real property.

Foreclosure   A procedure whereby property pledged as security for a debt is sold to pay the debt in the event of default in payments or terms.

Forfeiture   Loss of money or anything of value, by way of penalty due to failure to perform.

Freehold   An interest that is not less than an estate for life, in real estate.

Front foot   A measurement of property made for sale or valuation purposes by which each "front foot" on the street line extends the depth of the lot.

Grace period   Additional time allowed to perform an act or make a payment before a default occurs.

Grant   A term used in deeds of conveyance of lands to indicate a transfer.

Grantee   The party to whom the title to real property is conveyed.

Grantor   The person who conveys real estate by deed; the seller.

Gross income   Total income from property before any expenses are deducted.

Guardian's deed   Issued to the person responsible for the estate of a minor or incompetent.

Habendum clause   The "to have and to hold" clause that defines or limits the quantity of the estate granted in the deed.

Hereditaments   The largest classification of property, including lands, tenements, and incorporeal property, such as rights-of-way.

Holdover tenant   A tenant who remains in possession of leased property after the lease runs out.

Hypothecate   To use something as security without giving up possession of it.

Incompetent   A person who, because of insanity, imbecility, or feeble-mindedness is unable to manage his or her own affairs.

Incumbrance   Any right to or interest in property interfering with its use or transfer, or subjecting it to an obligation. In connection with foreclosure property, the most likely encumbrances are mortgages and claims for unpaid taxes.

In rem   A legal proceeding taken against the property as distinguished from a proceeding against a person. Used in taking land for nonpayment of taxes, and so on.

Installments   Parts of the same debt, payable at successive periods as agreed; payments made to reduce a mortgage.

Instrument   A written legal document.

Interest rate   The percentage of a sum of money charged for its use.

Intestate   A person who dies before making a will, or whose will is defective in form.

Involuntary lien   A lien imposed against property without consent of the owner, e.g., taxes, special assessments.

Irrevocable   Incapable of being recalled or revoked; unchangeable; unalterable.

Jeopardy   To have one's property or liberty subjected to a possibly adverse decree of a court or agency.

Joint tenancy   Ownership of property by two or more persons, each of whom has an undivided interest with the right of survivorship.

Judgment   Decree of a court declaring that one individual is indebted to another, and fixing the amount of such indebtedness.

Junior mortgage   A mortgage second in lien (subordinate) to a previous mortgage.

Land, tenements and hereditaments   A phrase used in early English law to describe the entire range of immovable property.

Landlord   One who rents property to another.

Lease   A contract whereby, for a consideration, usually termed rent, one who is entitled to the possession of real property transfers such rights to another for life, for a term of years, or at will.

Leasehold   The interest given to a lessee of real estate by a lease.

Lessee   A person to whom property is rented under a lease.

Lessor   One who rents property to another under a lease.

Lien   A legal right or claim upon a specific property that attaches to the property until a debt is satisfied.

Life estate   The conveyance of title to property for the duration of the life of the grantee.

Life tenant   The holder of a life estate.

Lis pendens   A legal document, filed in the office of the County Clerk, giving notice that an action or proceeding pending in the courts affects the title to a property.

Listing   An employment contract between principal and agent, authorizing the agent to perform services (usually the sale) for the principal involving the latter's property.

Litigation   The act of carrying on a lawsuit.

Mandatory   Requiring strict conformity or obedience.

Marketable title   A title that the court considers to be so free from defect that it will enforce its acceptance by a purchaser.

Mechanic's lien A claim made to secure the price of labor done and materials furnished for uncompensated improvement.

Meeting of the minds Whenever all the parties agree to the exact terms of a contract.

Metes and bounds A term used in describing land by setting forth all the boundary lines together with their terminal points and angles.

Minor A person under an age specified by law; usually under eighteen years of age.

Monument A fixed object and point established by surveyors to establish land locations.

Moratorium An emergency act by a legislative body to suspend the legal enforcement of contractual obligations.

Mortgage An instrument in writing, duly executed and delivered, that creates a lien on real estate as security for the payment of a specified debt, which is usually in the form of a bond.

Mortgage commitment A formal indication, made by a lending institution, that it will grant a mortgage loan on property, in a certain specified amount and on certain specified terms.

Mortgage reduction certificate An instrument executed by the mortgagee, setting forth the status of and the balance due on the mortgage as of the date of the execution of the instrument.

Mortgagee The party who lends money and takes a mortgage to secure repayment.

Mortgagor A person who borrows money and gives a mortgage on his or her property as security for the payment of the debt.

Multiple listing An arrangement among members of the Real Estate Board of Exchange, whereby brokers present their listings to the attention of the other members. If a sale results, the commission is divided between the broker providing the listing and the broker making the sale.

Net listing The lowest price for which an owner will sell a property. The broker's commission will consist of whatever sum is paid over and above the net listing price. Otherwise, no commission is payable.

Nonsolicitation order An order issued by the secretary of state to brokers and salespersons, prohibiting them from soliciting any listings in a designated geographical area.

Notary public A person authorized to take acknowledgments to certain classes of documents, such as deeds, contracts, and mortgages, and before whom affidavits may be sworn.

Notice of default Letter sent to a defaulting party as a reminder of the default. It may state a grace period and the penalties for failing to cure the default.

Obligee The person in whose favor an obligation is entered into.

Obligor   The person who is bound by a promise or obligation to another; one who has been engaged to perform some obligation; one who makes a bond.

Obsolescence   Loss in value due to reduced desirability and usefulness of a structure because its design and construction become obsolete; loss because of becoming old-fashioned, and not in keeping with modern means, with consequent loss of income.

Open listing   A listing given to any number of brokers with commissions payable only to the broker who secures the sale.

Open mortgage   A mortgage that has matured or is overdue and, therefore, is "open" to foreclosure at any time.

Option   A right given for a consideration to purchase or lease a property on specific terms within a specified time; if the right is not exercised, the option holder is not subject to liability for damages; if exercised, the grantor of option must perform.

Partition   The division made of real property among those who own it, in undivided shares.

Party wall   A wall built along the boundary between two properties.

Performance bond   A bond used to guarantee the specific completion of an endeavor in accordance with a contract.

Personal property   Any property that is not real property.

Plat book   A public record containing maps of land showing the division into streets, blocks, and lots and indicating the measurements of the individual parcels.

Points   Discount charges imposed by lenders to raise the yields on their loans.

Police power   The right of any political body to enact laws and enforce them, for the order, safety, health, morals, and general welfare of the public.

Power of attorney   A written instrument (documented) duly signed and executed by an owner of property, which authorizes an agent to act on behalf of the owner.

Prepayment clause   A clause in a mortgage that gives a mortgagor the privilege of paying the mortgage indebtedness before it becomes due.

Principal   The employer of an agent or broker; the broker's or agent's client.

Probate   Court proceeding to establish the will of a deceased person.

Procuring cause   Legal term used in real estate to determine whether a broker is entitled to a commission.

Proration   Allocation of closing costs and credits to buyers and sellers.

Purchase money mortgage   A mortgage given by a grantee in part payment of the purchase price of real estate.

Quiet enjoyment   The right of an owner or a person legally in possession to the use of the property without interference.

Quiet title suit   A suit in court to ascertain the legal rights of an owner
to a certain parcel of real property.

Quitclaim deed   A deed that conveys simply the grantor's rights or
interest in real estate; generally considered inadequate except when
interests are being passed from one spouse to the other.

Real Estate Board   An organization whose members consist primarily
of real estate brokers and salespersons.

Real Estate Owned   Property acquired by a lender through foreclosure
and held in inventory; commonly referred to as REO.

Real estate syndicate   A partnership formed for a real estate venture.
Partners may be limited or unlimited in their liability.

Real property   Land, and generally whatever is erected on or affixed
thereto.

Realtor   A term used to identify active members of the National Association of Real Estate Boards.

Recording   The act of writing or entering in a book of public record
instruments affecting the title to real property.

Recourse   The right to claim against a prior owner of a property or note.

Red lining   The refusal to lend money within a specific area for various
reasons. This practice is illegal because it discriminates against the
creditworthy who happen to live there.

Redemption   The right of a mortgagor to redeem property by paying a
debt before sale at foreclosure; the right of an owner to reclaim his
or her property after it has been sold to settle claims for unpaid
taxes.

Release   The act or writing by which some claim or interest is surren-
dered to another.

Release clause   A clause found in a blanket mortgage which gives the
owner of the property the privilege of paying off part of the debt,
and thus freeing part of the property from the mortgage.

Rent   The compensation paid for the use of real estate.

Restriction   A limitation on the use of property that is specified in the
title deed.

Revocation   An act of recalling (cancelling) a power of authority con-
ferred, as the revocation of a power of attorney, a license, an
agency, and so on.

Right of redemption   Right to recover property transferred by a mortgage or other lien by paying off the debt either before or after
foreclosure; also called "equity of redemption."

Right of survivorship   Right of the surviving joint owner to succeed to
the interests of the deceased joint owner. This right is a distin-
guishing feature of a joint tenancy or tenancy by the entirety.

Right-of-way   The right to pass over another's land.

Sales contract   A contract by which the buyer and seller agree to terms of sale.

Satisfaction piece   The receipt for a mortgage that has been paid off.

Second mortgage   A mortgage made by a home buyer in addition to an existing first mortgage.

Setback   The distance from the curb or other established line, within which no buildings may be erected.

Special assessment   An assessment made against a property to pay for a public improvement.

Specific performance   A remedy in a court of equity compelling a defendant to carry out the terms of an agreement or contract.

Statute   A law established by an act of a legislature.

Statute of limitations   A law that limits the time within which a criminal prosecution or civil action must be started.

Stipulations   The terms within a written contract.

Straight-line depreciation   A definite sum set aside annually from income to pay costs of replacing improvements.

Subdivision   A tract of land divided into lots or plots.

Subletting   To let (rent) to another the property one is renting.

Subordination clause   A clause in a mortgage that gives priority to a mortgage taken out at a later date.

Sui juris   Having legal ability to handle one's own affairs.

Surrogate's Court (Probate Court)   A court that deals with wills and the settling of estates.

Survey   The process by which a parcel of land is measured and its area ascertained; also, the blueprint showing the measurements, boundaries, and area.

Tax sale   Sale of property after a period of nonpayment of taxes.

Tenancy in common   An ownership of realty by two or more persons, each of whom has an undivided interest, without the right of survivorship.

Tenancy by the entirety   An estate that exists only between husband and wife, with equal right of possession and enjoyment during their joint lives and with the right of survivorship.

Tenancy at will   A license to use or occupy lands and tenements at the will of the owner.

Tenant   One who is given possession of real estate for a fixed period or at will.

Testate   Where a person dies leaving a valid will.

Title   Evidence of the ownership of land.

Title company   Firm examining title to real estate and/or issuing title insurance.

Title defect   Unresolved claim against the ownership of property that prevents presentation of a marketable title. Such claims may arise from failure of the owner's spouse, or former part owner, to sign a deed; current liens against the property; or an interruption in the title records of a property.

Title insurance   A policy of insurance that protects the holder from any loss caused by defects in the title.

Title report   Document indicating the current state of the title, such as easements, covenants, liens, and any other defects. The title report does not describe the chain of title. See also *Abstract of title*.

Title search   An examination of the public records to determine the ownership and encumbrances affecting real property.

Torrens title   A system provided by state law for the registration of land titles whereby the ownership and encumbrances can be readily ascertained from an inspection of the Register of Titles without the necessity of a search of public records.

Transfer tax   A tax charged under certain conditions on the property belonging to an estate.

Trust deed   Conveyance of real estate to a third party to be held for the benefit of another. It is commonly used in some states in place of mortgages that conditionally convey title to the lender.

Trustee   (1) One who holds legal title to property in trust for the benefit of another person, and who is required to carry out specific duties with regard to the property, or who has been given power affecting the disposition of property for another's benefit. (2) Loosely, anyone who acts as a guardian or fiduciary in relationship to another, such as a public officer toward constituents, a state toward its citizens, or a partner to a co-partner.

Trustor   One who creates a trust, often called the settlor.

Undivided interest   Ownership of real estate by joint tenants or tenants in common under the same title.

Unearned increment   An increase in value of real estate due to no effort on the part of the owner.

Usury   The lending of money at a rate of interest greater than that permitted by law.

Valid   Having force, or binding force; legally sufficient and authorized by law.

Valuation   Estimated worth or price. The act of valuing by appraisal.

Variance   The authorization to improve or develop a particular property in a manner not authorized by zoning.

Vendee's lien   A lien against property under contract of sale to secure a deposit paid by a purchaser.

Verification   Sworn statements before a duly qualified officer to the correctness of the contents of an instrument.

Violations   Acts, deeds, or conditions contrary to law or permissible use of real property.

Void   To have no force or effect; that which is unenforceable.

Voidable   That which is capable of being adjudged void, but is not void unless action is taken to make it so.

Waiver   The renunciation, abandonment, or surrender of some claim, right, or privilege.

Warranty deed   A conveyance of land in which the grantor guarantees the title to the grantee.

Will   The disposition of one's property after death.

Without recourse   Words used in endorsing a note or bill to denote that the future holder is not to look to the endorser in case of nonpayment.

Wraparound loan   A new loan encompassing any existing loans.

Zone   An area set off by the proper authorities for specific use; subject to certain restrictions or restraints.

Zoning ordinance   Act of city or county or other authorities specifying type and use to which property may be put in specific areas.

Index